The History of Siberia

Siberia has a long and fascinating history, quite distinct from that of Russia. This vast region – covering 40 per cent of the landmass of Eurasia – was at one time part of the Mongol Empire, and was only settled relatively late by the Russians. Today it contains many non-Russian nationalities, and is increasingly important because of its huge energy reserves. This book provides a comprehensive account of the history of Siberia, spanning several millennia from the earliest human settlement to the twenty-first century. It describes how a rich, diversified set of cultures emerged, not only fully capable of living in the harsh conditions, but also displaying impressive artistic achievements. It goes on to show how Russia's thirst for furs and empire brought its intrepid *conquistadores* to establish a river-borne colonial system that dominated the north and east from the mid-seventeenth century. The development of a rich agricultural and mining economy by the First World War, based on railway and steamship enterprise, was disrupted by the cataclysmic events of the Russian Revolution, whose ensuing civil war was decided on Siberian soil. The book depicts the heroic and barbaric endeavours to develop the region's massively rich resources under Stalin, and under the later more benign Soviet leadership, demonstrating how ruinous the Marxist planning system was for Siberia's fragile ecology. The book also shows how the Siberian population is now levering itself up from the crisis of the 1990s to build the treasure house for Russia's renewed emergence in the post-Communist era. Overall, this book is an important resource for anyone seeking to understand the history of Siberia.

Igor V. Naumov is head of the History Department in Irkutsk State Technical University in Siberia. Born in Irkutsk, he specializes in Siberian history and Russian military history, and is the author of over 40 publications.

David N. Collins was formerly head of the Department of Russian and Slavonic Studies, and Director of the Centre for Canadian Studies at the University of Leeds. He is published widely on Siberian and Canadian history.

Routledge Studies in the History of Russia and Eastern Europe

The History of Siberia

Igor V. Naumov
(Edited by David N. Collins)

Routledge
Taylor & Francis Group

LONDON AND NEW YORK

First published 2006
by Routledge
2 Park Square, Milton Park, Abingdon, Oxon OX14 4RN

Simultaneously published in the USA and Canada
by Routledge
270 Madison Ave, New York, NY 10016

Transferred to Digital Printing 2006

*Routledge is an imprint of the Taylor & Francis Group,
an informa business*

Typeset in Helvetica and Times New Roman by
Florence Production Ltd, Stoodleigh, Devon
Printed and bound in Great Britain by
the MPG Books Group

British Library Cataloguing in Publication Data
A catalogue record for this book is available from the British Library

Library of Congress Cataloging in Publication Data
Naumov, I.V. (Igor Vladimirovich)
   The history of Siberia/Igor V. Naumov; edited by
   David N. Collins. – 1st published.
      p.cm. – (Routledge studies in the history of Russia and
      Eastern Europe)
   Includes bibliographical references and index.
   1. Siberia (Russia)–History. I. Collins, David Norman.
   II. Title. III. Series.
   DK761.N34 2006
   957–dc22   2006011413

ISBN10: 0–415–36819–7 (hbk)
ISBN10: 0–203–02798–1 (ebk)

ISBN13: 978–0–415–36819–3 (hbk)
ISBN13: 978–0–203–02798–1 (ebk)

Contents

Illustrations

Tables

Preface

The aim of this book is to acquaint the reader with the history of Siberia, an enormous swathe of contemporary Russia, covering the whole northern part of the Asian continent.

The author's intent has been to survey the entire history of Siberia beginning with the emergence of early humanity and ending in the twenty-first century. The account throws light on the main stages and key events occurring in this region over thousands of years. The text is based on a course of lectures delivered by the author to students attending Irkutsk State Technical University (ISTU).

The material is divided into chronological parts, each of them covering a specific period in Siberian history. The parts are in turn subdivided into chapters, the internal structure being determined by the need to present a full account of widely varying issues in different periods. The first part introduces the reader to the general concept of 'Siberia' and depicts the natural and climatic conditions that influenced its history. It also presents a brief account of the main stages in the development of the study of Siberia, demonstrating how knowledge was accumulated, and ends with the condition of contemporary Russian historiography relating to the region.

The author is sincerely glad that western readers interested in Siberia will now also have a chance to learn more about the history of this severe yet beautiful land.

The author is most grateful to all those who helped to write this book, especially to Dr Artur Kharinskii of ISTU for his valuable recommendations and comments on the pre-Russian period in the history of Siberia. He is also very grateful to Tatiana Verkhoturova and Leonid Ginsburg of Irkutsk State Linguistic University for their help in translating the book, and to Dr David Collins who has edited the translation for the English edition.

The author would be interested to hear readers' responses, opinions and comments to assist future revisions of the text. These should be sent to Dr Naumov at the following address: Lermontov Street, 83, Irkutsk, Russia, 664074.

Ivor V. Naumov

Editor's note

The form of transliteration used for Russian words is a modification of the simplified Library of Congress system, using 'ya', 'ye', 'yu' for initial palatalized vowels, and 'yo' for a stressed 'e'. No apostrophe is included to represent the soft sign. This is done to aid pronunciation by non-speakers of Russian. A few exceptions have been made for commonly accepted terms such as Moscow, Nicholas I, etc.

Editor's preface

The English language literature on Siberian history is extensive, so a word of explanation for adding to it might be appropriate.

Professor Naumov's *History of Siberia* is being published in English translation for several reasons. For a start, his account stands virtually alone as being written by a native-born *Sibiriak*. Professor Naumov was educated in Siberia, has lived there most of his life and dedicated himself to studying and teaching about his native land. His work therefore bears a stamp of authenticity, particularly since he drew on researches into this fascinating region conducted by dedicated Siberian enthusiasts from a range of disciplines while preparing the present wide-ranging study.

I was eager to edit this history as a means of paying homage to the scholarly endeavours of my colleagues beyond the Urals whose works have been of great assistance to me during my twenty-odd years teaching about Siberia in the University of Leeds. Unearthing remote archaeological sites, travelling by helicopter or on horseback to conduct ethnographic fieldwork, searching archives and libraries, often under tremendous difficulties, not least the trammels of Soviet censorship, they have provided us many examples of how true scholarship can thrive *in extremis*. I remember with fondness my days in the Rare Books section of the Novosibirsk Library perusing remarkable Old Believer manuscripts gathered on summer expeditions into the taiga; I am so glad that on my visit to the regional museum in the Altai – the first foreign scholar they had had – I was welcomed with open arms and chocolates. Thank you, for glimpses of true hospitality!

I trust, together with Professor Naumov, that this volume will inspire a future generation of researchers in the English-speaking world to work on the inexhaustible riches of Siberian regional history, anthropology, geography and social studies.

David N. Collins

Abbreviations

BAM	Baikal Amur railway
CER	Chinese Eastern Railway
CPSs	Committees of Public Safety
FER	Far Eastern Republic
GKChP	anti-Gorbachev State Committee on the Extraordinary Situation in the USSR
GNTPB	State Scientific-Technical Public Library
IDG	Interregional Deputies' Group
ISTU	Irkutsk State Technical University
MTS	machine tractor station
NEP	New Economic Policy
PRA	People's Revolutionary Army
RF	Russian Federation
RSDWP	Russian Social Democratic Workers' Party
SDs	Social Democrats
SRs	Social Revolutionary Party
TPR	Tuvan People's Republic
VTsIK	Soviet Supreme Central Executive Committee
VTsIK SSSR and VtsIK RSFSR	All-Union and Russian Republic Soviet Central Executive Committees
VTsSPS	All Union Trades Union Congress

Part I

The country known as 'Siberia'

1   General information

'Siberia' is a name of Tartar origin. The term has been known since the thirteenth century, when the Mongols conquered the area and named it. On coming to the region the Russians adopted the same name, calling it the *Sibirskaia zemlitsa* (land) or 'Siberia' for short. The name is being used in this book to refer to the whole northern part of the Asian continent, covering a vast territory of about 13 million square kilometres, approximately 40 per cent of the territory of Asia.

Siberia has natural[1] borders: in the west the Ural Mountains (the Urals), in the north the Arctic Ocean, in the east the Pacific Ocean and in the south the Kazakh and Mongolian steppes. Geographically the country consists of three large regions: western Siberia covering the territory from the Urals to the Yenisei River; eastern Siberia stretching from the Yenisei to the mountains of the Pacific watershed; and the Far East including the Pacific Ocean littoral and the adjoining territory. The natural and geographical conditions of Siberia have greatly influenced the history, culture and way of life of the Siberian population.

In terms of its physical relief, Siberia is subdivided into four geomorphological areas: the west Siberian Lowland, the mid-Siberian Plateau, the mountains of south Siberia and the mountains of the Far East. This geomorphological structure has influenced the climate and the quality of topsoil.

Siberia lies within moderate and cold continental climatic zones. It is isolated from the warm influence of the Atlantic Ocean by Europe and the Urals and from the warmer air of central Asia by the mountains of south Siberia and the Far East. It is open only to the north, allowing the intrusion of cold air from the Arctic. Therefore the winter in Siberia is cold. However, though short, the summer is hot. The annual precipitation is not large, the average being 200–300 millimetres. The southern mountainous area and the Pacific Ocean coast are the exception where this index exceeds 1,000 millimetres. The winter is especially low in precipitation, which accounts for the widespread permafrost in Siberia.

The soils are predominantly acidic podsols, not very good for agriculture. Only in south-western Siberia, in the forest-steppe zone, are there fertile black earth (*chernozem*) belts. There are also some small 'islands' of black-earth further east, in southern Siberia.

Siberia is a land of rivers. Its main system consists of four great rivers: the Ob, the Yenisei, the Lena and the Amur with a large number of greater and lesser tributaries. Besides these, there are other very big rivers: the Indigirka, the Kolyma, the Olenek, the Khatanga and the Yana. Lakes are also plentiful, the largest of which is Baikal. The large number of water resources compensates for the severity of the climate and the poverty of the soil, and creates the necessary conditions for human habitation. In fact, Siberia is a very rich land. Over 90 per cent of Russia's known natural resources are located here.

The flora and fauna of Siberia can be divided between five landscape zones[2]: the tundra, the forest-tundra, the *taiga* (huge coniferous forests covering over half of Siberian territory), the mountain *taiga* and the wooded-steppe. Historically these landscape zones have determined the main activities of Siberia's inhabitants.

The population of Siberia is over 30 million. Its overwhelming majority consists of the descendants of those who came from European Russia and other regions of the former Russian Empire and the Soviet Union. They represent various ethnic types, cultures and religions. The indigenous population numbers less than one million people. Ethnically, it belongs to the Mongoloid race, but is linguistically divided into six language groups:

- *Turkic* (the most numerous) – the Tartars, Yakuts, Tuvinians, Khakass, Altaians, Shor, Dolgan and Tofalar (Karagass[3]);
- *Mongolian* – the Buriats;
- *Tungus-Manchu* – the Evenk (Tungus), Even (Lamut), Nanai (Gold), Ulchi, Udegei, Orok, Oroch and Negidal;
- *Samodii* – the Nenets, Nganasan (Tavgii), Enets and Selkups (Ostiak-Samoieds);
- *Yugrian* – the Khanti (Ostiaks) and Mansi (Voguls); and
- *Palaeoasiatic*[4] – the Chukchi, Koriak, Ket, Aleuts, Yukaghir, Siberian Eskimos (Inuit), Nivkhi (Giliak) and Itelmen (Kamchadals).

The native Siberian populations differ from each other in cultural and economic terms.

2   The study of Siberia's history

Unlike other regions of the Eurasian continent Siberia began to be studied a relatively short time ago. The reason for this was the difficulty of access to the area, particularly its central and northern parts. Therefore, historians writing in ancient times pictured the territory of Siberia as a vast, uninhabited and cold desert where so-called 'hyperborians', unreal fantasy creatures, dwelt.

Nevertheless, some information about Siberia and its inhabitants did reach the 'civilized world'. In particular, it can be found in *Geography*, written at the beginning of the first century CE by Strabo, an ancient Greek historian. In the seventh century the Gothic historian Jordanes wrote in his work about the origin and deeds of the Goths (see *The Gothic History of Jordanes*, Cambridge, 1966) that in the east, beyond the Ural Mountains, there was the land of the Yugra people who dwelt in the forests and whose chief occupation was hunting; the land of Ugra was rich in furs. In particular, Jordanes noted the abundance of the 'silver sable' whose fur was highly esteemed in Europe.

The famous Chinese historian Ssu-ma Ch'ien gave more information about Siberia than other ancient historians. In his famous work *Shi Tsi* (see *The Grand Scribe's Records*, ed. W. Nienhauser, Bloomington, 1994), written in the late second or early first century BCE, he left a detailed description of the 'Empire of the Huns', their history and population, which also touched on some parts of southern Siberia.

In the Middle Ages, the world-famous European explorers Plano Carpini (Friar Pian del Carpine), Wilhelm von Rubruk, Marco Polo, and the famous Arabian historians Asad Gardizi, Rashid ad-Din, Ibn Batuta, and others wrote about the peoples of Siberia. Though none of them had visited Siberia, they made a detailed description of its nature and inhabitants from the evidence of those who had been there. Thus, Gardizi, for example, wrote in the eleventh century about the Yenisei Kirghiz and a mysterious Siberian people, the 'Furi'. All of these descriptions were inaccurate. They contained a good deal of invention, but, nevertheless, they still communicated the first information (even if it was vague) about Siberia. Much more detail about the history of the south Siberian peoples is contained in medieval Chinese chronicles; it is from Chinese sources that experts learn about the history of ancient Siberian states and peoples.

The ancient Russians (*Rus*) also knew about Siberia. It was first mentioned in the eleventh century in the still extant *Novgorod Chronicles*. There is some information about Siberia (the Land of Yugra) and its people in the *Lavrentiev Chronicle* (the second half of the fourteenth century) and in the *Ipatev Chronicle* (early fifteenth century). These chronicles are one of the main sources for the study of ancient Russia. They describe the marches of the Novgorod people into the 'Land of Yugra and Samoiad', and the 'Yugra and Samoiad' peoples too. Siberia became an object of systematic studies only after its unification with Russia.

As early as the seventeenth century, when Siberia had not yet been completely conquered, the *Siberian Chronicles* emerged. They were remarkable examples of historiography. In these accounts the explorers involved in the conquest of Siberia (*zemleprokhodtsy*) sought to tell about their heroic deeds, and about the lands and peoples they had discovered and conquered.

In 1621, by order of the first Siberian bishop, Kiprian, survivors from Yermak's expedition were gathered in Tobolsk, and *Tales of Siberian Marches* (*Napisanie, kako priidosha v Sibir'*) were compiled which have not survived. They were used as a basis for subsequent chronicles. The chronicle *About the Seizure of the Kingdom of Siberia* was written in 1630. Kiprian's former secretary, Savva Yesipov, compiled his chronicle *About Siberia and the Seizure of Siberia* in Tobolsk in 1636 (it is now called the *Yesipov Chronicle* or the *Kiprian Chronicle*). In the middle of the seventeenth century the tale *About the Conquest of the Siberian Land* (the *Stroganov Chronicle*) was written on the basis of earlier chronicles and some documents belonging to the Stroganov family. In 1680 *The History of Siberia* was published. It was written by Yuri Krizhanich (Križanic), a church figure, exiled to Siberia. At the very end of the seventeenth century the cartographer and historian Semion Remezov compiled a *History of Siberia* on the basis of earlier chronicles, as well as his famous *Book of Drawings of Siberia*, the country's first geographical atlas.

The Siberian chronicles were not historical works in the full sense of the term. The authors wrote down every bit of information they happened to hear or learn about Siberia, the Siberian peoples and historic events. Nonetheless, they are of great value as contemporary sources of information about the history of Siberia of the sixteenth and seventeenth centuries. All later researchers of this epoch, including present-day scholars, have needed to use them.

Scholarly study of Siberia began in the eighteenth century after Peter the Great's reforms. In the middle of the eighteenth century, the academician **G.F. Müller** wrote a most valuable two-volume work, *The History of Siberia*, in which he gathered and generalized all information about Siberia known by that time. Müller's work became an outstanding event in Russian and international historical science. It is precisely this work that is the starting point of scientific historiography of Siberia.

The study of Siberian history was vigorously pursued between the second half of the eighteenth century and the beginning of the twentieth century. During that period quite a few general historical works on Siberia came out. Perhaps

Gerhard Friedrich Müller (1705–83) was born in Germany and studied at Leipzig University. In 1725 he was invited to Russia to work in the Academy of Sciences. He was in charge of academic publications, and in 1731 became a professor of the Academy. In 1733–43 he was the chief of the team despatched by the Academy to participate in the Great Northern Expedition. He travelled throughout Siberia from the Urals to Nerchinsk and Yakutsk, examining the archives of many Siberian towns. He discovered, gathered and brought to St Petersburg a vast amount of valuable historical material, known today as 'Müller's 38 Dossiers'. In 1745–6 he worked on the *General Map of the Russian Empire* which was drawn up using the results of the Great Northern Expedition. In 1748–9 he published his fundamental work *A Description of the Kingdom of Siberia*. In 1748 he became a Russian citizen. In the Academy he concentrated on studying history and became one of the authors of the 'Norman Theory of the Origin of the Russian State'. He initiated the establishment of a Department of History in the Academy and was the author of many historical works including the two-volume *History of Siberia*. He died in St Petersburg.

the most significant and interesting of them were published at the end of the nineteenth century. These consist of a two-volume work by P.A. Slovtsov, *An Historical Survey of Siberia* (1886 and 1888), and a five-volume work, *An Historical Essay on Siberia*, by V.K. Andrievich (1889), as well as *A Chronological List of the Most Important Data on the History of Siberia* (1884) by I.V. Shcheglov. In addition to works of a general nature, a large number of major and minor works were published devoted to specific issues in Siberian history.

On the whole, by 1917 researchers had investigated the history of the annexation of Siberia to Russia and its exploration by Russians relatively well. The pre-Russian period in the Siberian history had been investigated far more sketchily: scholars had only just started searching for and gathering relevant historical sources and material.

The study of Siberian history was continued in the Soviet era. After 1917 a vast number of books and articles came out, devoted to various aspects of it, and they contained a large quantity of previously unknown facts. Soviet historians were particularly successful in researching the ancient history of Siberia, from the Stone Age to the arrival of the Russians. This great work was headed by academician **A.P. Okladnikov**, who, on the basis of new archaeological finds and the thorough investigation of ancient sources, succeeded in restoring the history of many Siberian peoples, both those surviving till the present-day and some who had died out a long time ago.

The high level achieved in the study of Siberian history was reflected in a fundamental five-volume work *The History of Siberia* prepared by the Siberian branch of the Academy of Sciences (1968–9). In addition, a large number

Alexei Pavlovich Okladnikov (1908–81) was born in the village Anga, Irkutsk Province. He graduated from Irkutsk Teacher Training College and later completed a postgraduate course in Leningrad State University. From the end of the 1920s to the early 1930s he was engaged in Young Communist League (*Komsomol*) work in Irkutsk. Between 1938 and 1961 he worked in the Leningrad branch of the Archeological Institute of the USSR Academy of Sciences undertaking archaeological investigations in Siberia. From 1961 to 1966 he was Head of the Humanities Department in the Institute of Economy of the Siberian branch of the USSR Academy of Sciences. From 1964 he was an Associate Member of the USSR Academy of Sciences, becoming a full member in 1968. He was the founder of the Institute of History, Philology, and Philosophy at the Siberian branch of the Academy of Sciences in Akademgorodok, being its first director between 1966 and 1981. He founded the Siberian School of Archaeology, making a number of outstanding archaeological discoveries proving the existence of ancient civilizations in Siberia. He was the author of many works on the archaeology and history of Siberia and the adjoining regions.

of new, interesting and weighty historical works on Siberian themes were published after its publication.

Nevertheless, Soviet Siberian historiography suffered from a grave short-coming that adversely affected the results and quality of its historical researches. As is well-known, the Marxist party's class approach to history was used as the foundation for the whole of Soviet historical work. Its corner-stone was the theory that class struggle was the major motivational force in history. Activities of various classes were assessed in accordance with this theory as either 'reactionary' (negative) or 'progressive' (positive).

The class approach to history led Soviet researchers to a distorted representation of many aspects of Siberian history. Most attention was paid to the class struggle; its scale, significance and results were artificially overestimated. Class struggle was looked for and 'found' even where there was no place for it, for example, among the peoples of the Siberian north who had a tribal social system. Another vivid example of the influence of the class struggle approach on Siberian historiography is the way the Russian Orthodox Church's role in exploring Siberia was treated. Since from the Marxist point of view the Church was an organization for the class oppression of the workers, historians primarily searched for and overstressed negative facts about its activities. The enormous constructive role played by the Orthodox Church in the economic and, particularly, the cultural development of Siberia was either ignored or just mentioned in passing. Similarly, the work of many prominent Siberian historical figures was assessed in contradictory ways.

The class approach had a particularly negative effect on research into the Soviet period of Siberian history. The greatest number of errors and misrepresentations of historical truth was made in regard to the events of the Russian

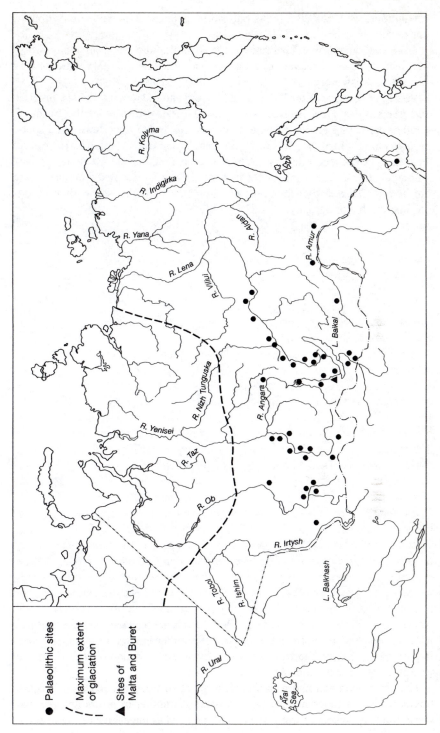

Figure 2.1 The Palaeolithic era in Sibera

Palaeolithic sites
Maximum extent
of glaciation
Sites of
Malta and Buret

R. Kolyma
R. Indigirka
R. Yana
R. Lena
R. Aldan
R. Viliui
R. Amur
L. Baikal
R. Nizh Tunguska
R. Angara
R. Yenisei
R. Taz
R. Ob
R. Irtysh
R. Tobol
R. Ishim
L. Balkhash
R. Ural
Aral Sea

revolutions, the Civil War, industrialization, collectivization and other important themes.[1]

In sum, though Soviet historians made advances in researching many historical issues, the interpretation of Siberian history within the Marxist framework proved unsatisfactory.

After the collapse of the Communist system and ideology in Russia, Siberian historians did a great deal of work during the last decade of the twentieth century correcting earlier mistakes and throwing light on the 'unstudied spots' in the region's history. However, this task is far from complete. A uniform conception of Siberian history has yet to be created. Nowadays, there is a lack of major generalizing works on the history of Siberia presented with due regard for both the latest achievements in research and the findings of earlier periods in Siberian historiography.

Part II
Siberia in antiquity

3   Siberia in the Stone Age

The Stone Age is understood as a period in the history of humanity between the emergence of man and the time when metal began to be used. Stone Age people used stone, wood and bone as tools. The Stone Age[1] is subdivided into:

- *the Palaeolithic era* (the old Stone Age) – from 2.5 million to 10,000 years ago;
- *the Mesolithic era* (the middle Stone Age) – from 10,000 to 8,000–7,000 years ago; and
- *the Neolithic era* (the new Stone Age) – from 8,000–7,000 to 6,000–5,000 years ago (the fourth to third millennia BCE).[2]

Siberia was not the place where humanity originated, since its climate has been severe throughout human history and the life of ancient people was entirely dependent on the environment.

The earliest history of humanity went on against a background of global natural changes, which affected it greatly. The period in the history of Earth connected with the emergence of man, the Anthropogenic era, consisted of three stages:

- *the Aeopleistocene* (the beginning of Pleistocene) – the pre-glacial epoch, lasting from the emergence of man (2.5 million years ago) to 600,000 years ago;
- *the Pleistocene* – the glacial epoch (the period of extreme cold), lasting from 600,000 years ago to 10,000 years ago; and
- *the Holocene* – the present natural geographic environment, which set in about 10,000 years ago.

The Pleistocene era was not entirely cold. It had glacial periods alternating with warmer times, in which the ice retreated; each period manifesting itself in various ways in different regions of the planet. In Siberia the glaciation occurred on a considerably smaller scale than in Europe and North America.

The emergence of ancient man in Siberia was conditioned particularly by the fact that some regions on Earth became unfit for habitation and people were forced to look for new places to settle. The southern part of Siberia became one of those. There was no ice sheet here, and the rich vegetation and wildlife (mammoths, woolly rhinoceroses, cave bears, deer, etc.) created favourable conditions for life, notwithstanding the severe climate. The migration of human beings into Siberia lasted throughout the Stone Age. It was a slow, lengthy and continuous process. People migrated into Siberia from Eastern Europe and also from central Asia.

According to the data we have at present, early humans appeared in Siberia about 100,000 years ago.[3] Palaeolithic camping sites have been found in many regions of the southern part of Siberia. The best-studied and well-known sites are at Malta and Buret in the River Belaia area, in Irkutsk Oblast.

In Siberia, Palaeolithic people led a semi-nomadic life. They lived in small settlements and used animal bones and skins as building materials. They made shallow depressions in the ground in which they anchored mammoth ribs as a framework. The ceilings and floors were made from deer antlers tied together. That structure was tightly wrapped with skins and there was a hearth in the centre of the dwelling.[4] The Palaeolithic people were mostly hunters and gatherers, with collective forms of social organization prevailing. Their tools were stone scrapers, knives, spearheads, wooden sticks, bone needles and awls, etc.

They also had a well-developed art. At the Malta and Buret campsites archaeologists found small female statuettes made from bone (about 30 per cent of the total world findings of this type). The statuettes personified the cult of the woman and fertility. The Palaeolithic people practised polygamy, whereby the father of the child was unknown and the family origin was traced from the mother. It was on the woman's fertility that the continuation of each family depended. Women, therefore, were highly honoured. Besides the statuettes, many decorations made from bone have been found at Palaeolithic sites, including necklaces and amulets. Apparently, the ancient people attached a particular significance to them: they were believed to protect hunters and bring luck.

In the late Palaeolithic and Mesolithic eras humans gradually spread throughout the whole of Siberia. This dispersion was caused by changes in natural and climatic conditions. With the advent of the Holocene, the southern and central parts of Siberia were gradually covered with forests. Mammoths and woolly rhinoceroses, the principal game for the early hunters, migrated still farther northward in search of pastures; the people were obliged to follow them. During the Mesolithic period tools were improved: the bow and arrow and fishing harpoon were invented; far finer stone tools were processed.

The environment of early man in Siberia had completely changed by the beginning of the Neolithic period (8,000–7,000 BCE). All the big animals – mammoths and woolly rhinoceroses – had died out, and the present-day landscape had been formed. The changes made the people look for new ways of life since their former mode of existence no longer allowed them to provide for themselves.

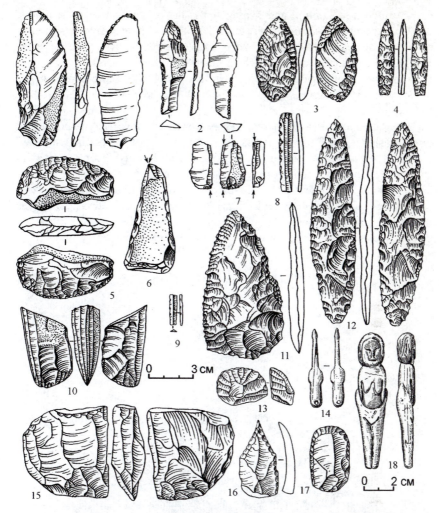

Figure 3.1 Late Palaeolithic tools. 1–12 from Diuktai Cave, 13–18 from Malta. 1. Retouched blade; 2, 6–7 chisels; 3, 4 and 12 spear heads; 5 scraper; 8 and 9 micro blades; 11 double-bladed knife; 10 and 15 wedge-shaped tools; 13 and 17 scrapers; 16 hole piercer; 14 and 18 bone figurines of birds and women

During the Neolithic period revolutionary changes took place in human history. The ancient people:

* considerably improved stone processing techniques – they learned to drill and polish stone – and developed new tools (stone axes, cutters, etc.);
* discovered means of manufacturing ceramics (pottery appeared and was used for cooking and the preservation of food);

- invented new hunting and fishing tools (the canoe, fishing rods, hooks, etc.) and developed improved forms of bow and harpoon;
- domesticated animals (dogs, sheep, etc.);
- started cultivating the land, which diversified their diet; and
- improved dwelling construction technique (marked by more extensive use of wood in building).

As a result, these ancient people created conditions for a more secure and stable existence and further progress. In Siberia, the Neolithic period witnessed a gradual cessation of early human economic uniformity. People started to engage in whatever activities provided them with the best means of subsistence. Groups in different parts of Siberia practised different occupations to support life, either hunting or fishing, depending on the natural conditions of a given area. However, Neolithic people in Siberia did not raise livestock or cultivate the land owing to the severe climatic conditions.

Figure 3.2 Reconstruction of tepee-style dwelling at the Malta site

4 Siberia in the Bronze Age

The Bronze Age[1] arrived in Siberia in the second half of the third millennium BCE (about 4,500 years ago) when people mastered the art of making objects from metal, and their lives underwent important changes. The Bronze Age in Siberia lasted about 2,000 years, until the second half of the first millennium BCE.

The Bronze Age in Siberia did not evolve in a homogeneous fashion. The population made a gradual transition from the new Stone to Bronze, the changes coming earliest in southern Siberia, in the mountains and foothills of the Altai, the Kuznetsk Alatau, the Saian and Transbaikalia where there were easily accessible non-ferrous and precious metal deposits (copper, tin, silver, gold, etc.), and favourable natural conditions (fertile river valleys, alpine meadows and wooded-steppes). In the northern part of Siberia and the Far East, where there were no accessible non-ferrous metal deposits, people continued to live in the Neolithic period, and would only rarely get the occasional imported metal object.

Archaeology has revealed that during the Bronze Age there was a succession of cultures in southern Siberia; they have been named after the location of the respective discoveries.[2]

The first Siberian Bronze Age culture known of at present is the *Afanasevo* culture (second half of the third millennium – middle of the second millennium BCE). It was located between the Altai and Saian mountains, in the meadow and steppe areas in the foothills, where it was easy to discover copper ore outcroppings and to move on to husbandry and cultivation of the land.

The Afanasevo people were the first in Siberia to use metals and objects made from them. They obtained soft metals (copper, tin, silver and gold) in native form, then processed them by cold forging and made decorations – bracelets, necklaces, etc. Metal casting technology was unknown to them; therefore, the Afanasevo people made more extensive use of stone than metal tools. From stone they made axes, hoes, tips for spears, arrowheads, knives, etc.

The second accomplishment that distinguished the Afanasevo people from other inhabitants of Siberia was their transition to livestock breeding and arable farming. They bred all the major species of domestic animals: sheep, cows and horses. Their knowledge of farming was limited, based on the use of

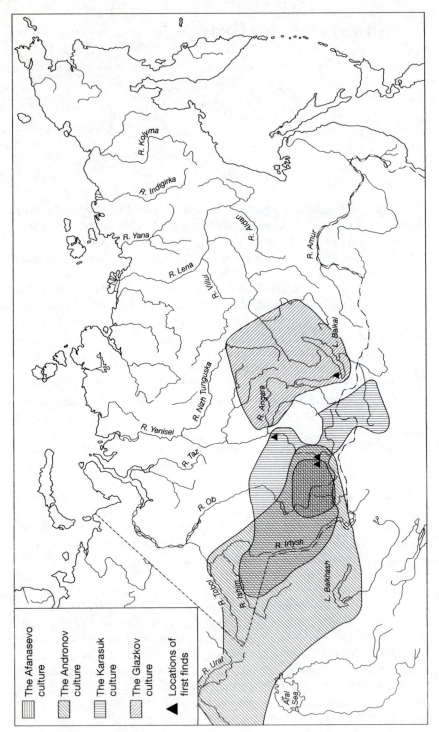

Figure 4.1 Siberia in the Bronze Age

pickaxe-like digging sticks (mattocks). However, they were unable to support themselves entirely by farming and livestock-raising. The hunting and gathering traditional for ancient man still played a significant role in their lives.

The people of the Afanasevo culture had a semi-nomadic mode of life. They lived in small family settlements. The predominant type of dwelling was a

Figure 4.2 Bronze Age Siberia. 1–5 from the Karasuk culture; 6–17 from the Glazkov culture. 1–2 Bronze daggers; 3–5 bronze decorations (horse brass, ring, pin); 6 and 7 reconstruction of human clothing; 8 unidentified; 9 piercer; 10 and 13 scrapers; 11 knife; 12 compound fish hook; 14 straightener for arrow shafts; 15 compound knife; 16 and 17 adzes

semi-dugout hut (a hole in the ground over which a small wooden frame was erected). Racially the Afanasevo people were Europeoid.

In the middle of the second millennium BCE they were replaced by the *Andronovo* culture in southern Siberia. The Andronovo culture (mid-second millennium – end of the second millennium BCE) covered a far larger area – from the Saian to the Urals.

The Andronovo people mastered metal smelting. They mined non-ferrous and precious metals by excavating shallow pits using stone tools, then smelted the ore in special furnaces dug into the ground, and cast it in stone moulds prepared in advance. After moulding, the outer surfaces of the metal items were subject to additional forging. During the forging, the metal was consolidated and the blades were sharpened. From the metal, the Andronovo people made various tools (axes, needles, knives, etc.), weapons (arrowheads and spearheads) and also decorations. The development of metallurgy gradually led to a reduction in the use of stone and it was finally abandoned altogether.

In this period livestock breeding was further developed. The Andronovo people, like their Afanasevo predecessors, raised all major species of livestock. Their main form of livestock was cows, which gave skin, meat and dairy products.[3] Sheep were second in significance. Their fleeces were used for making sheepskin coats, and the wool was also spun. The Andronovo people practised semi-migratory livestock breeding, with summer and winter pastures and harvested fodder for winter. Because of livestock-raising the traditional occupations of early humans – hunting, fishing and gathering – gradually lost their significance around this time.

In this period the art of ceramics was further developed. Instead of primitive pots, the Andronovo people made ornamented items more perfect in shape and quality.

The people of the Andronovo culture lived in settlements. The main type of dwelling was a big rectangular semi-dugout hut up to 150 square metres in size. The earthen walls (no less than one metre high) were lined with stone slabs and a small frame was built on top. There were hearths in the centre of these dugouts and there were plank beds along the walls. It appears that several families of the same clan lived in them together.

It would seem that the social elevation of males began at this period. Men gradually monopolized all basic occupations of the time – livestock-raising, metallurgy, handicraft and warfare. As a result, their role in society increased and that of the woman was reduced, limited to housekeeping and bringing up children. This was caused by a general rise in the standard of living.

At the end of the second millennium BCE the Karasuk culture replaced the Andronovo culture. The *Karasuk* culture (late second millennium – early first millennium BCE) is considered the high point of the Bronze Age in Siberia, when the art of metal-casting reached its peak. The people of this culture cast various metal items (tools, household objects, weapons, decorations, etc.).

In the period of the Karasuk culture, livestock-breeding rose to first place among the occupations of the south Siberian people. It provided all the necessities for people's lives (food, wool and leather). Livestock herding was cyclic or semi-migratory: the livestock were kept indoors in winter and pastured in the open air during the summer. The Karasuk people, like their predecessors, lived in settlements and lived in spacious semi-dugout dwellings.

The Karasuk people mastered the art of horse riding. They started making a simple bridle for horses (without hard bits), but saddles were not used as yet. Horse riding enabled people to become more mobile, which encouraged wider inter-ethnic relationships. They therefore had widespread relations with their neighbours. Karasuk metal articles were distributed throughout many parts of Siberia up to Yakutia and other contiguous territories.

In eastern Siberia the people maintained the mode of life of their predecessors during the Bronze Age – fishing, hunting and gathering. Nonetheless, the use of metal changed their lives considerably. The Bronze Age culture of the eastern Siberian tribes has received the name Glazkov. The *Glazkov* culture (seventeenth to thirteenth centuries BCE) flourished between the River Yenisei and Lake Baikal. In addition to this, small local cultures existed at the same time in Transbaikalia, where there were a considerable number of open deposits of non-ferrous and precious metals.

The people of the Glazkov culture first cold-forged metal discovered in its natural form, and then later mastered casting techniques. They produced knives, needles, fishing hooks and other tools, weapons and decorations. However, their form was less sophisticated than that produced by the cultures of the Altai-Yenisei region.

The use of metal allowed them to make considerable improvements to their fishing tools, such as hooks. Consequently, fishing became more effective and became the main occupation of the Glazkov people. Fishing, hunting and gathering dictated a semi-nomadic mode of life. The Glazkov people built light transportable dwellings of the *chum* type (a kind of a tepee made of skin or bark).

Socially, the Glazkov people were going through a process analogous to that of the Altai-Yenisei cultures. The main tendency was towards an elevation of the role of men in society. Glazkov burial ceremonies testify to this: widows were forcibly killed and put in the grave with their dead husband. Some graves with Shamanic attributes have been found at Glazkov burial sites, indicating the birth of Shamanism.[4]

5   Siberia in the Scythian period

The first millennium BCE in the history of the Eurasian steppe peoples has been named the Scythian era.[1] During this period people inhabiting a vast territory from the Danube to Transbaikalia and Manchuria shared common features in their material and artistic culture, as well as their social systems.

In the Scythian period Siberia's inhabitants gradually mastered the art of iron working. Items made of iron and ancient iron mines have been found in many regions of Siberia. Consequently, there were considerable changes in the way of life and domestic economy of the southern Siberian peoples. Several very large archaeological cultures have been discovered here. The best-known and most thoroughly studied of these are the Tagar, Pazyryk and 'Slab-Grave' cultures. Meanwhile, the way of life of the northern Siberian tribes and the tribes of the Far East differed little from that of previous epochs.

The *Tagar* culture (flourished in seventh to second centuries BCE) covered the region of the Minusinsk Basin in the upper reaches of the Yenisei River. Livestock breeding constituted the economic basis of this culture, whose people combined semi-settled and migratory types of herding. Their ability to ride horses allowed the Tagar people to develop a migratory cattle herding system, using all-year pasturage on the steppe lands in their territory. On the remaining parts of their territory, the Tagar people employed the old semi-settled, cyclic type of livestock herding. Agriculture was further developed during the Tagar culture period. Although the mattock remained the main tool, people started building and using irrigation systems to water fields in the Minusinsk Basin. In this culture metallurgy gradually began to turn into a separate industry. Bronze casting was developed to an exceptional perfection. The artefacts made by Tagar master craftsmen were distributed throughout Siberia, central Asia and Eastern Europe. From the fifth century BCE the people of the Tagar culture mastered the art of producing iron, from which they made the most necessary items for life, such as axes, weapons, knives, mattocks, etc.

The combination of settled and migratory livestock breeding and the mastering of iron production led to improvements in housing. The Tagar people used two types of dwelling: a light collapsible one, the *yurta*,[2] and a solid one. They began to build log huts, instead of semi-dugouts, containing open hearths.

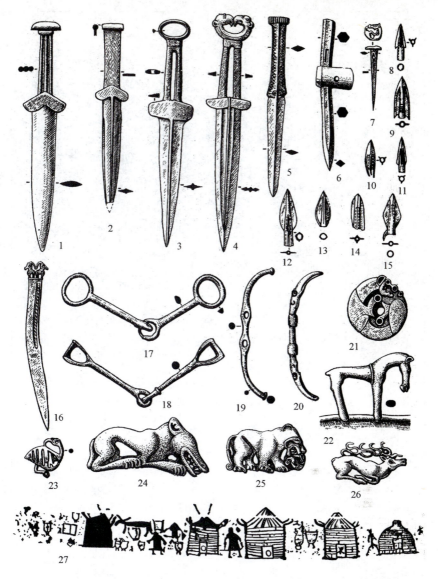

Figure 5.1 The Tagar culture. 1–5 daggers; 6 stamp; 7 nail; 8–15 arrow heads; 16 knife; 17 and 18 horse bits; 19 and 20 harness sections; 21, 23–26 horse brasses; 22 handle for cooking pot; 27 petroglyphs

The Tagar people created a highly developed artistic culture. Their art was of an applied nature and used the 'Scythian-Siberian animalistic style'.[3] They reached a very high level in the production of animal figurines and various decorations, using gold, bronze, bone, horn and wood as working materials. Tagar rock paintings survive to this day.

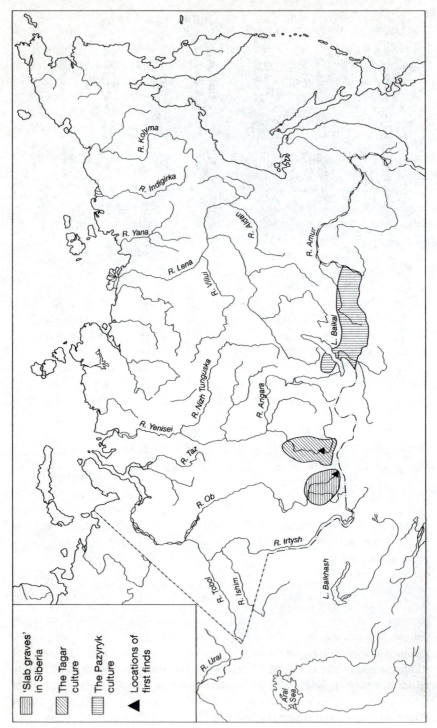

'Slab graves' in Siberia

The Tagar culture

The Pazyryk culture

▲ Locations of first finds

R. Kolyma

R. Indigirka

R. Yana

R. Aldan

R. Amur

R. Lena

R. Vilui

L. Baikal

R. Nizh Tunguska

R. Angara

R. Yenisei

R. Taz

R. Ob

R. Irtysh

L. Balkhash

R. Tobol

R. Ishim

R. Ural

Aral Sea

Figure 5.2 Siberia in the Scythian period

The process of social stratification became much more marked among the people of the Tagar culture. Like other Siberian peoples they lived in a kinship system. At the same time, wealthy kinsmen and the tribal elite achieved special prominence: huge *kurgany*[4] were built over their graves. The largest Tagar tumulus, the Salbyk *kurgan*, was 11 metres high with a base 500 metres in diameter. Around it there was a ring of huge, six-metre vertical stone slabs, each weighing 20–50 tons. A noble warrior, with his slaves and wives, was buried in the tumulus. The Tagar people were of the Europeoid anthropological type.

The *Pazyryk* culture (fifth to third centuries BCE) was located in the Altai. Like the Tagar people, the people of the Pazyryk culture were livestock breeders. However, they had progressed to migratory livestock breeding which influenced their life significantly. The Pazyryk people raised all kinds of livestock, which gave them food (meat and milk products) and clothing. They made fabrics and felt from wool and they sewed footwear, overcoats and household items from leather. The transition to migratory livestock breeding gave the horse a more important role as a form of transport in the life of the people. Horse breeding gradually became an independent industry. The Pazyryk people bred and used two main breeds of horse: a short and hardy type and a tall, lean-legged type, both from central Asia. They invented the saddle[5] and improved the harness making it possible to cover long distances faster.

The transition to migratory livestock breeding made for a mobile way of life, too. The light, collapsible felt *yurta* became the dominant type of dwelling. Migratory livestock breeding and nomadic life caused the emergence of carts for transportation: the Pazyryk culture people knew about the wheel and

Figure 5.3 Tagar burial mound excavations

employed two kinds of carts: square, box-like carts to carry cargo, drawn by oxen, and light chariots for moving people, in this case drawn by horses.

The migratory livestock breeding and nomadic life of the Pazyryk people caused inter-ethnic relationships and contacts to expand, even including distant peoples. The Pazyryk tumuli contained objects from Persia (a carpet, fabrics), central Asia (coriander seeds, southern timber species, the remains of horses) and China (silk, bronzes, mirrors). The most valuable of these is the Persian carpet, which is the oldest relic of carpet manufacturing. Its distinguishing feature is very fine work (the carpet contains 1.25 million knots). The Roman emperor Hadrian paid 108 tons of bronze (four million *sestertii*[6]) for a similar carpet in the first century AD.

The Pazyryk people, like the Tagars, developed metal production further, reaching a very high level in bronze casting. They also mastered the art of iron production, from which they made tools, household items and weapons.

The Pazyryk people also reached a very high level in the applied arts in the 'Scythian-Siberian animalistic style'. They made sculptures of animals, as well as bas-reliefs and silhouettes, on metal, bone, wood, skin, furs and felt, which they used to decorate many objects. The Pazyryk people also tattooed pictures of animals on their bodies.

The transition to migratory livestock breeding and a nomadic life, the accumulation of large numbers of livestock and the mastering of metal production caused an increase in the role of war. Wars were waged for livestock and profitable pastures, gradually becoming an inseparable part of nomadic life. The frequent battles contributed to improvements in methods of warfare and weapons. Cavalry became the main armed force. In battle, the Pazyryk warriors mainly used bows; the arrows had triple-bladed heads, making them steadier in flight. Besides this, they used long daggers with embossed hilts.[7] Protection from enemies was ensured by shields fashioned from wooden boards secured together with strips of leather.

The Pazyryk people were in an active process of social stratification. They had a clan system. Wealthy kinsmen and tribal noblemen achieved distinction judging by the large mounds in the Pazyryk Valley and on the Yukok Plateau, which were erected above the graves of the chiefs of clans, tribes and tribal alliances. The most famous of them is the Great Pazyryk mound, consisting of a large hill built from earth and stones, around 2,000 cubic metres in volume. Beneath it there was a chamber, 200 cubic metres in volume, in which a grave had been built surmounted with a layer of about 500 logs. The chief of a tribe or a tribal union had been buried in this tumulus in a wooden sarcophagus made of larch, together with his wives and slaves, 14 horses and a large number of varied objects (a chariot, saddles, carpets, pottery, clothing, decorations, weapons, etc.).

The 'Slab-Grave' culture (thirteenth to third centuries BCE) covered a very widespread territory in the steppes and wooded steppes, including land to the west of Lake Baikal, Transbaikalia to the east of it, Eastern, Central and Inner Mongolia. In this culture, a wall made of vertical stone slabs as high as one to two metres was built around the burial place (hence the name). The economy of the Slab-Grave culture was also founded on nomadic herding. Its people raised livestock of all kinds which they used for food and clothing. However, sheep and horses prevailed in their herds, being the most common species for a nomadic form of livestock-raising. The combination of nomadic herding, a wandering lifestyle, and a vast territory of settlement led to significant mobility and to the development of inter-ethnic relationships and contacts with other peoples. Archaeological findings provide evidence of such relationships with the inhabitants of the steppe and wooded-steppe zone of Eurasia, from China to ancient Scythia (on the northern shore of the Black Sea).

This nomadic mode of life with its accumulation of large herds of livestock caused an enhanced military element in the life of the Slab-Grave Culture people. Like the Pazyryk people, they fought wars for livestock and profitable pastureland, and such warfare gradually became an inseparable part of life. The fact that knives and weapons are the most common archaeological arte-facts retrieved from the Slab-Graves points to the significant role of warfare in their culture. Their society was also in the process of social stratification, but to a less pronounced degree than in the Tagar and Pazyryk cultures. Slab graves also vary in their size and the quantity of relics.

The people of this culture also made progress in developing metal produc-tion, which was encouraged by rich and open deposits of copper, tin, lead and silver (in Transbaikalia, in particular). They built mines and smelting furnaces.

Figure 5.4 A slab grave

Ore was mined with the help of stone tools; picks, wedges and spades. Moulds were also made from stone, shale being used most frequently. Gradually, the people of this culture mastered the art of iron production and the metal was used for tools, household objects and weapons.

In common with other peoples of southern Siberia the people of the Slab-Grave culture reached a very high level in the applied arts, using the 'Scythian-Siberian animalistic style'. They decorated weapons, pieces of clothing, horse harnesses, large numbers of household objects, etc. with animal drawings. They used gold, silver, copper, horn, bone, wood and skin. A significant artistic peculiarity of the Slab-Grave culture of the earlier period are the 'deer stones' – vertically placed, quadrangular, hewed stones with drawings of running deer on them. In the second half of the period, these stones apparently lost their significance and began to be used as grave walls. Rock paintings from this culture have survived too. The Slab-Grave people were of Mongoloid anthropological type.

Figure 5.5
A deer stone

6   Siberia in the period of the Huns

The end of the first millennium BCE and the beginning of the first millennium CE have been called the 'period of the Huns' in Siberian historiography. Originally, the Hunnic tribes inhabited the territory of the present-day Chinese province of Inner Mongolia (the ancient Ordos). The Huns were destined to play a significant role in the history of many Eurasian peoples, including those in Siberia. In their mode of life, the Huns were typical livestock breeders. They lived in felt *yurtas*, they had a well-developed material and artistic culture and they were warriors. According to their anthropological type, they are referred to as Mongoloids.

Dwelling beyond the northern boundaries of China, they travel with their livestock from pasture to pasture. As regards livestock they keep mainly horses, cattle, and small horned cattle [sheep and goats]. To an extent they raise camels, donkeys, wild asses, and horses of the best breeds. They migrate from place to place in search of more grass and water. They feed on livestock, they are dressed in its skins; they cover themselves with woollen and fur garments.

(Ssu-ma Ch'ien, an ancient Chinese historian, first century BCE)

In 209 BCE the unification of 24 Hunnic groups into a single military tribal confederacy occurred, which later received the name 'the Hunnic Empire'. The founder of this empire was the *shan-yü*[1] **Modae**. The Hunnic tribal union took over the territory of the former Slab-Graves culture.

The Hunnic Empire had the embryo of a state structure. The *shan-yü* had advisers and interpreters (most frequently they were captured Chinese commanders and officers). The Hunnic tribes making up the nucleus of the Empire were divided into two wings: the western and eastern. Subsequently conquered peoples also entered the confederation under the control of governors appointed by the *shan-yü*. These peoples paid the *shan-yü* unsystematic tribute which he divided proportionally between all the Hunnic tribes; the entire spoils of war were divided according to the same principle. The Huns did not interfere in the life of the conquered peoples unless they were disloyal to them. Modae

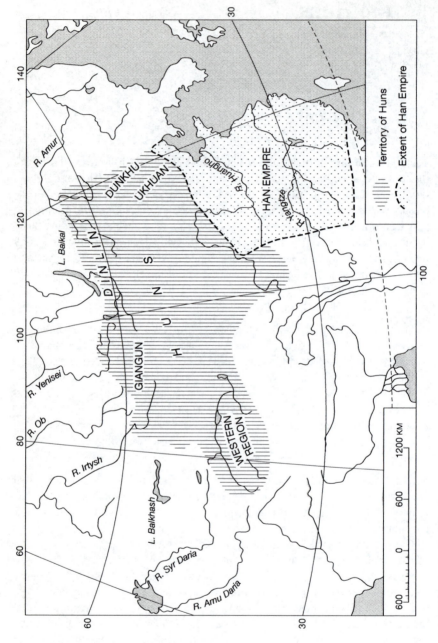

Figure 6.1 Siberia in the period of the Huns

Modae (birth date unknown – 174 BCE) was the founder of the Hunnic Empire, *shan-yŭ* in 209–174 BCE. He was very cruel and strong-willed. He seized power by a plot, having murdered his father, his younger brother and many relatives. He formed a powerful Hunnic army. In 200 BCE he won a victory in war against China and forced the latter to pay tribute (he also married a Chinese princess). He conquered many tribes in central Asia and southern Siberia. Numerous legends are associated with his name.

formed a strict military hierarchical system: all of the tribal chiefs were the *shan-yŭ*'s military commanders and hence obeyed him implicitly. Yet they were fully independent in managing their own tribes.

Warfare became the strongest point of the Hunnic Empire and *Shan-yŭ* Modae and his successors contributed a great deal to its development. The Huns invented a complex bow up to 1.5 metres in size, capable of shooting farther and having a higher force of impact than previous types. They used massive, three-bladed iron arrowheads with notches, which inflicted additional injuries while being extracted from the body. Besides this, the Huns fixed a peculiar 'psychological weapon' on their arrows, behind the tips. These were hollow bone balls called 'whistlers', which produced a terrifying sound in flight. Bows and arrows became their main weapons. In addition, iron daggers, spears with iron tips, and wooden shields were used.

Modae created a united army, numbering up to several tens of thousands. All men capable of fighting were included. The army was organized on the basis of a convenient and simple decimal system (tens, hundreds, thousands, etc.), which was later used by all nomadic states. Cavalry was the shock force of the army. It was divided into four corps according to the horses' coats (black, bay, white and grey), which also had a psychological effect on the enemy. The Hunnic army had strict discipline. Improvements in military organization and weapons made it possible for the Huns to perfect a war tactic based on high mobility, surprise and all-out attacks.

They advance while they have good fortune; they retreat when they have bad luck, and are not ashamed of being routed. They artfully decoy the adversary to surround him. Seeing the adversary they rush for spoil like a flock of birds, but when defeated scatter like broken tiles, disperse like clouds.

(Ssu-ma Ch'ien, an ancient Chinese historian, first century BCE)

The Huns' military achievements made their army unconquerable. Warfare became a significant part of their existence. *Shan-yŭ* Modae and his successors fought a number of triumphant wars against China.[2] The Huns succeeded in conquering a vast territory from Manchuria in the east to the Tien Shan Mountains in the west, and from the Great Wall of China in the south to Lake Baikal in the north. The southern regions of Siberia, Transbaikalia, the Upper Yenisei (present-day Tuva [Tyva] and Khakassia) and the Altai, also became part of the Hunnic Empire.

Early Chinese sources called the population of the Altai-Yenisei region the *Dinlin*. The Huns conquered the Dinlin (some of whom moved northward and eastward). The Huns then re-settled the *Gyangun*, Mongoloid tribes from central Asia, in the vacated lands. This area received the name 'Hiagas'. Hiagas was headed by Chinese governors. It differed from the rest of the Huns' Empire: its population not only engaged in nomadic cattle breeding, but also developed a semi-settled lifestyle, using irrigation to grow crops.

Continuous warfare gradually weakened the Huns, and in the first century CE their empire broke up. A considerable proportion of them migrated towards Europe.

The Hunnic dominance had a considerable influence on the development of the peoples of Siberia, who adopted quite a few innovations from them. In particular, the Huns had more advanced methods of iron working. These methods enabled them to produce a variety of improved iron artefacts. Under their influence the Siberian peoples increased iron production. Thus, a large iron-producing centre emerged on the western bank of Lake Baikal among a people who have been called the 'Yelgin Culture'.

In time Hunnic dominance led to iron artefacts gradually replacing bronze in the life of the Siberian peoples. Various household items, tools and weapons of Hunnic origin became widespread among them. For instance, they began using the horse saddle everywhere, which eased riding. The elaborate Hunnic bow also became widely used. Their ceramic vases and other objects made on the potter's wheel were also very popular.

The Huns influenced the Siberian peoples' art too: a Hunnic form of the 'Scythian-Siberian animalistic style' became widespread. One example is the Hunnic belt-plates with depictions of fighting animals which became popular with the Siberian population. A remarkable relic of the Huns' culture is the burial ground of their emperors, located in Ilmovaia pad near the city of Kiakhta, which contains around 30 burial mounds. Archaeologists have found many valuable items of Hunnic and Chinese origin.

The dominance of the Huns strengthened the influence of Chinese culture and the presence of Chinese people in Siberia. Before they arrived on the scene, Chinese objects such as silks and bronze looking-glasses were scarce in the region; during the time of the Huns their number and variety considerably increased. In addition to fabrics, wooden lacquered objects, ceramics and metal articles were also introduced from China. The Huns also founded several Chinese settlements in Siberia. The most famous of them is the town of Ivol'gino on the outskirts of Ulan-Ude. The Chinese settlers built a fortress here with four banks 1.5–2 metres high and four ditches of the same depth. Inside there were dwellings in a square of about 200–300 metres; some of them were even equipped with an ancient Chinese heating system (the flue from the stove went down the walls along the perimeter of the dwelling). The population of the settlement engaged in making iron and bronze, as well as in agriculture and livestock breeding.

It was during the period of the Huns that the Mongoloid anthropological type became firmly established among the population. The merging of the Gyangun tribes with the remnants of the Dinlin created a new people – the Yenisei Kirghiz who were to play a significant role in the history of Siberia. The emergence of new Turkic speaking tribes 'Tu-Gyu', also greatly influencing Siberia, was another effect of Hunnic dominance.

Part III

Siberia in the first millennium and in the first half of the second millennium CE

7   The Turks in Siberia

The Yenisei Kirghiz State

At the beginning of the first millennium CE the reign of the Huns in Siberia came to an end. New nomadic tribes, called by the Chinese the Syanbi and after them the Zhu-Zhan, came to take their place in central Asia. The Syanbi and Zhu-Zhan periodically made raids on the south Siberian lands, and the native tribes were in subjection to them.

In the fifth century, the nomadic Tu-Gyu (Tu-Kyu) tribes moved to the Altai from central Asia. A Tu-Gyu tribal confederation gradually came into existence; they formed a coalition of tribes inhabiting the Altai region.

In 552–5 CE the coalition, led by the chief of the Tu-Gyu tribal confederation **Tumyn**, defeated the Zhu-Zhan State and formed a new nomadic state, the Turkic Kaghanate, which occupied a vast territory, comprising southern Siberia, Transbaikalia and the Altai-Yenisei region.

The Turkic Kaghanate united nomadic tribes into a state. It had a more complex structure than the Hunnic Empire and its sequel, the nomadic tribal confederacies of Syanbi and Zhu-Zhan. The Kaghanate was headed by a Kaghan,[1] who was elected for life from among Tumyn's nearest kinsmen. The Kaghanate's nucleus was the *Horde*, which acted as its headquarters. It included the Kaghan's family, warriors and servants with their families. The Horde's

Tumyn (birth date unknown – 553 CE), in 535, united the Altai Turkic Tu-Gyu tribes and became their chief. In 536 he helped the central Asian nomadic Zhu-Zhan State in a war against the Uighur tribes and virtually conquered the latter. Subsequently, he asked for the hand in marriage of the daughter of the Zhu-Zhan State's ruler but was refused in an insulting manner. In addition, the Zhu-Zhan demanded that Tumyn become their vassal. Tumyn, in reply, killed the Zhu-Zhan ambassadors and became China's ally, the latter being interested in defeating the Zhu-Zhan who were in the habit of making devastating raids on its lands. In 551 Tumyn married a Chinese princess. In 552 he waged a war against the Zhu-Zhan, defeated them, and destroyed the Zhu-Zhan State. At the same time he took an official title, Kaghan (Il-khan), and formed a new nomadic state – the Turkic Kaghanate.

troops were headed by *Begs* (military commanders). The subjugated tribes were ruled by *Yagbu*, the Kaghan's local governors. These tribes paid tribute to the Kaghan on a regular basis. The tribute was collected by special officials – the *Tarkhans*.

The Turkic Kaghanate had its own written language known as the Orkhono-Yenisei (Orkhon-Türk) script, which was carved on rocks, metal and wood.[2] A remarkable relic of Turkic culture, this writing system was based on the ancient Aramaic alphabet; it arose in the fifth century and was used in southern Siberia, Mongolia and Kazakhstan. With the disappearance of the Turkic Kaghanate it gradually passed out of use. The Yenisei Kirghiz used this written language longer than anyone else.

Figure 7.1
An example of Orkhon
Turkic writing

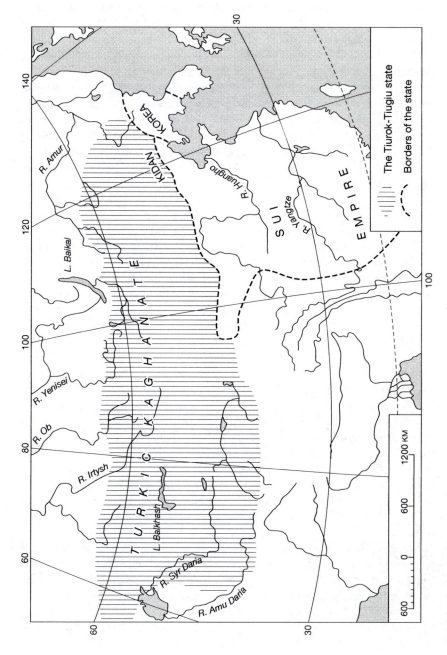

Figure 7.2 The Turkic Kaghanate

The Turkic Kaghanate did not last very long. It split up as a result of a power struggle in the 580s into the west Turkic and the east Turkic Kaghanates, the latter including the territories of southern Siberia. The east Turkic Kaghanate existed as such, except for a short period,[3] until 745 when it was destroyed by the Uighur tribes.

The Turkic, and later, the east Turkic Kaghanates significantly influenced the development of the south Siberian peoples. In the sixth and seventh centuries Turkic material culture spread over almost all southern Siberia, bringing more advanced weapons, horse harnesses, etc. For instance, the Turkic people were the first to start using stirrups, which made horse riding – this important part of nomadic cattle breeders' life – considerably easier. During the ancient Turks' dominion over southern Siberia the Turkic language and writing spread and separate Turkic speaking peoples began to emerge (the Altaians, Shor, Tuvinians, Kirghiz, Kurikan and others).

Finally, the first independent Siberian state, the Kirghiz Kaghanate, arose under the influence of the ancient Turks. It was set up by the Yenisei Kirghiz after the east Turkic Kaghanate broke up in the middle of the eighth century.[4]

The Yenisei Kirghiz[5] emerged from the Gyangun Mongoloid nomadic tribes, who had been driven from central Asia to the Upper Yenisei by the Huns in the first century BCE, merging with the Dinlin, Europeoid tribes of cattle breeders and farmers. Anthropologically, the Kirghiz were of Mongoloid physical type but, by some accounts, they had red hair, rosy complexions and blue eyes. They lived along the Yenisei River from the Saian Mountains to present-day Krasnoiarsk.

The Yenisei Kirghiz state structure was similar to that of the Turkic Kaghanate, with the Kaghan, *Begs*, rank and file soldiers (*Baturs* and *Oglans*) and *Tarkhans*. They also used the ancient Turkic written language.

The economy of the Yenisei Kirghiz was based on nomadic cattle breeding. However, it was not quite typical for nomads. Arable farming, which had earlier fallen into decline in southern Siberia, experienced a revival in the Kirghiz Kaghanate, adopting more advanced techniques: instead of using mattocks they started to employ ploughs. Also, they used irrigation in the dry areas of the Minusinsk Basin. Their chief grain crops were barley, millet, wheat and hemp. Iron sickles were used for reaping. According to Chinese chroniclers, the Yenisei Kirghiz land cultivation and crop growing skills were quite advanced.

The Kirghiz Khaganate had well-developed crafts; their craftsmen made various types of household utensils, work tools and ornaments. Pottery and jewellery-making were particularly prominent. The egg-shaped 'Kirghiz vase', for instance, was widely known in central Asia and southern Siberia.

The Kirghiz Kaghanate maintained regular trade links with the Arabs, Chinese, Tibetans, Uighurs and many Siberian peoples. Camel caravans plied between central Asia and the Kaghanate on a regular basis. The trade was mostly in the form of barter and covered such expensive items as could be afforded only by people of high rank. The Kirghiz bought silk fabrics, bronze

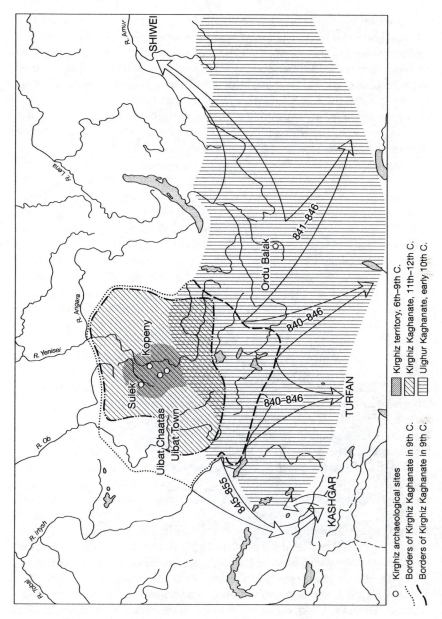

○ Kirghiz archaeological sites

▨ Kirghiz territory, 6th–9th C.
▧ Kirghiz Kaghanate, 11th–12th C.
▤ Uighur Kaghanate, early 10th C.

∙∙∙∙ Borders of Kirghiz Kaghanate in 9th C.
╌╌ Borders of Kirghiz Kaghanate in 9th C.

Figure 7.3 The Yenisei Kirghiz state

mirrors, articles made of lacquered wood, horse harnesses (especially richly inlaid examples) and sold items made of antlers and metal, as well as the furs which they obtained from the peoples of northern Siberia in exchange for metal objects.

Kirghiz society practised customs and traditions common among nomads of the day. For instance, bridegrooms paid *kalym* for their wives-to-be (i.e. the bridegroom had to pay money or other material assets to the girl's parents). Usually *kalym* took the form of a number of cattle. After their wedding women had their necks tattooed, whereas men were tattooed on their faces. On their household farms the Kirghiz used slave labour on a limited scale. These slaves were captured in battle. Defaulting debtors were also turned into slaves. Their favorite pastimes included wrestling, camel and horse racing. Like all Siberian peoples, the Kirghiz practised Shamanism.

Figure 7.4 Kirghiz (on right) and Mongol warriors

As was typical of nomads of their time, the Yenisei Kirghiz were good warriors. They built an army of almost 80,000. Its backbone was the cavalry. With this army they subdued many local tribes and subjected them to tribute. The northern tribes paid it in the form of furs; the southern in the form of cattle. The Kirghiz Kaghanate covered a vast area from west of Lake Baikal to the Altai.

In 840 they defeated the central Asian Uighur tribes and their Kaghanate and established their dominion over the territory of present-day Mongolia. In the tenth century the Kirghiz were driven from Mongolia back to the Yenisei. However, some of the Yenisei Kirghiz did not go back there, but went to settle in the foothills of the Tian-Shan in the territory of present-day Kyrgyzstan.

The Yenisei Kirghiz state existed until the early thirteenth century when it was destroyed by the Mongol conquerors.

8 The Mongols in Siberia
The Siberian Khanate

Very important events took place in central Asia in the early thirteenth century which affected the future development of many Eurasian peoples including those of Siberia.

In 1206 the chief of one of the Mongol nomadic tribes **Temüjin** (Genghis or Chinggis Khan) was successful in uniting all Mongol tribes into one Mongol State. The Transbaikal Steppe[1] became one of its territories.

From this moment the epoch of great Mongol conquests began which left a deep imprint on world history. Its end result was the creation of the great Mongol Empire.

> It was the concept of empire that became the distinctive feature, leading the Mongols ahead of the spirit of conquest, and overcoming the primitive mentality of feudalised tribal society. The Mongol emperors waged their wars with the evident objective of achieving universal peace and international stability. If this objective were to be attained, the price for mankind's security would be lasting service of the state by each and all ... The Mongol Empire was, in the understanding of the Mongol leaders, God's vehicle to bring order to the world.
>
> (G.V. Vernadskii, Russian historian)

Siberia became the Mongols' first conquest. In 1207 Chinggis Khan sent his troops north under the command of his elder son Jochi to subjugate the 'forest peoples'. Jochi was able to do so in the space of three years. The only exception was the remote northern tribes. Most of Siberia became part of the Mongol Empire.

The Siberian peoples offered little resistance to the Mongols, and some of them (for instance, the Khanti) accepted Mongol rule outright. However, the Mongols met with strong resistance from the Yenisei Kirghiz. In 1207–9, after a number of fierce battles, the Mongols destroyed the Kirghiz Kaghanate. But in 1204 the Kirghiz started an uprising and drove the Mongols out. It took a number of new campaigns and a lot of hard effort before they finally subdued the Kirghiz in 1270. In order to preclude any future resistance from them, the

Temüjin (1162²–1227) was the founder of the Mongol Empire and elder son of Yesugei, the head of the Bordzhighin family. When he was 10, Temüjin lost his father. His family became subject to persecutions and he ended up a vagabond. Later in his adolescence he became a vassal of Toghrul, the chief of the Kerait Mongol tribes. He took an active part in tribal factional struggle, from which he emerged a victor. By 1204 he had effectively brought all the Mongol tribes under his control. In 1206 the tribal chiefs' assembly, the *Kurultai*, elected him the first all-Mongol Khan and conferred on him the title of Genghis Khan (which means 'the one who embraces'), under which name he later became known by throughout the world. Temüjin carried out a number of significant reforms, which led to a gigantic empire being built. He developed into a great diplomat and military commander, introducing many innovations into the strategy and tactics of the day. Temüjin could skilfully divide his enemies and set them against each other. He planned each military campaign very carefully by closely studying the local terrain, natural conditions, the population and the country he was going to invade, which enabled him to carry out devastating attacks.

Mongol Khan Kublai had a large number of the Kirghiz resettled in central Asia in 1293. From there they later migrated to the Tian-Shan, where their fellow tribesmen had been living since the tenth century.

In 1224 Chinggis Khan divided the Mongol Empire into four *uluses* (i.e. provinces) which he gave to his sons to rule. Siberia was divided among three of his sons. The area west of the River Ob became part of Jochi's *ulus* (the future Golden Horde). The area from the Ob to the Saian Mountains became part of Jagatai's *ulus*. The areas immediately to the west of and beyond Lake Baikal became part of Ugedei's *ulus* (the Mongols' home *ulus*).

The Mongols collected tribute from the Siberian peoples. The tribes who lived in the *taiga* (i.e. coniferous forest) paid it in the form of furs, while those from the steppe and wooded-steppe areas gave cattle and the products of their crafts. They also had to supply fighting men for the Mongol army.

Mongol rule greatly influenced the development of the Siberian peoples and, particularly, their material culture. This influence was many-sided. On the one hand, the Mongols were a contributory factor in involving the Siberian peoples in international exchange: it was the Mongols who were the first to raise international awareness of Siberian furs. The northern Siberian tribes managed to domesticate the reindeer, which changed their lifestyle and influenced its quality. They changed from being itinerant hunters and fishermen to nomadic herders. Many Mongol words passed into the Siberian peoples' languages, and the areas around Lake Baikal were settled by Mongol speaking tribes.

On the other hand, owing to Mongol influence, the southern Siberian peoples abandoned arable farming. By the time the Russians came to Siberia in the sixteenth and seventeenth centuries, farming was almost non-existent.

The Mongols were a contributory factor in causing the Siberian peoples' crafts to decline and some of those crafts were completely lost. With the vast Mongol Empire in place from Hungary to Korea and Vietnam, Siberia began to receive a large number of goods from China, central Asia and Eastern Europe (items made of metal, textiles, etc.). In terms of quality, these goods were often superior to local ones and were cheaper in cost when exchanged for furs. As a result of such competition some of the Siberian crafts, particularly in the *taiga* and northern areas, began to decline and even disappear. For example, the Khanti, Evenk and some other peoples lost the art of metal production.

After the break-up of the Mongol Empire in the second half of the fourteenth century, west Siberia became part of the Golden Horde, Tuva became part of the Mongol state, and Cis- and Transbaikalia remained in nominal subjection to the Mongol khans. Those Kirghiz who still remained on the Yenisei founded four independent khanates there: the Altysarskii, Alyrskii, Yezerskii and Tubinskii.

In the fifteenth century, after the Golden Horde distintegrated, a struggle erupted between the Kazan Khanate, the Nogai (Kazakh) hordes and the central Asian khanates for control of west Siberia. This led to the foundation of an independent Siberian Khanate in the late fifteenth century, which gradually

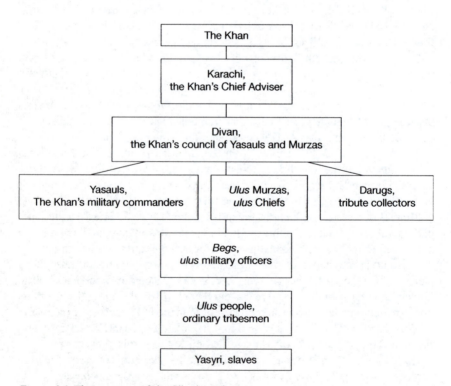

Figure 8.1 The structure of the Siberian Khanate

expanded over almost the entire territory of western Siberia. Initially, the new state had its centre in the town of Chimga-Tura on the site of present-day Tiumen. Later, it was moved to the town of Kashlyk (Isker or Sibir) on the Irtysh River.

The Siberian Khanate consisted of *uluses*, which, as vassals, were in subjection to the khan. They were obliged to take gifts to him and to supply troops if he went to war. Other than that, the *uluses* were independent. The nucleus of the khanate was formed by the Siberian Tatars[3] who made up the majority of the inhabitants of the *uluses*.

The subjugated Siberian peoples – the Khanti, Mansi, Nenets and others – paid *yasak* (i.e. tribute) to the khan in the form of furs. As far as their internal activities were concerned, they were free to do as they liked. The Siberian Khanate used slave labour on a limited basis (only at household level).

The Siberian Tatars professed Islam, although it was not their state religion. The rest of the Siberian peoples practised Shamanism.

The Siberian Khanate had a structure typical of the Mongol states, hence throughout its existence it was very politically unstable. Its *uluses* were often at war with each other, which weakened the khanate's unity.

Two families, those of the Sheibanids and the Taibugins, competed fiercely for possession of the title of khan. The Sheibanids were descended from the Inner Asian ruler Timur (Timurids) and the Taibugins were descended from the khans of the Golden Horde. The Siberian Khanate was founded by a Sheibanid whose name was **Ibak**. In 1495 he was murdered by the Taibugins who ruled until 1563. In 1563 power in the Siberian Khanate was seized by Kuchum, a Sheibanid, who was the last khan.

Ibak (year of birth unknown – 1495) was the founder of the Siberian Khanate, from the Sheibanid family. He managed to bring the disunited Siberian Tatar tribes together. His rule saw an expansion of the Khanate's territory to cover almost all West Siberia. He attempted to reconcile the Sheibanids with the Taibugins and to end the infighting (to this end he gave his sister in marriage to Mara, the head of the Taibugin family). In 1495 he was murdered as a result of a plot by the Taibugins.

9   The peoples of Siberia on the eve of Siberia's annexation to Russia

To conclude the review of the pre-Russian period of Siberian history a summary needs to be given of the Siberian peoples the Russians met in their advance eastwards.

According to Siberian historians, the population of Siberia in the late sixteenth century, just before the Russians arrived, was slightly more than 200,000. In the north of Siberia, in the tundra from the Ural Mountains to the east there lived (in the order cited here): *Samoieds*[1] (the Nenets, Enets, Dolgan and Nganasan) whose total population was about 8,000; *Yukaghirs* – about 5,000; *Chukchis* (Chukchis and Siberian Eskimos (Inuit)) – about 7,000; slightly south of the Chukchis there lived the *Koriaks* – about 10,000; and on Kamchatka there lived *Kamchadals* (Itelmen) – about 12,000.

The peoples who lived in the *taiga* forest area from the Ural Mountains eastwards (in the order cited here): *Voguls* (Khanti) and *Ostiaks* (Mansi) – about 18,000; *Ostiak-Samoieds* (Selkups) – about 3,000; *Kets* – about 2,000; *Tungus* (the Evenk, Even and Negidal) – about 30,000; and *Yakuts* (Sakha) – about 30,000. There were also some small tribes in the Amur River region – the Nanai, Ulchi, Udeghei and others – about 5,000.

In the steppe and wooded-steppe territories from the Ural Mountains eastwards: the *Siberian Tatars* – about 25,000; *Teleuts* (Kalmyks) – about 8,000; *Kirghiz* – about 8,000; small Turkic speaking tribes of the Saian Mountain area (Tofalar and others) – about 2,000; *Brats* (Buriats) – about 25,000; *Daur* and *Diucher* – about 10,000.

Economically, the Russians subdivided the Siberian peoples into three groups: sedentary, reindeer herders and nomadic.

The *sedentary* group included those who led a sedentary lifestyle along the Siberian sea coast from the Urals to the Amur River. They were tribes who hunted sea animals (walruses, seals, etc.).

The *reindeer herders* (or itinerants) included those who lived in the *taiga* and forest-tundra area. This group covered all the tribes whose activities included hunting, fishing and reindeer herding.

The *nomadic* group lived in the steppe and wooded-steppe areas. This group included all those tribes whose chief activity was cattle breeding.[2]

Figure 9.1 A Samoied encampment

Socially, the life of almost all the Siberian peoples was organized on a kinship basis. Only the Siberian Tatars and the Yenisei Kirghiz had a higher level of social structure. All the Siberian peoples used slave labour but only on a limited scale.

Most Siberian peoples' religion was Shamanism. The Siberian Tatars, among whom Islam began to take hold, constituted the only exception apart from the Buriat Mongols, who adopted the Mongolian form of Buddhism.

Wars played an important part in the lives of all Siberian peoples. In spite of Siberia being only sparsely populated, the Siberian peoples' roving lifestyle inevitably compelled them to fight for new territories (pastures, hunting and fishing grounds, sea mammals' breeding grounds, etc.).

Armed conflicts constantly took place between tribes and clans with the result that more powerful groups subjugated and gradually assimilated weaker ones.

Part IV

The annexation of Siberia to Russia

10 The Russian penetration into Siberia

It was evidently in the early eleventh century that the Russians learned that there was a vast land stretching from the Ural Mountains eastwards. The first mention of Siberia in the still extant *Novgorod Chronicles* was made in 1032. The Russians named it *Yugorskaia Zemlitsa* (Yugor Land or Yugra). This name covered all the territories they knew of east of the Pechora River, including the northern part of western Siberia. The Russians were attracted to Siberia by its furs.

The Feudal Republic of Novgorod attempted to cultivate relations with Siberia from the eleventh to the fifteenth centuries. As early as the twelfth century the Novgoroders began to refer to Yugor Land as *Yugor Province*, thereby staking claim to it. But in actual fact this territory had never been part of their state; they visited it only occasionally and for brief periods.

The Novgoroders established two main routes to Siberia. Both of them started off in the town of Velikii Ustiug on the Sukhona River. The first route went along two tributaries of the Northern Dvina River, the Sukhona and Vychegda, then portaged over dry land to the Pechora River. It continued along its tributary, the Usa, and over the Ural Mountains (the so-called Yugor Pass) to the lower reaches of the River Ob. The second route went down the Northern Dvina and then along the coast of the White and Kara seas to the mouth of the Ob.

The contacts the Novgoroders maintained with Siberia were of two kinds: trade relations and military campaigns. They traded iron artefacts and textiles for furs. A special trade association, *Yugorshchina*, was set up in Novgorod in the fourteenth century to trade with Siberia. However, in the main the contacts were in the form of military campaigns whose object was to collect tribute and to plunder the local population. Such incursions by the Novgoroders often met with resistance from the Yugra people who, according to the chronicles, succeeded in defeating and wiping out expeditions from Novgorod in 1187 and 1193.

After Novgorod had been annexed by the newly emerging centralized Russian state in 1478, its government, located in Moscow, tried to lay claim to Yugor Land as well.

In 1483 Prince Ivan III sent a large expeditionary force to Siberia under the command of Prince Fyodor Kurbskii. They proceeded through the Kama River region, over the Urals and reached the River Ob by means of the rivers Tavda, Tobol and Irtysh. As a result of this campaign the tribal chiefs of Yugor Land submitted themselves as vassals to Russia and undertook to pay tribute in the form of furs. However, all contact with these tribes ceased after the departure of the Russians.

In 1499–1500 Ivan III sent another large force of men under the command of Prince Semion Kurbskii. They took the route known to the Novgoroders – through the Yugor Pass. The Russians reached the lower reaches of the Ob, seized over 40 local settlements, collected plentiful tribute and returned.

The Russian government did not follow up the above actions. Both campaigns ended up as one-off events without any serious consequences for Siberia.

11 The Yermak expedition

The subjugation of Siberia

The Russian government turned its attention to Siberia once more in the second half of the sixteenth century. This was in response to activities undertaken by the Siberian khans.

In 1555 the Siberian Khan Yediger, being frightened by the defeat of the Kazan Khanate, had suddenly decided to send his ambassadors to Moscow to acknowledge himself a vassal of Russia and promised to pay a yearly tribute of 1,000 sable skins.

Kuchum, the new Siberian khan, stopped paying tribute and banned all contacts between west Siberia and the Russians. On his orders the Russian ambassador in the Siberian Khanate, T. Chubukov, was murdered in 1573. In the same years Siberian Tatar troops under the command of Kuchum's nephew Mametkul made an incursion into the Kama River region. Following this a conflict between Russia and the Siberian Khanate became inevitable.

In 1574, in response to Kuchum's hostile activities, Tsar Ivan the Terrible granted the Stroganovs, hunter-merchants (*promyshlenniki*) from near the

Kuchum (dates of birth and death unknown) was the last khan of the Siberian Khanate, ruling from 1563 to 1598. A representative of the Sheibanid family, in 1563 he defeated the army of the Siberian Khan Yediger with support from the Nogai and seized power. In 1573, when reports of the Crimean Tatars' successful attack on Moscow reached him, Kuchum severed relations with Moscow and attempted to establish his authority over Bashkiria (which had recently been annexed by Russia). In 1582 he was heavily defeated by Yermak's troops and spent the following 16 years resolutely fighting the Russians to restore his Siberian Khanate and, meanwhile, continuing his internal power struggle with the Taibugins. In 1585 he succeeded in luring Yermak into an ambush in which the latter was killed. In 1597 Tsar Fyodor Ivanovich proposed that Kuchum acknowledge Russian rule and stop fighting on condition that he would retain his control over the Siberian Tatars (which meant being the tsar's vassal). He declined. In 1598 Kuchum's headquarters were destroyed; he fled to central Asia, where he died.

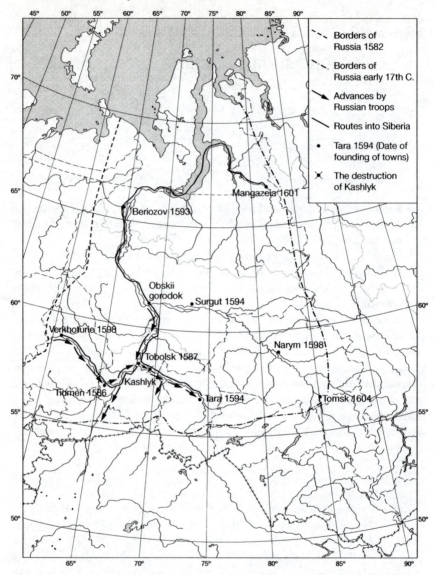

Figure 11.1 The Yermak campaign and the annexation of western Siberia

Urals, a Royal Licence which authorized them to recruit troops and send them to Siberia. Also, he granted the Stroganovs lands to the east of the Urals, allowing them to build outposts along the Irtysh and the Ob rivers, and decreed that any future population of such outposts would be allowed to fish and hunt tax free. Ivan the Terrible's decision to issue this licence was mainly due to the fact that the Russian government was then involved in the arduous Livonian

War and did not have the means for waging a direct campaign against the Siberian Khanate. That was why they decided to resort to the help of the rich hunter merchants, the Stroganovs.

In 1579–81 the Stroganovs assembled a large force of Cossacks to go to Siberia under the command of Chieftain (*Ataman*) **Yermak**.

Figure 11.2
Yermak

Yermak (year of birth unknown – 1585) was a Cossack *ataman* who played an outstanding role in the destruction of the Siberian Khanate and the annexation of Siberia to Russia. Yermak's biography is not very well-known. According to some sources, he was a Cossack from the Don River; other accounts suggest that he had come from Priuralie (i.e. the area along the western side of the Ural Mountains). Yermak participated in the Livonian War; later he lived as a brigand on the Volga. In 1579 at the Stroganovs' invitation he came to them with his band of men. He assumed charge of preparing an expedition to Siberia and later headed this expedition. He proved himself an outstanding organizer, military commander and statesman. He won a number of victories over the Tatars. When he took Kashlyk, Yermak sent a report and gifts to Ivan the Terrible with the result that the tsar issued a decree about incorporating the 'Siberian Land' into Russia. In 1582–4 Yermak succeeded in completely and effectively eliminating the Siberian Khanate, which opened the way into Siberia for the Russians. In summer 1585, in a time of famine, it was brought to Yermak's attention that a group of tradesmen from Bukhara were coming up from the south on their way to Kashlyk with a caravan of food (this information was a trap by Kuchum). Yermak set off to meet this fictitious caravan with a party of 150 men. During the night of fifth to sixth of August 1585 he died when caught in the Tatars' trap. According to legend, Yermak had to swim in order to reach the boats and escape from the Tatars. He drowned in the Irtysh River under the weight of his own armour. Yermak has become a legend.

In September 1582[1] Yermak's party (540 men) set off on their expedition, crossed the Ural Mountains and reached the town of Chimga-Tura by means of the rivers Tagil and Tara, where they defeated the troops of the local *murza* Yepancha. Soon Yermak was joined by *Ataman* Ivan Koltso's party (300 men) and continued the expedition down the the Tura, Tobol and Irtysh rivers advancing on Kashlyk, the capital of the Siberian Khanate.

An important battle between Yermak's men and Siberian Tatar troops (about 10,000 in strength) took place in the latter days of October not far from Kashlyk. At the height of the battle the Tatar commander Mametkul was wounded and had to leave the battlefield. Panic ensued in the Tatar ranks. Their Vogul and Ostiak conscripts fled and the Tatars were defeated. The Russians won the victory thanks to their use of firearms unknown to the Tatars, who thought the firearms were some kind of magic and panicked.

The conquest of Siberia was in many ways similar to the conquest of Mexico and Peru: a handful of people, shooting fire, overwhelmed thousands wielding arrows and spears.

(N.M. Karamzin, Russian historian)

On 26 October 1582 Yermak took the capital of the Siberian Khanate – the town of Kashlyk. Khan Kuchum fled to the south with his family and close retinue. By destroying the Siberian Khanate, Yermak opened up the possibility for the Russians to explore Siberia; herein lies the historical significance of his expedition.

The defeat of the Siberian Tatars and the flight of Siberia's ruler Kuchum had a strong impact on the Siberian peoples. The chiefs of the Vogul and Ostiak (the Khanti and the Mansi) tribes and many Tatar *murzas* hastened to appear before Yermak with rich gifts and declarations of their acceptance of Russian rule. In December 1582 Yermak sent *Ataman* Ivan Koltso to deliver the gifts and his report of the victory over Kuchum to Moscow.

When he received Yermak's report, Ivan the Terrible gave the order to annex the 'Siberian Land' to Russia and to dispatch a force of 300 'serving men' (*sluzhilye liudi*, i.e. salaried soldiers and officials) under the command of the military governors Semion Bolkhovskii and Ivan Glukhov. They arrived in Kashlyk in the summer of 1584.

Yermak continued his campaign against the Tatars in 1583–5 and inflicted a number of defeats on them, two of which were quite serious. In the spring of 1583 he defeated a large force of Tatars on the Vagai River and captured Mametkul, Kuchum's commander-in-chief and nephew. One year later the Tatars, under the command of *Murza* Karachi, made an attempt to besiege Kashlyk, but it was a complete failure. On a dark March night Yermak's Cossacks launched a surprise attack on the besieging party and killed most of them. Those who survived fled in panic.

Figure 11.3 Yermak taking tribute (a miniature from the *Remezov Chronicle*)

In the autumn of 1584, after these defeats, Kuchum changed his military tactics against the Russians. He decided no longer to engage in large-scale battles, but to use guerrilla tactics instead, in order to carry out surprise attacks on small Russian parties out collecting *yasak* (i.e. fur tribute). The Tatars were successful in destroying a number of such parties. The Cossack *Ataman* Ivan Koltso, Yermak's closest assistant, became a victim of these tactics when he fell into an ambush and was killed. In the winter of 1584–5 Kuchum's new tactics led to famine with the result that many Russians died, including the military governor Semion Bolkhovskii. However, during the summer of 1585 Kuchum succeeded in ambushing and killing Yermak.

Following Yermak's death the remaining Russian troops (about 150 men in all) under the command of Ivan Glukhov and Cossack *Ataman* Matvei Meshcheriak abandoned Kashlyk and began to retreat towards the Urals. Soon they met with another Russian party headed by Military Governor Ivan Mansurov, joined up with them and returned to the Irtysh River. At its confluence with the River Ob they built a small fortress, Obskii gorodok, where they intended to spend the winter. This fortress existed until 1594.

The Russians' retreat led to a resurgence of old internicine struggles among the Tatars. Kashlyk was occupied by the troops of Seidiak, a Taibugin, who declared himself khan of the now defunct Siberian Khanate and began to fight Kuchum.

After its military setbacks of 1585 the Russian government changed its tactics for the subjugation of Siberia. They decided to establish permanent fortified outposts (*ostrogs*) and to subject the Siberian population to tribute (*yasak*) on a regular basis.

In the summer of 1586 a force of 300 *streltsi* (Russian professional soldiers) came to Siberia under the command of military governor Vasilii Sukin and were joined by the troops of Glukhov, Meshcheriak and Mansurov from Obskii gorodok. In July, Sukin's troops founded the *ostrog* of Tiumen on the site of the Tatar town of Chimga-Tura. This became the first permanent Russian settlement in Siberia.

In the spring of the following year, 1587, another force of *streltsi* (500 men) under the command of military governor Daniil Chulkov arrived in Siberia. They started from the Tiumen Ostrog, sailed down the Tura and Tobol rivers and founded the *ostrog* of Tobolsk opposite the mouth of the Tobol on the right hand bank[2] of the Irtysh River. This *ostrog* became the main Russian headquarters in Siberia.

With the Tobolsk and Tiumen *ostrogs* as their chief bases, the Russian parties headed by Chulkov, Mansurov, Meshcheriak and other commanders commenced a systematic advance on the Tatars with the result that Kashlyk was destroyed and burned to the ground, Seidiak was taken captive and the Tatars were defeated again. Only a few remaining scattered groups of Kuchum's men continued resisting. They raided the newly Russian territories and tried to collect tribute from the Siberian peoples. In 1598, when the Russians destroyed Kuchum's headquarters, the Tatar resistance broke and their organized struggle against the Russians ceased.

After Tobolsk had been founded and the Tatars had been finally defeated, the exploration of Siberia began to proceed with rapidity. In 1593 the *ostrogs* of Pelym and Beriozov were founded; others followed: in 1594 – Surgut; in 1598 – Verkhoturie and Narym; in 1601 – Mangazeia; and in 1604 – Tomsk. Most west Siberian territory had been incorporated into Russia by the early seventeenth century.

The Russians' advance through Siberia continued for the whole of the following century and was completed in the natural course of events when they reached the Pacific coast.

The exploration of east Siberia and the Far East was carried out by parties of explorers[3] who were primarily looking for new sources of furs. The chief result of their efforts was the annexation of Siberia to Russia.

The explorers carried resolutely on eastwards through the vastness of Siberia, braving the severe climate and total lack of roads, struggling through the impenetrable *taiga* forest, marshes, mountains and tundra. In 1619 they founded the *ostrog* of Yeniseisk which became a principal base for preparing expeditions into the Siberian interior. Some 13 years later in 1632 the explorers founded the *ostrog* of Yakutsk (Piotr Beketov), and the following year they reached the mouth of the Lena River (Ivan Perfilev). In 1639 they reached the shores of the Okhotsk Sea (Ivan Moskvitin), in 1644 Lake Baikal (Kurbat Ivanov)

Figure 11.4 Tomsk (a drawing by S.U. Remezov, late seventeenth century)

and in 1645 the Amur River (Vasilii Poiarkov). The second half of the seventeenth century saw active exploration of the areas to the immediate west and east of Lake Baikal and of Kamchatka. At that time the following *ostrogs* were founded: Albazin (1651), Nerchinsk (1654), Irkutsk (1661) and others.

As they moved eastwards the Russian explorers made some important geographical discoveries, namely:

* they discovered and explored the basins of the four great Siberian rivers (the Amur, Yenisei, Lena and Ob) and of many other substantial waterways;
* they discovered and explored the north-eastern extremity of the Asian continent, Chukotka and Kamchatka;
* they discovered the strait between Asia and America; and
* they explored large sections of the Siberian sea coast in the north and east.

Many of these famous explorers' names have gone down forever in Russian history: Vladimir Atlasov, Piotr Beketov, **Semion Dezhniov**, Kurbat Ivanov, Ivan Moskvitin, Ivan Perfilev, Vasilii Poiarkov, **Yerofei Khabarov** and others.

The Siberian peoples were not able to offer much resistance to the explorers because of their limited numbers, disunity and technical backwardness (they had no firearms).

It was only in the south where more numerous nomadic groups lived (Kirghiz, Buriats, etc.) that the Russians met with stout resistance. During the seventeenth century they had to fight almost continual wars with the Kirghiz

Semion Ivanovich Dezhniov (year of birth unknown – 1672 or 1673), was born in the town of Velikii Ustiug, and served as Cossack in Tobolsk and then Yeniseisk. In 1638–9 he arrived in Yakutsk, where he continued his service. In 1640–1 he participated in expeditions to the Amga and Yana rivers. In 1641–3 he went on a long expedition from Yakutsk to the Indigirka River and from there by sea to the mouth of the Kolyma River. He took part in founding the *ostrog* of Nizhnekolymsk. In 1643–8 he served as a tribute collector. In 1648–9 he took part in his most famous expedition as a tribute collector (it was a trading and hunting expedition, organized by the trading manager F.A. Popov). Dezhniov was, effectively, head of the expedition. He managed to sail from the mouth of the Kolyma River to the eastern coast of Siberia south of the Anadyr River. Thus the strait between Asia and America had been discovered. In 1649 he founded the *ostrog* of Anadyrsk where he worked as an administrator until 1660 and explored Chukotka. From 1660 he continued his service in Yakutsk. In 1667–8 he travelled from Yakutsk to the Olenek and Anbar rivers. In 1660s and early 1670s he headed two tribute delivery trips, taking furs and walrus tusks from Yakutsk to Moscow where he was promoted to the rank of Cossack *ataman*. The easternmost cape of the Asian mainland bears his name.

Yerofei Pavlovich Khabarov (year of birth unknown – 1671) was born into a family of peasants near the town of Velikii Ustiug. He came to Siberia in 1628 and settled on the Lena near the mouth of the Kirenga River where he took up farming, built a mill and a saltworks. In 1642 he came under severe criticism from the Yakutsk military governor, who accused Khabarov of abuses, confiscated his property and put him in jail. In 1645 he was released and decided to search for new lands fit for farming in the Amur Basin. In 1649 he took a group of volunteers (70 men) and went on a reconnaissance trip down the Olyokma River and its tributaries over the Stanovoi Mountain Range to the Amur River. In 1650–2 he led a campaign to subjugate the Amur region. He seized the Daur fortress of Albazin on the Amur River and subdued the local population by force of arms. During his Amur expeditions he showed himself to be both a cruel, strong-willed person and a talented military commander. He was an organizer of high intelligence and a keen observer. The reports of his expeditions were very informative. He made a sketch of the Amur River. He found lands fit for farming in the Amur Basin and had them put under cultivation which helped to supply east Siberia with bread. In 1653 he faced more accusations of abuse and his property was confiscated. In 1654 in Moscow, Khabarov was acquitted, promoted to the rank of *Boiar son* (an honourable title which was conferred on serving men for their contribution to the exploration of Siberia) and was appointed to serve as administrator in the Ust-Kut locality. He lived out his days in his village on the Kirenga River. The town of Khabarovsk was named after him.

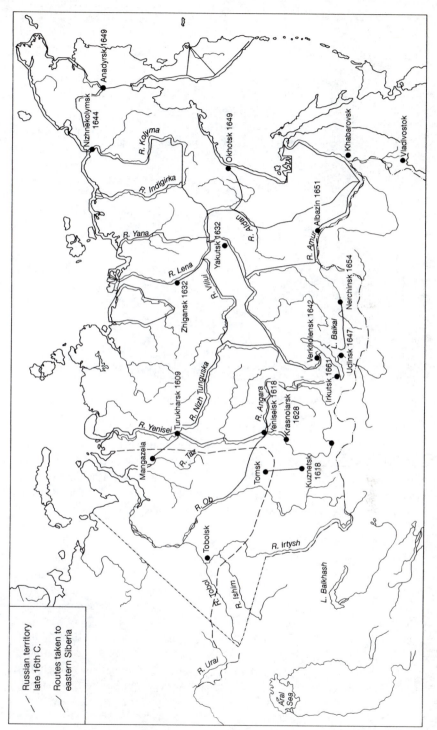

Figure 11.5 Expeditions by Russian explorers and the annexation of southern Siberia

Figure 11.6 Monument to Dezhniov on the cape named after
        him, far northeast Siberia

which prevented them from moving further south than Krasnoiarsk and Kuznetsk. The Buriats repeatedly rose up against Russian rule in the regions adjacent to Lake Baikal (1634, 1644, 1658, 1688 and 1698). Practically all the Siberian peoples staged uprisings, although on a smaller scale. The uprisings were mainly caused by the excesses of explorers and serving men.

12   The Russo-Chinese conflict of 1685–9

The Manchurian Qing Dynasty came to power in China in the middle of the seventeenth century. The new dynasty began to pursue expansionist policies in the north. The Chinese sequentially seized Inner Mongolia, East Mongolia (Khalkhu) and northern Manchuria.

The Russians' movement to the south and the Chinese movement to the north put the two expansionist forces on a collision course. The first armed conflict between them took place when Khabarov's troops advanced into the area near the Amur River (Priamurie) in 1652. In the following years such conflicts grew more frequent.

When the Russian government learned that the powerful Chinese state lay to the south of the Amur and Transbaikalia, they tried to establish friendly relations with it and to resolve border issues. A number of ambassadorial delegations were sent to China (F. Baikov – 1654–6; I. Perfilev – 1658–62; S. Ablin – 1666; I. Milovanov – 1670; and N.G. Spafarii (Spathary) – 1675–6), but they failed to produce any positive results. Initially, the Chinese government would not enter into any discussion at all; later they began to demand that the Russians pull out of the Amur region and hand over the Daurs with their prince Gantimur, who had earlier fled to Transbaikalia. The Chinese informed Spathary, the last ambassador, that they intended to receive no more embassies and to hold no more negotiations until the Russians met their demands. This led the Russian government to realize that the Chinese were going to try to implement their expansionist policies by force. So, the Russians took steps to shore up their defences in Transbaikalia and Priamurie by fortifying the *ostrogs* and reinforcing their garrisons.

China's active northward expansionist drive began in 1681, when they seized the areas around the Amur tributaries, the Zeia and Bureia. Fierce fighting broke out in 1685–6 for control of the Russian *ostrog* Albazin on the Amur. The Chinese decided to strike at Albazin as the main target because it was a centre for Russian farming, whose destruction would lead to a disruption of grain supplies throughout eastern Siberia. The Chinese emperor Kangxi took a very active part in planning the campaign into Russian territory.

In May 1685 a Chinese force (6,000 men and 100 cannon) besieged Albazin. Its garrison (450 men and three cannon), under the command of the Military

Governor Alexei Tolbuzin, repulsed the attack that took place in the beginning of July, but could not defend Albazin much longer (their ammunition had
run out and the walls of the *ostrog* had been destroyed by fire). They surren-
dered on 5 July on condition of safe passage to Russia. The Chinese razed
Albazin and returned to China.

By order of the Nerchinsk governor, Vlasov, the Russians returned to
Albazin after the Chinese had left. The new garrison was headed by Tolbuzin
and Afanasii Beiton. The fortress was quickly rebuilt with the experience of
the recent battle very much in mind. It was surrounded by a six-metre rampart
on which they built double timber walls. The space between the walls was
filled with earth and the outside wall was covered with turf and plastered with
a thick coat of clay to prevent it from catching fire.

When the Chinese government learned that Albazin had been rebuilt they
decided to send another expedition. In July 1686 a Chinese army (11,000 men
and 40 cannon) besieged the Russian fortress again. But the garrison (over
1,000 men and 18 cannon), under the command of A. Tolbuzin and A. Beiton,
repulsed all attacks. The Russians lost about 800 men and the Chinese about
2,500. In October 1686 the Russians managed to come to an agreement with
the Chinese about ending the siege and renewing peace negotiations. The
Russians ended up keeping Albazin. After their failed attempt to take this
fortress the Chinese sent the Mongol cavalry to attack the Transbaikal area,
but the attack was repulsed. In 1686 when reports about the commencement
of hostilities reached Moscow, the Russian government sent a force of 1,500
streltsi under the command of **F.A. Golovin**, who was also appointed ambassador plenipotentiary to China.

Fiodor Alexeevich Golovin (1650–1706) was a prominent Russian statesmen
and Boiar son. His aristocratic background, good education and ability helped
him to distinguish himself and secure important government posts. In 1686 he
was appointed ambassador plenipotentiary to China. In 1688 he directed the
defence of Transbaikalia against Mongol troops. In 1689 he signed the *Nerchinsk
Peace Treaty* with China on terms favourable to Russia. When he returned from
Transbaikalia in 1691, Golovin was received by Peter I who granted him the title
of Boyar and made him a provincial governor. Later he became one of the
closest associates of Peter I. He participated in the Azov campaigns of 1695–6
and in the 'Great Ambassadorial Delegations' to Europe in 1697–8. From 1699
he was in charge of the Armoury, the Mint and the Department for Little Russia
(Ukraine); then he was president of ambassadorial affairs and chief admiral of
a fleet under construction. He directed Russian foreign policy and participated
in the Northern War against Sweden as commander-in-chief of the Russian
army. He was the first Russian general field marshal and the first winner of
Russia's highest award, the St Andrew's medal. Golovin died during talks with
Prussia.

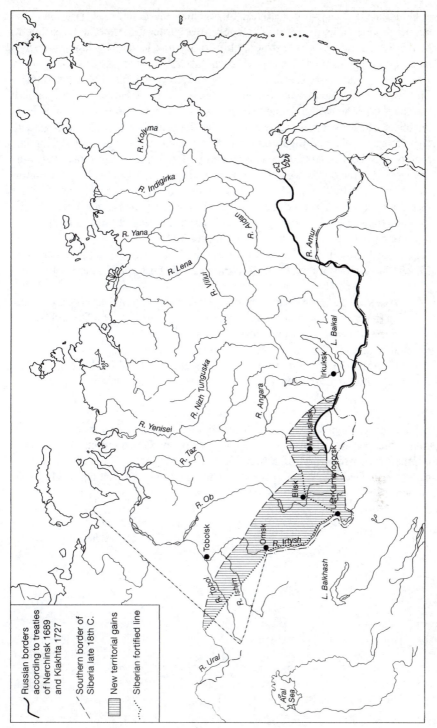

Legend:

- Russian borders according to treaties of Nerchinsk 1689 and Kiakhta 1727
- Southern border of Siberia late 18th C.
- New territorial gains
- Siberian fortified line

R. Kolyma
R. Indigirka
R. Yana
R. Aldan
R. Lena
R. Viluj
R. Nizh Tunguska
R. Angara
R. Yenisei
R. Taz
R. Ob
R. Irtysh
R. Ishim
R. Tobol
R. Ural
R. Amur
L. Baikal
L. Balkhash
Aral Sea
Irkutsk
Minusinsk
Bisk
Ust-Kamenogorsk
Omsk
Tobolsk

Figure 12.1 The Russo–Chinese border and the annexation of southern Siberia

Golovin was set two objectives: to organize the defence of Transbaikalia and to conduct talks with China to resolve the border dispute. The Department of Ambassadorial Affairs instructed him to try and have the boundary designated along the Amur River and to keep Albazin under Russian control.

In July–August 1689 Russo-Chinese negotiations took place near Nerchinsk. The Russian delegation was headed by Golovin; the Chinese group was led by Songotu, head of the Chinese emperor's Chamber of Foreign Affairs. The language of the negotiations was Latin. Catholic missionaries, who regarded Orthodox Christians as their competitors in missionary matters, acted as interpreters for the Chinese. At the beginning of the negotiations the Russians proposed that the border should run between Russia and China along the Amur River and its tributary the Argun. The Chinese counter proposal was for it to run along the watershed of the Stanovoi Range, and then along Lake Baikal (thereby the whole of Transbaikalia and Priamurie would fall to China). Intense diplomatic controversy arose over these proposals.

After difficult talks and mutual concessions Golovin and Songotu signed the *Nerchinsk Russo-Chinese Peace Treaty* on 29 August 1689. This treaty:

- established the Russo-Chinese border from the Sea of Okhotsk along the Uda River, the Stanovoi Range, then along the Gorbitsa, Shilka and Argun rivers (no border was marked west of the Argun);
- stated that the fortress of Albazin should be dismantled; and
- prohibited the Chinese from colonizing the left hand bank of the Amur (they only had the right to collect tribute from this territory).

Although the Russian diplomats failed to achieve all their objectives, the signing of the *Nerchinsk Peace Treaty* was very important to Russia. The treaty paved the way for Russia and China to develop their relations. It signified international recognition of Siberia becoming part of Russia and that China had relinquished all claims to Siberia. Thus the treaty assured peaceful development of Siberia as part of Russia.

13 The administration of Siberia

Upon its incorporation into Russia, a system to administer Siberia was gradually established.

In the sixteenth century the new territory came under the Ambassadorial Department. In 1599 the administrative responsibility was transferred to the Department of Kazan Affairs whose jurisdiction covered the eastern part of Russia (the former Kazan and Astrakhan Khanates). However, Russia's rapid movement to the east soon required a separate department to be set up to administer Siberia.

A special administrative body – the Siberia Office (*Sibirskii prikaz*) – was formed in 1637 by order of Tsar Mikhail Fiodorovich. It functioned from 1637 to 1708 and again from 1730 to 1763. It was headed, as a rule, by representatives of prominent Russian Boiar families who were close to the tsar. In the seventeenth century the Siberia Office was headed by: B.M. Lykov (1637–43), Duke N.I. Odoevskii (1643–6), Duke A.N. Trubetskoi (1646–62), Boiar R.M. Streshnev (1663–80), Duke I.B. Repin (1680–97), and a senior clerk from the Boiar's Council (*dumnyi diak*) A.A. Vinnius (1697–1703).

The Siberia Office handled matters of administration (the appointment and dismissal of military governors, supervision of their activity, judicial functions, etc.); the provision of supplies; defence; taxation; control over Siberian customs; the receipt, storage and sale of furs; diplomatic relations with China, Jungaria and the Kazakh Hordes.

The office was divided into territorial sub-departments (*razriadnye stola*) and chambers (*palata*). The sub-departments were involved in the actual administration of the Siberian territories. At the end of the seventeenth century there were four of them: Tobolsk, Tomsk, Yeniseisk and Lensk. The chambers concerned themselves with matters of finance and furs.[1] The Siberia Office had three chambers – pricing, trade and treasury. The first was responsible for the receipt and pricing of furs and other kinds of tribute coming from Siberia. The second chamber's responsibility was to select merchants to trade in government-owned furs and to supervise such merchants' operations. The third chamber administered all the office's financial affairs. The sub-departments and chambers were headed by clerks (*diaki*). The clerks[2] had a staff of deputy clerks (*podiachie*).

All Siberia, like the whole of Russia, was divided into counties (*uezdy*) for ease of administration. The vast size of Siberia soon made it necessary to introduce an additional administrative unit immediately above county level. Thus at the end of the sixteenth century the Tobolsk territory (*razriad*) was instituted which included all the counties in Siberia. The Tobolsk military governor (*voevoda*) became chief military governor of Siberia and the military governors of the other Siberian *ostrogs* were to report to him.

The military governor of Tobolsk had general oversight of Siberia's defence and the provision of supplies. His opinion took precedence in matters of foreign policy and foreign trade. Normally, the persons appointed to this post were of high rank, close to the tsar, but who had fallen into disfavour for one reason or another. The most prominent Tobolsk military governors of the seventeenth centuries were **Yu.Ya. Suleshev** (1623–5) and **P.I. Godunov** (1667–70).

> **Yu.Ya. Suleshev** came from a noble family of Crimean Tatar *beys* who had taken up service with the Russians. During his term in office in Siberia he implemented a number of significant reforms to improve Siberia's status. He organized the first census of the population and arable lands, establishing a clear ratio between the peasants' personal farming plots and the size of the government-owned plot which they had to work. Also, he harmonized the serving men's salary scales.

As Siberia was further explored and settled more territories were instituted: Tomsk (1629), Lensk (1639), Yeniseisk (1677) and more counties were formed.

Tobolsk retained its dominant role as a territory after the others had been established. The Tobolsk military governor's position was also regarded as more important than that of the other territories.

Territorial military governors (*voevody*) were appointed by the Siberia Office, as a rule, for a three-year term. They directed the activities of the county military governors (supervision, appointment of temporary replacements if a county military governor died or fell ill, dismissal of those county military

Table 13.1 Territorial subdivisions of Siberia in the seventeenth century

Territories	Counties
Tobolsk	Beriozovskii, Verkhoturskii, Pelymskii, Tarskii, Tobolskii, Turinskii, Tiumenskii
Tomsk	Ketskii, Kuznetskii, Narymskii, Surgutskii, Tomskii
Lensk	Ilimskii, Yakutskii
Yeniseisk	Albazinskii (until 1689), Yeniseiskii, Irkutskii, Krasnoiarskii, Mangazeiskii, Nerchinskii

P.I. Godunov focused on Siberia's defence to counter the threat of attacks by nomads from the south. He initiated the construction of fortifications and Cossack settlements (*stantsii*) along the border in the steppe areas of west Siberia, and the stationing of Dragoon regiments, the latter manned by non-Russians. He supervised the compilation of the *Drawing of Siberia* – the first known map of the region – which summed up the Russians' geographic knowledge of Siberia of that time and represented an important landmark in the history of Russian cartography.

governors who were guilty of abuses, etc.) and dealt with all matters pertaining to the administration of their respective territory (tribute and tax collection, supplies, courts, maintenance of law and order, constructions of new outposts, etc.). The *voevoda* had the exclusive right of correspondence with the Siberia Office. He administered the territory through the departmental chamber (*prikaznaia palata*) which was a body for administering the territory. The chamber was composed of county sub-departments (*stola*) and its structure mirrored that of the Siberia Office. The chamber was headed by two clerks who were appointed centrally. The sub-departments were headed by deputy clerks.

The counties were administered by county military governors who were also appointed by the Siberia Office, as a rule, for a term of three years. The county military governor had the authority to appoint and dismiss administrators and tribute collectors; he was responsible for the state of affairs in his county and dealt with all the administration within his jurisdiction (tribute and tax collection, supplies, law and order, courts, etc.). He administered the county through the county hall (*sezhaia izba*), which consisted of committees responsible for different areas of life: the tribute collection committee, the bread committee, the finance committee, etc. The county hall was headed by a clerk and the committees were headed by deputy clerks.

The Siberian counties consisted of Russian areas (*prisudki*) and 'tribute paying' (*yasachnye*) localities. The Russian areas covered an *ostrog* or residential settlement (*sloboda*) with its adjacent villages. Such areas were headed by an administrator who was appointed by military governors or elected by the public. The population of the areas formed themselves into communes (*obshchiny*) and elected community leaders (*starosty*). The tribute paying localities comprised local tribes (or '*yasak*-paying people') who were obliged to pay tribute. Such localities were headed by tribal chiefs who ran the life of the tribes according to their traditions and customs. In the seventeenth century the Russians did not interfere in the Siberian peoples' affairs other than to stop tribal wars.

The Siberian military governors had greater power than their counterparts in Russia. The Siberia Office instructed them to govern 'according to their discretion and the will of God'.

The extensive powers of the military governors and the vast distance which separated them from the capital city created a fertile ground for abuses. The system devised to provide income for the Russian administration also encouraged maladministration. In the seventeenth century a so-called 'feeding' system (*kormlenie*) was in operation in Siberia whereby the military governors and administrators received no salaries from the government. Also, they were strictly prohibited from engaging in business activity. Instead, they were to live off gifts. As a result of this, abuse by the Siberian administration assumed large proportions. Practically all Siberian military governors and administrators of the seventeenth century were guilty of abuses, particularly in the form of pay-offs and bribes. Especially prevalent was the practice of taking bribes from serving people in return for the favour of appointing them as tribute collectors. At the end of the century, for instance, the Yakutsk military governors received over 6,000 roubles worth of bribes annually (a fortune by the standards of that time).

The Russian government tried to do something to at least limit the abuses of the Siberian administration. It took the following steps:

- held enquiries (*syski* – calling suspects to Moscow to interrogate and investigate them);
- dismissed multiple offenders; and
- searched military governors and administrators at the Verkhoturie customs on their way back to Russia and seized part of their possessions.

However, the measures failed to produce any noticeable results.

The abuses of Siberian military governors, administrators and other officials frequently occasioned mass public unrest[3] and uprisings, in which both Russian and indigenous populations participated. There were a few hundred cases of such unrest and uprisings during the seventeenth century. They took place practically over the whole of Siberia – from Verkhoturie to Yakutsk and Nerchinsk. In Tomsk and Yakutsk they were more frequent than anywhere else. The biggest uprising took place in Transbaikalia in 1696. The protesters staged a march on Irkutsk and laid siege to it to express outrage at the abuses of the local Military Governor Savelov. As a rule, the Russian government had to exercise tolerance towards such protests and tried to settle them amicably.

14 The exploration of Siberia

The annexation of Siberia to Russia drastically changed the course of Siberia's historical development. The Russians brought their skills, economic practices, culture and mode of life and began vigorous exploration of the new land.

Population growth had a potent influence on the nature and rate of exploration. The subjugation of Siberia was paralleled by a mass migration (by the standards of that time) of Russians to the region. In the sixteenth and seventeenth centuries this process evolved in the following three forms: voluntary, government-initiated resettlement and exile.

Voluntary migration was of two kinds: legal migration (by permission of the government), which included most of the voluntary migrants, and illegal migration by various categories of runaway peasants. The majority of these migrants were peasants.

Government-initiated resettlement meant sending people from Russia to settle in Siberia for 'permanent residence' by order of the tsar. This type of resettlement mainly affected serving men, but peasants were also affected to a certain extent.

Exile played a notable part in settling Siberia. By that time Siberia had already become a place of exile for criminals, political offenders, participants in public protest demonstrations and foreign prisoners of war[1] (Poles, Swedes, Turks and Crimean Tatars). The first people to be exiled to Siberia, in 1592, were those involved in events that led up to the death of Prince Dmitrii in Uglich in 1591. The exiles joined the ranks of serving men and 'burden bearing' (*tiaglye*) people. There were three types of exile: 'service', 'urban' and 'farming'.

As a result of the active resettlement policy the Russian population in Siberia steadily increased. By the early eighteenth century Russians already made up more than half of the Siberian population: at a time when the total population; was 500,000, more than 300,000 were Russian. Although some parts of Siberia were settled more actively than others, about 80 per cent of the Russian settlers lived in west Siberia. By the late seventeenth century the Siberian population (especially the Russians) began to increase more as a result of natural growth.

The Russian population in Siberia fell into three social categories: 'burden bearing people' (*tiaglye liudi*), 'itinerant people' (*guliashchie liudi*) and 'service men' (*sluzhilye liudi*).

The burden bearing group included those who had to bear the 'burden' (*tiaglo*): a combination of government taxes and work and service duties that these people had to perform for the government.

The itinerant group included those who came to Siberia of their own volition (including runaways) and who had no special skills and made their livings doing whatever jobs they could get. The government tried to deal with these people by either getting them into 'service' or having them join the burden bearing group. The itinerants represented a recruitment source for all the population divisions.

The serving men included all those who were in the service of the government. Their responsibilities were not strictly defined. The most important of them was military service and tribute collection. Besides this, they guarded trade routes, caravans, warehouses, government institutions and groups of exiles. When necessary, they were to perform various types of work and services such as construction, shipbuilding, etc. For their work, the rank and file members of this group were paid wages in the form of money (4–8 roubles per year), grain in the form of 30–50 *pudy* of oats or rye per year, and salt (one to two *pudy* of salt annually).[2] The wages were paid very irregularly. Higher ranking members of this group were paid 10–12 roubles, 60–80 *pudy* of grain and three *pudy* of salt. The serving men made up the majority of the population in Siberian towns and *ostrogs* in the seventeenth century.

By the end of the seventeenth century the main Russian population group in Siberia was peasants who constituted over 50 per cent of its population. The Siberian peasants were subdivided into 'black plough' (*chernososhnye*) peasants and 'monastery' (*monastyrskie*) peasants. The black plough peasants (87 per cent of all agricultural workers) enjoyed personal freedom and bore their 'burden' in the interests of the government. They were divided into arable peasants and tax paying peasants in a ratio of 4:1. The arable peasants worked the so-called 'Tsar's Ten' (*gosudareva desiatina*) and the tax paying peasants paid an annual rent in cash or in kind – 40 Altyns (1 rouble and 20 kopecks) or 20 *chetverts*[3] of rye and 20 *chetverts* of oats per male peasant. Monastery

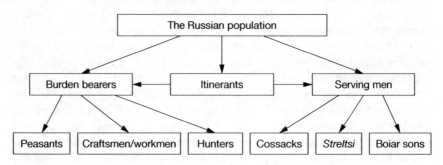

Figure 14.1 The social composition of the Russian population in Siberia in the seventeenth century

peasants, as the name implies, settled on lands which belonged to monasteries and were dependent on them. Apart from their principal occupation, all Siberian peasants had various work duties to perform: they had to participate in government construction projects, help with the transportation of cargoes, provide accommodation for serving men, etc.

In the seventeenth century the more urbanized 'craftsmen and workmen' (*posadskoe naselenie*) population group in Siberia was also predominantly involved in farming, but it also had to perform its craftsmen and workmen duties which were not at all clearly defined. This group just had to do whatever work the military governor deemed necessary, be it construction, repair, the manufacture of goods and products, transportation, etc.

The group called 'hunters' (*promyshlenniki*) consisted of those who trapped animals to obtain furs. It had to pay tax to the government, the value of which varied greatly. This population group had shrunk considerably by the end of the seventeenth century as a result of a decline in sable hunting. Some of them went back to Russia; others stayed in Siberia and joined the ranks of peasants, craftsmen or serving men.

The majority of people in the category of serving men were Cossacks, who were subdivided into foot Cossacks (*peshie* – the majority) and mounted Cossacks (*konnye*). The Siberian Cossacks were recruited from different population groups. All foreign prisoners of war were enlisted as Cossacks. There were not many *streltsi* in Siberia and by the end of the seventeenth century they were all sent back to Russia. A special population group among the serving men was represented by 'Boiar sons' who were the top of the hierarchy in this

Figure 14.2 A trap for ermine and sable

social group. A person was granted the title Boiar son for some special service regardless of their position. They held responsible jobs as government officials, garrison commanders and sometimes as military governors. Besides this they were given important missions to carry out (the command of military campaigns and security escorts, reconnaissance trips to explore new lands, diplomatic functions, etc.). Cossack *atamany* and *streltsi* commanders (colonels) were appointed from among this social group. From 1684 the Boiar sons were granted the aristocratic title of 'Siberian noblemen' (*sibirskie dvoriane*).

Farming became a dominant occupation among the Russian population in Siberia. The subjugation and exploration of Siberia would have been impossible without farming because its products constituted the staple diet of the Russians (a lack of these products had often resulted in famine during the initial stage of exploration).

During the seventeenth century the Siberia Office took steps to develop farming in Siberia which included:

- nationalization of all land in Siberia;
- resettlement of peasants to Siberia;
- allocation of the 'Tsar's *desiatina*'; and
- benefits (including tax breaks) for peasants (*lgoty*).

Land was provided to the peasants based on a 4:1 ratio. The peasants had to give the government the products harvested from one out of every four *desiatinas*[4] free of charge.

Working the 'Tsar's *desiatina*' was similar to the forced labour serfs in European Russia had to put in on their landowners' fields. Peasants from areas difficult to reach paid the annual tax in kind or money, as mentioned above. The peasants were given food aid and loans of money to help them settle in a new place. The size of the loans varied – from 10 roubles in Verkhoturie county to 30 roubles in the Lena Territory.

Russian peasants brought their traditional crops and techniques with them. The chief crop was rye. They also grew barley, wheat, peas, buckwheat, millet, and vegetables such as cabbages, turnips, carrots, onions, garlic, etc. Russian peasants practised plough-based farming. In the first decades of Russian domination in Siberia the fallow cultivation (*perelozhnaia*) system was used; later the farmers gradually changed over to three-field crop rotation.

A characteristic feature of Russian farming in Siberia was that it spread along the main route from west to east through the river valleys: Tura, Tobol, Irtysh, Ob, Ket, Yenisei, Angara, Ilim, Lena, Shilka, Argun and Amur.

In spite of the formidable challenges facing farmers, agricultural development made it possible for the Siberian Office to gradually reduce the quantity of food supplies imported into Siberia. As time went on Siberia became self-reliant in terms of food, thus establishing itself on a par with European Russia.

The second most important occupation of the Russians in Siberia consisted of small industries (*promysly*) involving the harvesting of natural products;

some of the more prominent of these included fur hunting, fishing and salt production. The Russians introduced their skills and techniques into these occupations as well. For example, in hunting, they began to use dogs and traps, and began to hunt in groups (*arteli*).[5] This enabled them to harvest more furs. In the seventeenth century the Russians' share in the local fur harvest accounted for about 60 per cent. In fishing they used long sweep-nets (up to 100 *sazheni*[6] long). For salt production they began to build salt works.

The Russians' hunting activities were characterized by irresponsible attitudes. Thus, the sable was almost wiped out during the seventeenth century, and in 1684 the Siberia Office had to ban sable hunting in the Yeniseisk and Lensk territories.

The third important occupation of the Russians was construction. A good deal of building was necessary in Siberia in the late sixteenth and seventeenth centuries. The principal construction material was timber. They used it to build *ostrogs*, administrative and industrial buildings, warehouses, churches, houses and boats which at that time were the main means of travel.[7] The main type of Russian dwelling was the *izba* (a strong single storey wooden house) which was built of round logs (35–40 or more centimetres in diameter) as opposed to tepees, yurts and dugouts. *Izba* windows were covered with mica. Inside these cottages they built Russian stoves in which they burned firewood 'white' style (i.e. when smoke escapes through a chimney as opposed to to 'black' style when it escapes through a hole in the roof) and laid floorboards. Next to their *izbas* the Russians always built their steam bath houses (the *bania* – which was hitherto unknown to the Siberian population).

In the late seventeenth century they started to use stone for construction in Siberia. The Cathedral of St Sophia, erected in Tobolsk in 1686, was the first stone building.

Another significant activity among the Russian population was trade and crafts. Trade was important in that it kept Siberia supplied with what its people needed. Initially all items for daily use and work tools were imported from Russia: cloths, shoes, tableware, firearms, tools, agricultural utensils, etc.

In 1597 the government imposed a customs duty on imports to Siberia to the amount of 10 per cent of their value for the Russians and 5 per cent for Bukharan merchants and established customs posts (*tamozhni*) on Siberia's borders and between its territories. So, when goods crossed from one territory to another within Siberia, the duty had to be paid as well. The customs were headed by heads of customs (*tamozhennye golova*) appointed by the military governors. Heads of customs inspected goods, priced them and assessed the customs duty. The customs enabled the state to control trade, control being extremely important because the government had imposed a monopoly on trade in furs. But on the other hand the customs impeded trade. In 1687 the Siberia Office abolished the internal customs and duties between the territories. Only the customs on the borders remained in Verkhoturie (on the border with Russia at the Urals watershed), in Tobolsk (for trade with central Asia), in Irkutsk (for trade with Mongolia) and in Nerchinsk (for trade with China).

Figure 14.3 Cathedral of St Sophia in Tobolsk, 1686

The establishment of customs had positive results for Siberia as well. The levies led to an increase in the price of imported goods and therefore stimulated the growth of local crafts. Gradually it made Siberia less dependent on imports. There were 386 items imported from Russia to Siberia in the early seventeenth century as against 170 in the late seventeenth century, and more than a quarter of this total was imported in very limited quantities.

Russian exploration of Siberia led to permanent settlements coming into being: towns, *ostrogs*, *slobodas* and smaller *malodvorkas*. The seventeenth-century Siberian town consisted of an *ostrog* with a residential area around it. The *ostrog* was a four-, six-, or eight-cornered timber fortress with a perimeter of 200–300 *sazheni* surrounded by two- to three-*sazhen*-high walls. There were towers built at the corners of the perimeter. The towers housed various offices. The *ostrogs* included the military governor's quarters, the departmental chamber or the county hall, guards' quarters, warehouses, a prison and a church. In case of danger the people from the residential area could shelter inside the perimeter of the *ostrog*. The term *sloboda* was applied in Siberia to large settlements numbering from a few dozen to a few hundred households. *Slobodas* were self-governing communities and were headed by an administrator. *Malodvorkas* were the most common type of Russian settlements in Siberia in the seventeenth century. They consisted of one or at most a few housholds.

The Russian Orthodox Church played an important role in the exploration of Siberia. Its role in this process was very special, since Orthodoxy contributed to the spiritual and cultural development of the population. The new land drew all kinds of fortune seekers and adventurers who had a very vague idea of Christian morality.

Figure 14.4 Walls of Yakutsk *ostrog* (early twentieth-century photograph)

People fight and stab each other in a state of drunkenness with impunity. The corrupt tribute collectors rip off local pagans, fasts are broken, couples join in matrimony without blessing from the Church. Cossacks take girls and women from Russia by fraud and from local pagans by force and live in sin with them without baptizing either their wives or their children. They treat the wives like slaves and sell and lend them to others commercially for pleasure; frenzied and blinded by lust they sometimes wed their mothers' daughters and sisters – a practice unheard of among the pagans who do not know the true god.

(Kiprian, the first archbishop of Siberia)

Such a deplorable religious and ethical situation as described above made it imperative for the Russian government and church leaders to set up an independent administrative arm of the Church in Siberia. The Diocese of Siberia was established in 1620 with its centre in Tobolsk. In 1668 it was reorganized into a metropolitanate. **Kiprian** became the first archbishop.

The Diocese had three main objectives in the seventeenth century:

* to disseminate Christianity among the indigenous Siberian peoples;
* to attend to the needs of the Christian population (including the performance of religious services and rites); and
* to raise the moral and cultural standards of the population.

The dissemination of Christianity was the chief objective of the Orthodox Church in Siberia. However, in spite of strenuous efforts by missionaries in the seventeenth century, they were not successful in accomplishing this objective. The main reason for their limited success was that they did not speak the languages of the Siberian peoples. Conversion to Christianity was performed

Kiprian Starorusennikov (year of birth unknown – 1635) was Siberia's first archbishop. Nothing is known of his background and adolescent years. In 1611 he was archimandrite (i.e. senior priest) of the Monastery of the Saviour in Novgorod. He visited Sweden for talks on Swedish intervention in Novgorod, was arrested and tortured 'for the fortitude with which he stood up for his country's interests'. In 1614 with the passing of the 'Time of Troubles' he was released and came back to Russia. He submitted an account of his time in Sweden to Tsar Mikhail Fyodorovich. In 1620 he was ordained Archbishop of Siberia and took over the Diocese of Siberia. In Siberia he worked to raise moral standards among the Russian and indigenous population, fought corruption among military governors, founded three new monasteries, securing royal stipends, land and fishing rights for them. He promoted farming in Siberia and founded two urban settlements. In 1622 Kiprian gave the order to find any surviving members of Yermak's expedition and write down their accounts. Thus, he made the first step towards studying Siberian history. In 1622 he was recalled from Siberia to Moscow and in 1625 he was ordained Metropolitan of Krutitskii for his contribution to the exploration of Siberia. From 1627 he was Metropolitan of Novgorod.

on a formal level, merely by baptizing them. The indigenous population continued to practise Shamanism as they had done before. But Orthodox missionaries were the first to begin studying the Siberian peoples. The accounts of their travels contained valuable information about the physical appearance, lifestyle, day-to-day practices, traditions and beliefs of the indigenous population. The clergy were also the first to begin to study the history of the annexation of Siberia to Russia.

The Church was actively involved in building churches and monasteries to attend to the population's religious needs. By the late seventeenth century there were 200 churches and 37 monasteries in Siberia.

The Church played a particularly significant role in the cultural and ethical development of the Siberian population. The clergy tried to remedy vice by sermon and enlightenment. As the most educated social group, they conducted classes for Siberian children (including those of the indigenous population) in church and monastery schools. The first Siberian library was opened in Tobolsk in the Bishop's residence in order to introduce the public to the riches of Christian culture. The library contained 77 books. Besides religious publications it had books on medicine, history and the *ABC Primer*. The Church frequently spoke up in defence of the Siberian public against the the excesses of military governors. In the seventeenth century it was through the clergy that complaints and petitions were submitted to Moscow to report injustices and cases of misappropriation by local government officials. The complaints went through the Church because apart from the territorial military governors only the clergy had the right to maintain direct correspondence with Moscow.

In the seventeenth century the Orthodox Church actively participated in the economic development of Siberia. It was mainly the monasteries that were involved in this activity: they received land from the government (called 'The Tsar's grants' – *tsarskie dachi*) on which they established settlements and industries. The monasteries invited farmers into their territory and gave them land to use on the basis of tillage and cultivation for the monastery as well as their personal use. Thus, by the end of the seventeenth century the Irkutsk Monastery of the Ascension had founded the Vvedenskaia and Baklashinskaia *slobodas* on the Irkut River, and the Badosskaia *sloboda* on the Belaia River. It also built a saltworks in Usolie-Sibirskoe and ran fishing operations on Lake Baikal. The economic activity of Siberian monasteries took many forms. Besides agriculture, they were involved in small industries, construction, etc. In the seventeenth century the monasteries supplied the population with salt. The Church in Siberia was one of the first in Russia to start using hired workers instead of forced labour, particularly in construction and small industries.

Figure 14.5 Siberian cavalry Cossack of the Line, 1808–12 uniform

The annexation of Siberia to Russia and its exploration by the Russians greatly influenced the development of the indigenous peoples. On the one hand, the subjugation of Siberia led to them being oppressed by the Russians. All the male Siberian native population was obliged to pay *yasak* to the government while they were of military serving age (approximately 15–55 years of age) and came to be known as '*yasak*-paying people'. The payment of *yasak* served to signify subjection. It was paid in the form of furs or in areas with no fur bearing animals or limited quantities of furs, it was paid in the form of cattle, skins, money, etc. The quantity of *yasak* varied from place to place. It ranged from one to 12 sable pelts per year or its equivalent. In the seventeenth century *yasak* collected by Russian collectors was an easier form of obligation than the labour and service duties the Russian population had to perform. But the *yasak* payment system exacerbated the numerous abuses by the Russians who cheated the '*yasak*-paying people' and stole from them. This led to many uprisings which were mercilessly suppressed by the Russian administration. In order to collect *yasak* more successfully the Russians widely used *amanaty*. These were high-ranking tribesmen who were taken hostage to induce the whole tribe to pay their fur tribute promptly.

On the other hand, the Russians prohibited inter-tribal and ethnic conflicts among the Siberian peoples. This resulted in their gradual consolidation. These people learned about things that had been unknown to them before (for example firearms) and gradually began to adopt some Russian work practices.

The seventeenth century saw some acceleration of ethnic changes among Siberia's native population owing both to the fact that they started to assimilate with the Russians and to their internal assimilation when one Siberian people was absorbed by another.

In conclusion, one can say that events in the seventeenth century laid the basis for the future development of Siberia as part of Russia.

Part V

Siberia in the eighteenth and the first half of the nineteenth centuries

15 Siberia's foreign policy situation

In the eighteenth and first half of the nineteenth centuries the Russian government's most important political objectives in Siberia were:

- to establish the Russo-Chinese border west of the Argun River and to further normalize relations with China;
- to annex to Russia Siberia's southern regions where conditions were quite favourable for human habitation;
- to protect Siberia against incursions by steppe nomads from the south; and
- to fully subdue the peoples in the north-east of Siberia (the Chukchi, Koriak, Kamchadal and others) and to ensure the security of that remote territory.

Renewed Chinese expansionist activity in Mongolia in the early eighteenth century raised the question of further demarcation of the Russo-Chinese border: Siberia's security depended on it. Peter I strongly believed that it was very important for the border issue to be completely settled. He sent envoys to China for talks on two occasions, in 1692 and 1719, but the Chinese evaded discussions. After Peter I's death in 1725 a new embassy headed by count **S.L. Raguzinskii** was sent to China.

After very complex and intense discussions he managed to reach an agreement. On 21 October 1727 S.L. Raguzinskii signed the *Russo-Chinese Kiakhta Peace Treaty* with representatives of the Chinese government (a delegation of three ministers). This treaty:

- re-confirmed, in general, the Russo-Chinese border determined in 1689 (Russia conceded a small area to China at the confluence of the Shilka and Argun rivers);
- designated the Russo-Chinese border from the Argun to the Yenisei (from the Argun to the Saian Mountains, then along the East and West Saian Mountains to the Yenisei River);
- established the procedure regulating Russo-Chinese trade (Kiakhta became a year-round location for border trade. Russian merchants obtained the right to go and trade in China once every three years;[1] Russo-Chinese trade was made tax-free;

Savva Lukich Raguzinskii-Vladislavich (year of birth unknown – 1738) was born in Bosnia into the family of a descendant of the Bosnian dukes and a prominent tradesman. His real name was Vladislavich. At the end of the seventeenth century his father fled with him to Raguza (today's Dubrovnik) and he received a double-barrelled family name and the title of Count of the Raguza Republic. In 1742 became a secret agent of Peter I in the Ottoman Empire and in Mediterranean countries. He was successful in completing difficult and responsible secret missions for the tsar. As a gesture of appreciation, Peter I bestowed generous estates and trade privileges on him. In 1708 he settled in Russia. In 1711 he participated in Peter's unsuccessful Pruth campaign. He was part of the group which organized a bribe to be offered to the Turkish commanders to let the Russian army out of encirclement and spare it from annihilation. In 1716–22 he was on diplomatic assignments in Venice and Raguza. He was one of the tsar's closest associates and after the death of Peter I he was sent to China as Envoy Plenipotentiary with the mission of informing the Chinese of the emperor's death and signing a new treaty with China. He conducted talks with the Chinese government over a period of two years, first in Beijing and later near the Kiakhta River. Raguzinskii demonstrated perseverance and resourcefulness (by bribing Chinese officials) and managed to negotiate the *Kiakhta Peace Treaty* on terms favourable to Russia. At the same time he had been gathering copious intelligence about China which led him to conclude that it would be inadvisable to go to war with the Chinese unless absolutely necessary. In the area where he conducted talks, Raguzinskii founded the Troitskosavsk (Kiakhta) fortress with a market place and customs post He returned to Russia in 1728 and was awarded the medal of Alexander Nevskii for the *Kiakhta Peace Treaty*. He was a very rich man and left a huge inheritance.

- granted the Russian Orthodox Church Mission in Beijing[2] the status of a permanent unofficial representative group; and
- allowed Russia to build an embassy, a market and a church in Beijing.

The *Kiakhta Peace Treaty* ensured Siberia's security against China, normalized relations between the two countries and contributed to the economic development of Siberia.

After the conclusion of the treaty the Russian government repeatedly tried to obtain China's permission to use the Amur as a convenient transportation waterway to the Pacific coast. In 1753 a special secret Nerchinsk expedition was even formed to explore the Amur. But in 1757 it was stopped at the demand of China owing to the beginning of China's period of self-isolation.

By the early eighteenth century the growing Russian population of Siberia and its successful exploration had created favourable conditions for the annexation of southern Siberia where warlike Turkic-speaking nomadic cattle breeders lived. At that time they were controlled by the Jungar Khanate. The territories to the south attracted the Russians by their fertile lands and stories of riches in the Altai, Kuznetsk and Saian mountains. The Russians' move south followed three routes.

The first route went up[3] the Yenisei. As early as 1692 bands of Cossacks under the exiled Ukranian colonel V.I. Mnogogreshnii inflicted a crushing defeat on the Yenisei Kirghiz who as a consequence stopped their regular incursions into the outskirts of Krasnoiarsk. In 1701 the Russians started their offensive and inflicted one more massive defeat on the Kirghiz. After this the Jungar khan (the Kirghiz were under his control) commanded them to move to the Tian-Shan where some people from their tribe already lived. Most of the Kirghiz obeyed and left. Their settlements ceased to exist. In 1707 the Russians founded the Abakan *ostrog*, and in 1709 the Saiansk *ostrog* – thus they had reached the Saian Mountains and secured the upper reaches of the Yenisei.

The second route went southwards to the headwaters of the Ob. In 1709 the Russians built the fortress of Bikatun (Biisk) at the confluence of the Biia and Katun rivers. When the Russians began to move south, the Jungar Khan Tsevan-Raptan launched hostilities against them, besieging Kuznetsk in 1709. In 1710 they stormed the Bikatun fortress and destroyed it. They carried out raids on Russian settlements but could not keep the south Siberian territories under their control. The Russians repulsed the Jungar attacks and continued moving up the Ob. In 1716 they built an *ostrog* at Berdsk; in 1718 they re-built the Bikatun fortress and reached the Altai Mountains.

The third and main route of the Russian advance south went up the Irtysh River. In 1715, a 3,000-man force under lieutenant colonel I.D. Buchholts began to move from Tobolsk southwards along the right-hand bank of the Irtysh. In 1716 the Russians built the fortress of Omsk. In 1718 they built one at Semipalatinsk, and in 1720 Major Likharyov's party built another fortress at Ust-Kamenogorsk.

By that time the Russians had managed to break the resistance of the south Siberian peoples and the Jungars, and succeeded in annexing the greater part of south Siberia. In the early 1760s, after China had conquered and destroyed the Jungar Khanate, Russia annexed the mountainous region of the Altai (Gornyi Altai).

After the annexation of Siberia's steppe and wooded-steppe zones the Russian government faced the task of providing for the defence of the newly acquired territories against attacks by southern nomads (the Bashkirs, Kazakhs, Jungars and Mongol-Oirats). To this end, a Siberian fortified line (*Sibirskaia ukreplionnaia liniia*) was built in 1720–60 from Cheliabinsk in the Urals to Kuznetsk. This line consisted of a system of small fortresses and redoubts which were built during the course of 50 years. It had a total of 124 fortifi-cations. The line consisted of three sections: the Ishim section which ran from the Ural River to the Irtysh River; the Irtysh section extending along the right bank of the Irtysh River; and the Kolyvano-Kuznetsk section which continued from the Irtysh to the Tom River. In the eighteenth century the Siberian fortified line was guarded by three infantry regiments and Cossacks (about 6,000 troops by the end of the century). In 1808 the Cossacks were formed into a Siberian Cossack Army. From then onwards the Cossack Army took over guard duties along the fortified line. The construction of the Siberian fortified line completed the incorporation of the fertile south Siberian areas into Russia and made it possible to explore them.

In parallel with the incorporation of south Siberia in the eighteenth century the Russian government took steps to finalize the annexation of the north-eastern part of Siberia. By the early eighteenth century Chukotka and Kamchatka were only nominally Russian. In practice, their population – the Kamchadals (Itelmen), Chukchi, Koriaks and other peoples – would not accept Russian rule and pay tribute.

A number of Russian military expeditions were sent to Kamchatka and the following Russian fortresses were built: the Bolsheretsk *ostrog*, the Niz-hnekamchatsk *ostrog* and a port at Petropavlovsk-Kamchatskii. After much resistance the Kamchadals and the Koriaks were subdued. As a result, their population dropped considerably (the Kamchadals – from 13,000 to 6,000; the Koriaks – from 13,000 to 5,000). The Chukchi offered even stouter resistance. Special military expeditions were organized to subdue them in 1730–1 and 1746–51, but they both failed and the Russians had to destroy the Anadyr *ostrog* and leave Chukotka. In the second half of the eighteenth century the Russians changed their tactics: instead of fighting, the Russians offered the Chukchi their friendship and began to trade with them (they exchanged Russian goods for Chukchi furs, sea animal skins, walrus tusks, etc.). The Chukchi later acknowledged Russian rule but still would not pay tribute.

The annexation of Kamchatka and Chukotka to Russia created conditions for Russian expansionism to advance towards America. In 1740–70 hunter merchants and explorers often visited the Aleutian Islands and Alaska. The hunter merchant **G.I. Shelikhov** made a significant contributuion to the explo-ration of Alaska. He founded the first permanent Russian settlement on Kodiak Island in 1784.

The above-mentioned Russian-American Company was set up 1799. It comprised all merchants interested in exploring and trading in Alaska. The government turned over all Alaskan hunting and fishing activities and the use of its resources to this company. The company headquarters were in St Petersburg under the Russian government's full control. In essence, it was a state company. The outfit responsible for shipping supplies to Alaska was based in Irkutsk. The company's executive manager who was vested with full authority was based in Alaska. The first and best-known executive manager was **A.A. Baranov.** The company organized expeditions, including scientific ones,[4] to Alaska and built settlements there, the main settlement was the port Novoarchangelsk (New Archangel).

In 1824–5 the Russian government secured international recognition of its lands in America. In 1824 a Russo-American Agreement was signed under which the United States recognized Alaska as Russian territory. By 1825 a

Figure 15.1
Chukchi warrior in armour

Grigorii Ivanovich Shelikhov (1747–95) was born in the town of Rylsk into a merchant family. He hunted and traded in furs. In 1775 he set up a trade company whose business involved hunting in the north-eastern part of Siberia. In 1784 he led a three-ship expedition to Alaska to study the potential for hunting sea animals there. In the same year he arrived at Kodiak Island, suppressed local resistance by force and founded the first Russian settlement in America where he stayed till 1787. He initiated many projects there such as building houses, encouraging the natives to embrace Russian rule, teaching them crafts and farming, giving them jobs in his company and even opening schools for their children. In 1778 he took 80,000 roubles' worth of furs to St Petersburg (a huge amount of money for that time) which caused a tremendous stir in Russian business circles and thereby contributed to the exploration of Alaska (eight million roubles' worth of furs had been harvested in Alaska by the end of the eighteenth century). Shelikhov wrote a detailed report of his expedition which was published. In 1791 he suggested that a Russian-American company be formed under the government's patronage to explore Alaska. But this suggestion was not acted on at the time (it was implemented after Shelikhov's death). He died and was buried in Irkutsk.

Alexander Andreevich Baranov (1746–1819) was born into a merchant family in the town of Kargopol. He was a hunter merchant. In the 1790s he visited Alaska and the Aleutians a number of times on hunting expeditions. In 1799–1818 he worked as Executive Manager of the Russian-American Company in Alaska. In 1801–3 he directed military activities aganst the Alaskan aborig- inal people (the Kolosh or Tlingit) to bring them into submission. He founded the first Russian settlements, built shipyards and workshops, organized hunting and exploratory expeditions. He sought to establish friendly relations with the Indians. In 1812 he acquired land in California, founded a Russian farming settlement there, named Fort Ross, and resolved the problem of food supplies to Alaska. He made an important contribution to the exploration of Alaska. He retired in 1818 and died on his way to his home town.

Russo-British Convention on Alaska was concluded which delineated the boundaries of Russian and British territories in North America.

Though geographically 'Russian America' (Alaska) was a land distinct from Siberia, administratively it was regarded as Siberian territory. Initially, it was made part of Irkutsk Province, and from 1822 it was part of the east Siberian Governor General's Territory.

16 The administration of Siberia

The Siberian reforms of 1822

The reforms of Peter the Great changed the administrative system in Siberia. In 1708, the Siberia Office and the territories were abolished and an all-Siberian Province (*guberniia*) was established with its centre in Tobolsk. The first Siberian governor was one of Peter I's associates, Duke M.P. Gagarin. The governor of the Siberian Province was appointed by the emperor's Cabinet (from 1741 – by the Senate) and approved by the emperor. The Governor of Siberia had the exclusive right of correspondence with the Russian government and the emperor and had almost unlimited authority in the province. He was vested with administrative, police, judicial, military, financial and economic authority. The governor administered the province through the gubernatorial administration (*kantseliariia*) which consisted of departments, each responsible for their respective area of activity.

In 1724 an important change took place on the administrative level. Because it was extremely difficult to administer this huge territory from a single centre, three smaller provinces – Tobolsk, Yeniseisk and Irkutsk – were established within the Province of Siberia. In parallel with this, the counties were re-named districts (*distrikty*). Each province was headed by a vice-governor who was appointed by the government in consultation with the governor and reported to the latter. The vice-governor had almost unlimited authority in his respective province. Similar to the governor of the Province of Siberia, he had administrative, police, judicial, military, and financial and economic authority in his area. The vice-governor administered his province through an administration whose structure mirrored that at gubernatorial level. In 1736 the most distant, and the largest province, Irkutsk, received administrative independence. Its governor started to report directly to the Russian government.

The provinces consisted of counties (*uezdy* – districts, 1724–30). They were headed by military governors (*voevody*, renamed commandants between 1708 and 1724) who were appointed by the governor; they reported to him and the vice-governor of their province. The military governor also had full authority at county level. The counties were administered through their respective administrations.

The lowest administrative-territorial unit was the *volost*. In eighteenth-century Siberia the *volosty* were subdivided into Russian and non-Russian.

Each Russian locality was headed by administrator (*prikazchik*) who was elected by the public or was appointed by the county military governor. He reported to the military governor, was accountable to him and bore responsibility for the state of affairs in his locality and for the proper execution of orders from his superiors. The administrator ran his *volost* through an administrative office (*prikaznaia izba*) also known as a local office or community office (*volostnaia izba* or *mirskaia izba*), which was a body of executive authority in the locality. Its staff, book keepers (*shchetchiki*) and scribes (*pisary*) were elected by the public at local and communal gatherings. The administrative offices established procedures which regulated the use of land, helped to settle land disputes, gathered statistics, issued passports to peasants, assessed and collected taxes from them, supervised the fulfilment of allotted work and services, presided over court hearings of petty civil and criminal cases which involved peasants, etc. The administrative office was supported with funds from the public living in the *volost*. The Russian *volosti* consisted of rural communities headed by elected community leaders, whose responsibility involved ensuring the correct functioning of their respective communities. The administration structure of non-Russian localities in the eighteenth century remained unchanged.

Some time previously, in 1722, bodies of municipal self-government had been set up in Siberia – magistrates' halls (*magistraty*) and town halls (*ratushy*). Magistrates' halls were set up in Tobolsk, in provincial centres and large county centres. The rest of the Siberian towns had town halls. Wealthy townsfolk and 'important and well-to-do residents' elected magistrates and town councillors from their own ranks (three to seven people). Magistrates' halls and town halls were in charge of the following matters: assessment and collection of taxes from the townsfolk, fulfilment by them of their allotted work and services, town development, court hearings of cases involving the townsfolk, the issue of passports, setting up schools, hospitals, etc. They reported to their respective administrations (gubernatorial, provincial or county) and were accountable to them and to chief magistrate in St Petersburg, communication with whom was carried out through the most influential Siberian magistrates' hall in Tobolsk. They were supported with money from the townsfolk.

In 1730, after Peter I had died, counties with military governors were restored to the administration system, replacing the districts, and so was the Siberian Office, which assumed the role of the Siberian governor's Moscow office. Its function was to sell furs and Chinese goods and to implement the Siberian governor's instructions.

The Siberian administrative system underwent a number of changes in the second half of the eighteenth century. In 1763 the government of Catherine II finally abolished the Siberian Office. In 1764 it divided the single Province of Siberia into two new provinces – Tobolsk and Irkutsk. In 1775 the system of provincial administration was changed. The new structure was based on the principle of separation of powers. The gubernatorial administration was

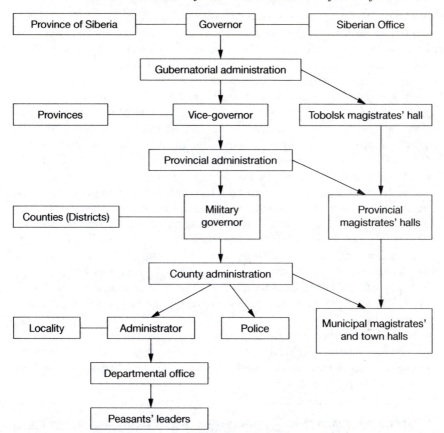

Figure 16.1 The administrative system in Siberia in the early eighteenth century

superseded by a number of independent institutions that reported to the governor:

- the province's administration office (*gubernskoe pravlenie*), which dealt with matters of administration;
- the government chamber (*kazyonnaia palata*), which dealt with the province's budget and government property;
- the treasury (*kaznacheistvo*), which collected and held government funds (taxes, duties, etc.);
- the department for education and health (*prikaz obshchestvennogo prizreniia*), which was in charge of colleges, schools, hospitals, orphanages, asylums; and
- the courts (with separate criminal and civil chambers).

The position of mayor (*gorodnichii*) was introduced in towns. The mayor's job was to maintain law and order. He was in charge of the courts, the police, prisons, fire departments, etc. Military governors were replaced by captains of police (*kapitan-ispravnik*) as administrative heads of counties.

In 1782 the Siberian provinces were abolished and three Siberian vice-regencies (*namestnichestva*) were established to replace them in Tobolsk, Kolyvan and Irkutsk. They were headed by governors general. Fifteen years later, in 1797, the viceregencies were abolished and the provinces were re-established. In 1803, in order to control the governors, a Siberian Governor Generalship was established with its centre in Irkutsk.[1] In 1804 the government established a third province in Siberia – Tomsk.

The frequent reorganizations of Siberia's administration system were, first, the result of looking for ways to develop an optimum system and, second, an effort to at least limit the abuses by the Siberian administrative officials.

Siberia's vast distances and the unlimited authority of the government and other bureaucrats resulted in stupendous misappropriation even by Russian standards. Almost all Siberian governors and other high-ranking officials ended up being dismissed from their jobs to be investigated and even imprisoned. The first Siberian governor, **M.P. Gagarin**, was executed for 'unheard-of misappropriation'.

In 1736 the same fate befell the Irkutsk Vice-Governor I. Zholobov. The government sought to fight such abuses by sending over inspectors (*revizory*), but this did not produce any noticeable results. A position vacated by one thief would be filled by another.

They were a multitude of predators who devoured the treasures of the province and plunged it into hopelessness and despair. All thought there would be no end to the suffering.

(I.T. Kalashnikov, Irkutsk resident, an early nineteenth-century writer, characterizing local government officials)

Matvei Petrovich Gagarin (year of birth unknown – 1721), a prince, served in Siberia from 1691, first as an assistant of the Irkutsk military governor, then in 1693–5 as military governor of Nerchinsk. Gagarin was placed under investigation on suspicion of embezzlement and corruption, but managed to escape serious punishment by paying a heavy fine. When he returned to Russia he secured himself a place among the closest associates of Peter I. In 1706–8 he was head of the Siberian Office and simultaneously in 1707–8 – *ober-komendant* (chief administrator) of Moscow. In 1708–17 he was governor of Siberia. In Siberia he formed an illegal organization of bureaucrats who were involved in producing illicit alcohol and vodka, smuggling goods into China, extorting bribes from members of the public and embezzling government funds, etc. In 1717 an investigation was carried out into this suspected malpractice. Colossal abuses were uncovered. He was sentenced to death and executed by hanging.

Of all the eighteenth-century governors **F.I. Soimonov** was among the most prominent and positive personalities; he did a good deal for the development of Siberia.

The continual abuses by the 'Siberian satraps'[2] finally made the government pay serious attention to Siberia. In 1819 Alexander I appointed as Siberian Governor General one of Russia's outstanding statesmen **M.M. Speranskii**.

Fiodor Ivanovich Soimonov (1692–1780), born into a noble family, graduated from the School of Navigation in Moscow and received training in Holland. In 1716–30 he served in the navy, carried out cartographic work in the Baltic and Caspian seas and compiled the first charts of these seas. In 1730–8 he served on the board of the Admiralty, in 1738–9 he performed the duties of Chief Prosecutor in the Senate, and in 1739–40 he was vice-president of the Board of the Admiralty. In 1740 he was accused of conspiring against Anna Ioannovna's favourite E.I. Biron and was sentenced to servitude in Okhotsk. In 1749 he was set free and lived in his estate near Moscow till 1753. In 1753–7 he was head of the Nerchinsk secret expedition to explore the Amur and its tributaries; in 1757–63 he was governor of Siberia and a privy councillor. During his term as governor of Siberia he acquired a reputation as a talented administrator who fought bribery and tried to accelerate the economic development of Siberia, especially in agriculture. In 1764–6 he was a senator and Catherine II's chief councillor for Siberian affairs. On his advice the Siberia Office was abolished and measures were taken to develop farming in Siberia (the rated norm of land allotments was established). In 1766 he retired on grounds of ill health. He wrote many scientific works including some about Siberia: *An Atlas of Nerchinsk, An Outline of Crop Growing in Siberia*, etc.

Mikhail Mikhailovich Speranskii (1772–1839) was born into the family of a village priest. In 1791 he graduated from St Petersburg Theological Academy (Main Seminary) and remained there as a lecturer. In 1792–1803 he was secretary of the Senate General Prosecutor's administration. He quickly came to prominence thanks to his outstanding abilities. In 1803–7 he was in charge of one of the departments in the ministry of the interior and took part in drafting all important laws. In 1808–12 he was state secretary and a close confidant of Alexander I. In 1809 he developed a 'State Reform Plan' which provided for a gradual move to constitutional government. His work prompted strong opposition from conservative members of the nobility. In 1812 on the eve of the war with Napoleon, Speranskii was accused of being a French spy and was exiled to Nizhnii Novgorod, and later to Perm. In 1816–19 he was Governor of Penza. In 1819–21 he was governor general of Siberia. He put together and implemented the Siberian Reform of 1822 and was in charge of the Siberia Committee. From 1821 he was a member of the State Council. In 1826–39 he was in charge of the project to codify the complete laws of the Russian Empire, for the implementation of which, he was awarded the St Andrew Medal and was granted the title of count (1839).

Figure 16.2 M.M. Speranskii

The emperor instructed him to carry out a thorough audit in Siberia and to present a Draft Programme of Siberian administrative reform. Speranskii did an excellent job of carrying out the audit, during which a mass of different violations were unearthed. Two governors and 48 high-ranking officials were put on trial; 681 officials were sacked for their abuses. Siberian bureaucrats had to pay over three million roubles worth of fines for malpractice and violations. Besides dealing with abuses Speranskii's audit aimed to achieve another goal, a major improvement of the region's administration.

The end result of this work was the enactment in 1822 of special legislation: ten legislative acts concerning Siberia, which became unofficially known as Speranskii's Siberian reform. This reform involved measures which radically changed the entire administrative system.

First, it provided for setting up a special Siberia Committee under the State Council. Its purpose was to coordinate the activity of government agencies in dealing with 'Siberian matters' and drafting resolutions on 'Siberian issues'. In 1838 Nicholas I abolished the Siberia Committee, but in 1852 he re-established it.

Second, the reform provided for a reorganization of the territorial administration system. Siberia was divided into eastern and western halves, and two governor generalships were established – east Siberian (centred in Irkutsk) and west Siberian (centred in Tobolsk, which was changed to Omsk in 1838).

The former included the Irkutsk Province, the newly formed Yeniseisk Province (centred in Krasnoiarsk), and the newly formed Yakutsk District (*oblast*)[3] and also special territorial border zones (*osobye pogranichnye upravleniia*) for Kamchatka, Okhotsk and Troitskosavsk).[4] The latter governor generalship included Tobolsk and Tomsk provinces and the newly formed Omsk Province.

Governors general were vested with full power – administrative, military, economic and judicial. Central offices (*glavnye upravleniia*) were established, which functioned as supervisory boards for the governorship general. They consisted of three officials appointed by the tsar from the ministries of the Interior, Justice and Finance, and three local officials to handle 'administrative', 'judicial' and 'financial' matters. The main purpose of the central offices was to supervise the performance of the governors general. Similar offices were set up for governors (their members were appointed by the governors general).

Third, the structure of municipal administration was changed. Magistracies and town halls were abolished. All towns were subdivided into large, medium and small. In large towns elected economic and administrative units known as *dumas* were established, consisting of a mayor (*gorodskoi golova*) and four deputies, as well as town courts and elected leaders (*starosty*) in each neighbourhood. In medium-sized towns elected units were established to manage economic and judicial affairs. They consisted of the town's judge and two deputies (*ratmany*),[5] as well as the *starostas* they had elected in each neighbourhood. Small towns were headed by elected town *starosty*. The principal functions of the new municipal administrative bodies remained the same. All bodies of self-government were strictly controlled by the provincial governors or other officials (*gorodnichie*) who were vested with administrative authority over the towns.

Fourth, a system for administering the indigenous Siberians (*inorodtsy*) was developed. All Siberian peoples were divided into three groups:

- *sedentary* (*osedlye inorodtsy*) – the Siberian Tatars, plus a few of the Altaians, Shor, Khanti and Mansi;
- *nomads* (*kochevye inorodtsy*) – the Buriats, Yakuts, Teleuts, most of the Altaians, Shor and others; and
- *itinerants* (*brodiachye inorodtsy*) – the hunter-gatherer or reindeer herding peoples of north and north-east Siberia and some small Saian tribes.

In terms of their rights and duties the sedentary non-Russians were placed on a fully equal footing with the Russians. A system of self-governing bodies and community leaders analogous to those in Russian peasant districts was instituted in their settlements. The nomadic non-Russians were granted traditional self-government – elective clan boards (*rodovye upravy*), plus steppe *dumas* which comprised a group of tribes. Their functions involved: collection and delivery of tribute; performance of government imposed work; and civil legal proceedings (based on customary native law). The 'itinerant non-Russians' retained their tribal self-government in the person of elders (*rodovye stareishiny*), who performed the same functions as the clan boards.

Speranskii's reforms re-affirmed the lands used by the indigenous peoples as rightfully theirs; it allowed them to trade, to send their children to government educational institutions, proclaimed religious tolerance, yet extended Russian criminal legislation to cover all indigenous Siberians.

Fifth, the reform provided for a reorganization of the Siberian exile system owing to the growing number of exiles. It clearly established the exile procedure. A series of 61 stopping places (*etapy*) were designated for exiles to eat, rest and recover during the long walk from European Russia, as were the location of camps, exiles' rights and duties, and surveillance regulations.

The Siberian reforms of 1822 broadly established the system for administering Siberia until 1917.[6] Only Siberia's administrative territorial division was changed after this reform.

Table 16.1 Territorial subdivisions of Siberia, 1700–1850

1708–24	Province of Siberia						
1724–64	Province of Siberia						
	Irkutsk Province		Yeniseisk Province		Tobolsk Province		
1764–82	Irkutsk Province			Tobolsk Province			
1782–97	Irkutsk Vicegerency		Tobolsk Vicegerency		Kolyvansk Vicegerency		
1797–1803	Irkutsk Province			Tobolsk Province			
1804–22	Siberian Governor General Territory						
	Irkutsk Province		Tomsk Province		Tobolsk Province		
1822–50	East Siberia Governor Generalship				West Siberian Governor Generalship		
	Irkutsk Province	Yeniseisk Province	Yakutsk Province	Special Border Zones Province	Tomsk Province	Tobolsk Province	Omsk Province

17 Socio-economic development

The settlement of Siberia continued intensively throughout the eighteenth century and the first half of the nineteenth century. Population growth was primarily due to resettlement from Russia, which was an overwhelming factor in the population increase. The resettlement was of two kinds: voluntary and involuntary.

The majority of resettlers were volunteers. They accounted for 85 per cent of the total number of resettlers. The volunteers received government loans to set up new homes and were exempt from taxes and work/service duties (except military service).

Involuntary resettlers were soldiers, assigned (*pripisnye*) peasants, some state peasants and the exiles who predominated in this group. A significant increase occurred in exile to Siberia in the eighteenth and early nineteenth centuries. The government began to use it not only for deportation but also for penal servitude involving forced labour (*katorga*). In this period 400,000 people were exiled to Siberia as opposed to a few thousand in the seventeenth century. Besides common criminals, the government exiled religious dissidents such as the Old Believers (*Staroobriadtsy*), national liberation activists (Poles, Lithuanians, Ukrainians, people from the Caucasus and others), prisoners of war and political opponents. The exiles made up around 9 per cent of Siberia's population by the mid-nineteenth century.

The annexation of new territories and voluntary migration were other factors contributing to population growth in Siberia. The majority of the population in south Siberia was ethnically Russian by the eighteenth century. China's expansionism at that time led to steppe nomads, unhappy with Chinese rule, migrating to Siberia voluntarily. In the 1730s about 30,000 Mongols moved to Transbaikalia, who gradually assimilated into the Buriats. About 100,000 Jungars (about 23,000 *kibitki*[1]) moved to Siberia and accepted Russian rule in the late 1750s after the destruction of the Jungar Khanate.

Lastly, natural population growth started to be more and more of a demographic factor in Siberia in the eighteenth and first half of the nineteenth centuries.

The south Siberian areas – best suited to human habitation – were settled more intensively than others. Besides those coming from across the Ural

Table 17.1 Siberian population growth, 1700–1850

Time period	Total population	Percentage of Russian total	Russian settlers	Siberian natives
Early eighteenth century	About 500,000	3.0	Over 300,000	Under 200,000
Late eighteenth century	1,200,000	3.3	850,000	350,000
Mid-nineteenth century	2,700,000	4.5	2,100,000	600,000

Mountains, people migrated internally – from north to south Siberia. People began to move from Verkhoturie, Tobolsk and Yeniseisk to the steppe regions along the Irtysh River, the Barabinsk steppe, the Altai and the Minusinsk Basin.

Over the period under review there was some increase in the number of people living in Siberian towns, especially in the south. Irkutsk, which became the trading and cultural 'capital', experienced particularly rapid growth. At the same time, north Siberian towns such as Yeniseisk, Verkhoturie, Tobolsk and others began to decline as a result of being situated on the outer limits of Siberia's socio-economic development. In the early eighteenth century the total urban population was about 80,000. At the end of the century it had grown to over 130,000. By the middle of the following century it was over 190,000. In the mid-nineteenth century eight Siberian towns had populations of 10,000 or more each: Irkutsk, population 28,000; Omsk – 18,000; Tobolsk – 16,000; Tomsk – 14,000; Barnaul – 11,000; whereas Tiumen, Petropavlovsk (on the steppes) and Krasnoiarsk had 10,000 each.

The population of Siberia came from diverse social backgrounds. It included all major social groups of the Russian population: peasants, the nobility, merchants, petty bourgeois, the clergy, Cossacks, craftsmen, exiles and the indigenous *inorodtsy*.

Predominant among the above groups were peasants, and their percentage in the overall population kept increasing. In the early eighteenth century peasants constituted about 60 per cent of the Russian population in Siberia; at the end of the eighteenth century they formed 82 per cent, and in the mid-nineteenth century they had increased their share to about 90 per cent.

Siberian peasants paid the following taxes:

- *government taxes* included the poll tax[2] and land tax (or rent), which in the mid-nineteenth century were respectively 3.5 and 8 roubles per year; and
- *local taxes* payable to the provincial and local municipal governments (to maintain roads, postal service, administration, prisons and schools), which in total amounted to about 5 roubles per year.

Apart from the above taxes all peasants were obliged to carry out such government imposed work and services as military service, 'road' service and conveyance service (i.e. transportation of government cargoes).

Based on their property status the peasants were divided into four groups:

- *rich* (over 50 *desiatinas* of arable land per male peasant, over 50 horses and over 40 cows);
- *sufficiently well-off* (30–50 *desiatinas* of arable land, about ten farm animals, including horses and cows);
- *average* (10–30 *desiatinas* of arable land, with three or four horses and two or three cows); and
- *poor* (less than 10 *desiatinas* of arable land, one or two horses or none and one cow or none).

The first group was quite small, constituting 3–5 per cent of all peasant households. Similarly, the last group was also fairly small, constituting only 10–12 per cent. The majority of the peasant households, about 85 per cent, came into the 'sufficiently well-off' or 'average' groups. Compared to their counterparts in European Russia, Siberian peasants were much better off.

In terms of their legal status, Siberian peasants were subdivided into state peasants, monastery (later 'economic') peasants and 'assigned' or 'Cabinet' peasants. Most of the agricultural population consisted of state peasants, as the former 'black plough' peasants came to be known. They enjoyed personal freedom, paid taxes and performed government imposed work and service duties. There were not too many monastery peasants in Siberia. The tax that they paid in kind for living on monastic lands was up to 20 per cent of the total harvest they produced. With the secularization of church-owned lands in 1764 this group became known as 'economic' peasants. As far as their status was concerned they were no different from state peasants.

The assigned (*pripisnye*) peasants were a special group. As their name indicates, they were officially designated to move to a certain location. They were sent to mines and factories in the Altai, Kuznetsk and Transbaikalia. Assigned peasants appeared in Siberia in the first half of the eighteenth century in connection with the construction of factories. They had the same work and service duties as state peasants. Apart from that they had to pay their respective factories in kind (providing them with food supplies) and to perform various types of work and services for them (delivering wood and coal for fuel; construction work; the transportation of factory cargoes; doing auxiliary jobs at the factories). After the factories were handed over to the ownership of the Royal Family, they were administered by the emperor's personal office, the Cabinet, and became known as Cabinet peasants. Their conditions were particularly difficult, hence their active participation in the Peasants' War of 1773–5 which was led by Ye.I Pugachov. After the Pugachov Revolt was suppressed, the government acknowledged the difficult situation of the Cabinet peasants. It banned unauthorized settlement in Cabinet lands and permitted the Cabinet peasants to have up to 100 *desiatinas* of good Altai land per male peasant. Hence the Cabinet peasants found themselves in a privileged position and their farms began to develop rapidly. By the mid-nineteenth century there were about 300,000 Cabinet peasants and their economic situation was better than that of the general Siberian agricultural population. It was this particular group that produced more rich peasants than any other. Conditions began to emerge in the Altai for 'farmer' style agriculture to develop.

Compared with the peasants, Siberia's other population groups were relatively small in number. By the mid-nineteenth century the total number of the Siberian nobility was only 150,000. Generally, the Siberian nobility had the status of so-called 'personal noblemen' (*lichnye dvoriane* – government officials and army officers) who earned their living from government jobs. Only those in the top rank of civil and military service (as a rule, not Siberian-born) were aristocrats by right of birth.

The merchants (*kuptsi*) were even fewer in number. As elsewhere in Russia, Siberian merchants were subdivided into three guilds. Initially, merchants could join any guild they liked regardless of how much capital they had. In 1775 the government of Catherine II introduced a scale which specified how wealthy a merchant needed to be to be able to join each guild (the first guild required not less than 10,000 roubles; the second – not less than 1,000; the third – not less than 500). These amounts were later repeatedly raised. The merchants of the first guild had the right to trade wholesale and retail both domestically and abroad. The merchants of the second guild had the right to trade domestically at trade fairs and in towns. The third guild merchants could trade on a limited scale within their counties. In the mid-nineteenth century there were only 7,000 merchants in Siberia, the overwhelming majority of whom (85 per cent) belonged to the third guild. The town with the largest merchant population was Irkutsk where over 700 lived. Many merchants actively gave to charity.

The Siberian clergy were also numerically limited. They were divided into 'black' clergy (monks) and 'white' clergy (married parish priests, etc.). However, this group was very influential by virtue of their occupation and their good education; they played an important role in Siberia's cultural development and exploration.

The petty bourgeoisie (*meshchane*), Cossacks and craftsmen (*masterovye*) formed a considerably larger part of the population. The first of these made up the bulk of the population in Siberian towns. They owned property, were engaged in farming, crafts and small-scale trade and worked for the merchants. They paid the poll tax, which in the middle of the nineteenth century exceeded 10 roubles, and local taxes which went towards supporting the police, the fire department, local government bodies and urban development. In addition, they performed their appointed work and services (military service and billeting, i.e. the provision of accommodation for troops).

The Siberian Cossacks had a duty to guard the borders, to keep order in the region and, if necessary, to fight when Russia was at war. They were in the service for life. When they were not on active duty they were farmers and engaged in hunting and related pursuits (*promysly*). The Cossacks were paid salaries and were exempt from taxes. In the eighteenth and early nineteenth centuries, they were divided into border patrol (*pogranichnye*) and urban

Cossacks. The border Cossacks guarded the southern frontier of Siberia, settling in stations (*stanitsy*, typical Cossack settlements). The urban Cossacks served in towns and the Siberian interior. In 1822 they were formed into Cossack regiments. In the mid-nineteenth century there were five urban Cossack regiments in Siberia: the Tobolsk, Tomsk, Yeniseisk, Irkutsk and Yakutsk regiments, plus and the Tobolsk Battalion of Foot. In 1808 the border Cossacks of the Siberian fortified line were formed into a Siberian Cossack Army (it had its headquarters in Omsk). By the end of the period under review it numbered 12 Cossack regiments, three half-battalions of infantry and a brigade of horse artillery. In the mid-nineteenth century the total Cossack population of Siberia was about 200,000, 45,000 of whom were on active service.

The craftsmen (*masterovye*) were skilled workers employed by Siberian factories to perform key jobs. They usually drew their recruits from the assigned peasants. The craftsmen's fairly privileged legal status resembled that of soldiers (they were fully controlled by their superiors, enjoyed free medical care, had a fixed wage whose size depended on each craftsman's position,[3] were tax-exempt, had the right to retire after 35 years' service, had the right to a pension and personal freedom, etc.). There were about 30,000 of these craftsmen in Siberia in the mid-nineteenth century.

The Siberian indigenous peoples formed another special population group. They pursued their traditional occupations and paid tribute. Their numbers slowly increased, but owing to immigration from Russia their share in the total population showed a downward trend. Social stratification processes were actively afoot among the Siberian non-Russians. The so-called 'Siberian princelings' (*sibirskie kniaztsy*), elders and tribal chiefs (toions, taishas, zaisans, shulengs, etc.) and also the shamans secured a dominant position. It was these high-ranking tribesmen who were elected as members of steppe *dumas* and tribal councils.

Regular population growth during the eighteenth and early nineteenth centuries created conditions for economic development in Siberia.

Agriculture was a leading sector of the Siberian economy. Considerable advances were made at this time in agricultural pursuits. The area of arable land increased significantly. In the early eighteenth century it was 130,000 *desiatinas*, but by the mid-nineteenth century it had reached 5.5 million *desiatinas*.[4] Accordingly the grain crop yields[5] rose from 64,000 tons in the early eighteenth century to 14 million tons in the mid-nineteenth century. The average yield was '6.5-fold', which was better than in European Russia. Siberia was completely self-sufficient in terms of food, and there was even a 300,000 ton excess of supply over demand. Agricultural tools were improved upon: many peasants abandoned the traditional Russian wooden ploughs in favour of more modern one or two metal shares.

The number of cattle also increased. In the mid-nineteenth century there were about 1.5 million horses, 1.7 million cows and bulls, 2.5 million goats and sheep plus 250,000 domesticated reindeer.

New types of agricultural production appeared in Siberia in the period under review: potato growing, sugar beet growing, tobacco growing, flax growing, melon growing and bee-keeping.

Siberian agriculture owed its development to a number of key factors. First, the main agricultural zone was located towards the south where there were better conditions for crop growing, particularly on the west Siberian steppes, in the Altai and the Minusinsk Basin. Second, it was affected by an increase in the agricultural population. Third, agricultural growth in Siberia was stimulated by the reforms of the 1760s, which were initiated by Governor F.I. Soimonov and implemented by the government of Catherine II. In 1762 the government abolished the 'Tsar's *desiatina*' in Siberia, since it prevented arable lands from growing in size, and the Imperial Manifesto of 1756 ordering a general land survey set the standard size of arable land allotments for peasants at 15 *desiatinas* per male peasant.

The second most important branch of the Siberian economy was the production of non-ferrous and precious metals. The eighteenth century in Siberia was marked by the advent of industry. Large deposits of non-ferrous and precious metals were discovered in Transbaikalia at the end of the seventeenth century and in the in the Altai in the early eighteenth century. In 1704 the first Siberian silver smelting works was built in Nerchinsk. Four years later four more smelters were built in the area. The first smelting works in the Altai – the Kolyvan smelter – was built in 1729 by the well-known entrepreneur **A.N. Demidov**.

Seven more mines and smelters – Barnaul, Pavlovsk (1763), Suzun (1763), Aleisk (1774), Loktevsk (1783), Gavrilovsk (1795) and Zmeinogorsk (1804)

Akinfii Nikitich Demidov (1678–1745) was the son of the well-known entrepreneur Nikita Demidov. He helped his father build metal manufacturing and processing plants from the late seventeenth century. After his father's death in 1725 Demidov continued his business. In 1726 he was granted the title of a nobleman for his successful efforts in developing the industry. After copper deposits were discovered in the Altai, he secured the right to build smelters there to produce copper. In 1729 he built the Kolyvan smelter and another was constructed at Barnaul in 1744. In 1735 he was accused of secretly using the Kolyvan smelter to produce silver instead of copper with the result that this smelter was confiscated by the government. In 1736 Demidov retrieved it by paying a large bribe to the empress's favourite, E.I. Biron, and resumed illicit silver production. In 1744 more charges were brought against him. In order to save himself and his smelters, Demidov requested Empress Elizabeth to transfer his Altai smelters from the jurisdiction of the government and provincial authorities into the jurisdiction of the empress's Cabinet. Elizabeth did so, but Demidov still lost his smelters.

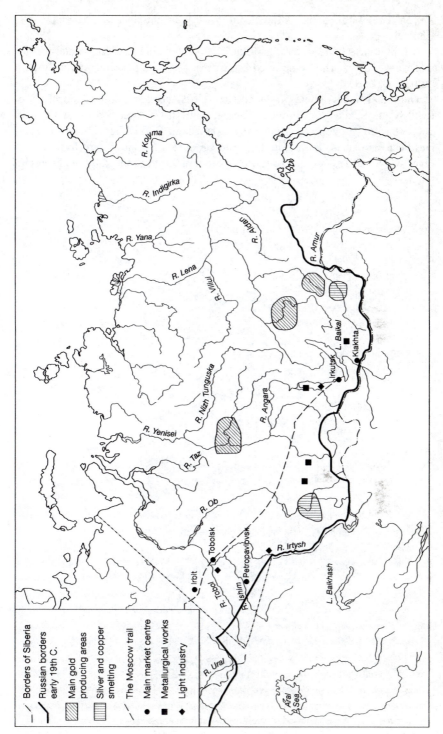

Figure 17.1 The economic development of Siberia, 1700–1850

Borders of Siberia
Russian borders
early 19th C.
Main gold
producing areas
Silver and copper
smelting
The Moscow trail
Main market centre
Metallurgical works
Light industry

R. Kolyma
R. Indigirka
R. Yana
R. Lena
R. Vilui
R. Aldan
R. Amur
R. Nizh Tunguska
R. Angara
R. Yenisei
R. Taz
R. Ob
R. Irtysh
R. Tobol
R. Ishim
R. Ural
L. Baikal
Kiakhta
Irkutsk
Irbit
Tobolsk
Petropavlovsk
L. Balkhash
Aral
Sea

– were later built in the Altai. From 1744 they belonged to the empress's Cabinet.

All Siberian smelters were manufactories which chiefly used manual labour and water power. They employed craftsmen, assigned peasants and a limited number of exiles.

The mines and smelters produced silver, gold, lead and copper. From 1766 to 1781 the Suzun plant minted Siberian coins from Altai copper. A total of 300,000 roubles' worth of coins was produced annually. After Siberian money had been abolished, the plant started to produce Russian money from 1781. Over 700 tons of silver and 16 tons of gold had been produced by the Siberian plants.

Figure 17.2 An iron foundry (eighteenth-century drawing)

In the 1830s–40s Siberia was gripped by a gold rush after deposits were discovered. The gold was produced by crews who used handmade equipment. Gold production increased almost 30 times during the course of 20 years, from 720 kilos in 1831 to 21 tons in 1850. Thanks to Siberian gold, Russia began to lead the world in gold production. In 1801 Russia accounted for 1 per cent of the world's gold production; in 1850 it accounted for 40 per cent. Siberia's share in Russian gold production was 70 per cent.

In the nineteenth century the Siberian smelters (especially in Transbaikalia) began to fall into decline as a result of the gradual depletion of the known resources and lack of equipment modernization.

Another industry which developed in Siberia was ferrous metallurgy. The manufacture of iron started in the mid-eighteenth century as an auxiliary activity in conjunction with Siberian silver and copper smelting works. Three iron-production mills were built in Siberia: Tomsk Mill in the upper reaches of the Tom River near Kuznetsk, the Irbinsk Mill in the Minusinsk Basin and the Petrovsk Mill in Transbaikalia. Apart from these mills, a few government works and some small private iron smelters were built in Siberia.

Generally speaking, the iron works were manufactories, i.e. they predominantly used manual labour. They produced equipment and instruments for the Altai and Transbaikal factories, household utensils and work tools. In the 1840s the technology to construct steam engines was introduced.

A more substantial metallurgical plant, the Nikolaevsk Iron Works, was built in the mid-nineteenth century on the Angara River. It had modern equipment and was capable of producing guns, artillery and shells.

Consumer goods, food and handicraft production were also part of the region's economy. However, in the eighteenth century there was only one relatively large light industrial facility in Siberia – Telma Cloth Mill near Irkutsk. It was built in 1736 by a trade company. In 1793 it came into government ownership. In the early nineteenth century two more factories were built – Tobolsk Linen Mill, which belonged to the merchant Kutkin, and Omsk Cloth Mill, belonging to the Siberian Cossack Army which specialized in preparing Cossack uniforms.

Salt production was a well-developed branch of the food industry. Siberia had a few large centres that produced salt in quantities sufficient to supply the population's needs for this product. The distilling industry was also well-developed. There were ten distilleries in Siberia in the early nineteenth century. By mid-century their output amounted to just over a million pails of alcohol (one pail, *vedro*, was 15 litres in volume).

The handicraft industry was quite widespread in Siberia. It covered a broad spectrum of public needs, including the manufacture of glass, crockery, goods made of leather, wood, mica, etc. By the mid-nineteenth century there were over 300 small handicraft manufacturing companies with an average workforce of five to ten each.

From the industrial standpoint, by the mid-nineteenth century, Siberia as a whole was a poorly developed region. Its share in Russian industrial output was only 1.5 per cent. There were slightly over 30 large manufacturing companies with a work force of over 500 in the whole vast area. Furthermore, by that time the equipment in most of them had become hopelessly obsolete. Siberian industry played a significant role only in the production of copper and precious metals.

In the eighteenth and first half of the nineteenth centuries the construction industry continued its development as an important branch of the Siberian economy. The scope of construction work increased noticeably as a result of population growth. The principal construction material was timber though stone and bricks were beginning to be used more often; in the early nineteenth century the percentage of such buildings in Siberia was a mere 3 per cent of the total. Later many new stone buildings were constructed mainly in large towns such as Irkutsk, Tobolsk, Tomsk, Barnaul and Omsk. Philanthropically minded Siberian merchants were particularly active supporters of stone construction projects.

Trade, both domestic and foreign, assumed a more prominent role in Siberia's economic life in the eighteenth and first half of the nineteenth centuries. The abolition of the Verkhoturie customs post and the lifting of customs duties on the movement of goods between Siberia and European Russia helped stimulate domestic trade. Annual trade fairs (*yarmarki*)[6] were a very popular way of doing business. At these fairs goods were traded wholesale during the one or two weeks each one took place. Trade fairs were held in many places in Siberia, but the largest took place in Irbit, where goods from Russia and central Asia were sold, and in Irkutsk, where merchants traded in Chinese goods. Apart from participating in trade fairs, Siberian merchants sold goods in town shops and market stalls; they also travelled to sell their goods in smaller towns.

Foreign trade started to grow as an important sector of Siberian economic development from the mid-eighteenth century. It was facilitated by the 1727 Russo-Chinese *Kiakhta Peace Treaty* and the lifting of the state monopoly on foreign trade in furs in 1762. Two permanent foreign trade establishments were opened in Siberia – one in Petropavlovsk to trade with central Asian and Kazakh merchants, and the other in Kiakhta to trade with China.

Russia's chief trading partner in the east was China. Therefore, Kiakhta became the centre of Siberian foreign trade, which by the late eighteenth century accounted for 8 per cent of the total volume of Russian foreign trade and 68 per cent of Russia's trade with Asian countries. Through Kiakhta furs (the main export), skins, cattle, cloth, iron and wheat were exported. Imports included silk (the main item), cotton, textiles, porcelain and glazed pottery. In the nineteenth century Russian textiles replaced furs as Siberia's leading export, and Chinese tea became the main import instead of silk.

Good communications were very important for Siberia's socio-economic development. A Moscow-Siberia highway (*Moskovskii trakt*) was built in the mid-eighteenth century. It went from Ekaterinburg through Tobolsk, Omsk, Tomsk and Krasnoiarsk to Irkutsk. The highway had smaller roads branching

Figure 17.3 Chinese tea arriving at the Kiakhta market

off from it: from Omsk to Barnaul and Kolyvan (to the Altai mines and smelters), and from Irkutsk to Nerchinsk and Kiakhta. It had bridges, corduroy roads (i.e. a surface made of thin tree trunks laid side by side, chinked with gravel and earth), river crossings and a coach service. The highway improved communications with European Russia and different Siberian regions (the upgrade meant that the government postal service now took only 34 days to get from St Petersburg to Irkutsk in winter).

In the mid-nineteenth century steamboats began to come into service. The first steamboat appeared on the Irtysh River in 1837, and in 1844 another came into service on the Angara River and Lake Baikal. In 1846 the 50 horse-power steamboat *Osnovo* with two barges in tow made the first round trip along the Tara, Tobol, Irtysh, Ob and Tom rivers from Tiumen to Tomsk.

The socio-economic development of Siberia in the eighteenth and first half of the nineteenth centuries had a growing influence on the lives of the indigenous peoples. Some of them began to adopt Russian practices in their economic activities and day-to-day lives. Thus, the Tatars and Buriats living near Lake Baikal gradually adopted a sedentary lifestyle and started to practise farming. In 1733 a decree by the Empress Anna Ioanovna abolished slavery among the Siberian peoples. This decree helped to normalize inter-tribal relations and contributed to a gradual cessation of devastating tribal wars, especially the Chukchi-Koriak and Chukchi-Yukaghir wars. Upon enactment of this decree, assimilation and consolidation processes among Siberian peoples began to gain momentum. A merging of the Turkic speaking tribes in the Altai in the eighteenth and first half of the nineteenth century gave rise to a new nationality – the Altaians (including the Teleuts and others). A similar process in the Yenisei

Basin led to the emergence of two other new nationalities, the Tuvinians and the Khakass. Another new nationality, the Dolgans, developed as a result of some Yakuts merging with groups of Tungus. The consolidation process continued between the Yakut and Buriat people.

Social stratification processes became more pronounced among the Siberian peoples during the period under review. A transfer of tribute collection responsibilities to tribal chiefs considerably reinforced their position and authority. The tribal chiefs became more and more conscious of their special status and began to ask to be granted rights associated with the status of nobility (as was proposed by the Yakut *toion* Arzhanov to Catherine II in 1789).

At that time too world religions, particularly the Russian Orthodox form of Christianity and Lamaistic Buddhism, gradually began to take over from Shamanism.

18 Cultural development and Siberian scientific expeditions

The reforms of Peter I opened the way for the development of primary school education in Siberia. There were two major types of schools in the eighteenth and first half of the nineteenth century: vocational and general education schools.

The appearance of vocational schools intended to meet the country's need for skilled professionals was the direct result of Peter the Great's reforms. There were five kinds of vocational training schools: military, mining, medical, theological and navigational (for seafarers).

Theological schools appeared in Siberia before any other vocational schools. Their chief objective was to train Orthodox clergy. The first such school was opened in 1703 in Tobolsk by the Siberian metropolitan Filofei Leshchinskii. The second theological school was established in Irkutsk in 1725. As Russia was an estate (*soslovie*)-based society, these schools were intended for children from families of the clergy. But it turned out to be impossible to follow this class segregation principle to the letter with the result that these schools taught many children from families other than those of the clergy. The length of training was strictly fixed. Their curriculum varied from school to school and depended on whether teachers for relevant subjects were available. For instance, in 1740 the students of the Irkutsk school learned how to read and write and studied the Old Church Slavonic and Latin languages, the basics of theology, the Book of Psalms and an Orthodox book of prayers, the *Chasoslov*.

The first theological schools in Siberia laid the basis for opening theological seminaries, which were vocational training schools of college rank. In 1743 the Tobolsk theological school was reorganized as a seminary, to be followed in 1780 by its equivalent in Irkutsk. The chief purpose of the seminaries was to train Orthodox clergy, but in practice their graduates followed careers as government officials, merchants, scientists, etc.

Seminary training lasted for eight years and the curriculum was comprehensive enough. It included applied subjects in order to equip students for service in remote and inaccessible places of Siberia, where a priest's work often went beyond performing strictly professional duties. Seminary students learned mathematics, reading, writing, history, geography, Latin, Greek, German, philosophy, rhetoric, singing by sight and basic medicine. Upon graduation the students were ordained as priests. In the middle of the nineteenth century the number of students at the Irkutsk seminary was 150. Two types of student support were provided. Children from deprived families were supported at government expense; children from rich families were educated at their own expense.[1]

Two-grade theological schools were set up in Tobolsk (1807), Irkutsk (1818) and later in other places in the early nineteenth century. They were elementary schools intended to train children for the seminary. The decision to start such schools for beginners was prompted by the fact that many seminary students lacked the basic training and skills to tackle the material in the seminary education programme. Graduates of the elementary schools could later go on to various church related jobs (as readers, sextons, etc.).

Another kind of theological school in Siberia was the missionary school. These were set up by Christian missions, monasteries and parishes to teach indigenous Siberian children and to disseminate Christianity. They existed for a relatively short period of time and had no definite curriculum. Everything depended on the knowledge and preferences of individual missionaries and the timescale of their mission's existence. The schools opened by the Kamchatka Orthodox Mission under archimandrite Ioasaf Khotuntsevskii in the mid-eighteenth century were among the best known. In 1760, 13 missionary schools were functioning on Kamchatka with a total of 284 students who learned reading, writing, arithmetic, drawing, singing and catechism.

The second type of vocational school to appear in Siberia was the military school. The first such institution opened in Tobolsk in 1713, becoming known as 'the garrison school'. Gradually these spread and were opened at other Siberian garrisons. By the late eighteenth century there were more than ten garrison schools in Siberia with a total of 7,000 students. The objective was to train junior army officers and to prepare low-ranking officials for the civil service. These schools were mainly attended by children from officers' and soldiers' families. The students learned arithmetic, geometry, reading, writing and military skills. In 1879 the Omsk Garrison School was reorganized into a so-called 'Asiatic school' whose students also learned the Chinese, Mongolian, Kalmyk and Tatar languages. At the end of the eighteenth century, garrison schools were re-named 'military orphans' departments'.

The Omsk Cossack School was opened in 1813. Siberia now had a professional military secondary school. It trained officers for the Siberian Cossack Army, urban Cossack regiments and border detachments. In 1846 it was reorganized into a Siberian Military School (*kadetskii korpus*).

The Great Northern Expedition of 1733–43 led to the establishment of schools for seafarers in Siberia, which became known as 'navigation schools' (*navigatskie shkoly*). By order of the head of the expedition, Vitus Bering, navigation schools were opened in 1735 in Yakutsk and Okhotsk. In 1745 a similar school was established in Irkutsk. The main function of navigation schools was to train specialists who would start to work for the Great Northern Expedition and would later navigate the seas that washed Siberia's shores.

Figure 18.1 The Siberian Cadet Corps building in Omsk

These schools taught arithmetic, geometry, reading, writing, drawing, cartography, geography, navigation, shipbuilding and architecture (the Irkutsk school also taught Japanese). Navigation school graduates became officers in the navy. In the second half of the eighteenth century these schools began to go into decline and in 1784 they were merged with general educational schools.

Industrial construction prompted the opening of mining and medical schools in Siberia in the second half of the eighteenth century. The first mining school was opened in Barnaul in 1753. By the end of the century there were seven of these, one of which was in Transbaikalia (Nerchinsk), and the rest were in the Altai. These schools trained mining specialists for the Siberian industial plants. Their students learned arithmetic, geometry, physics, reading, writing, German and mining. The best students were sent to the Mining College in Barnaul, which was opened in 1759. Being a vocational college, it trained mining technicians and had a five- to six-year curriculum. The best students were sent to St Petersburg to take their senior years at the Superior Mining School, and, on completion of three years' education, they received diplomas as mining engineers.

A medical school was opened in Barnaul in 1758. Known as a 'hospital' school (*gospitalnaia shkola*), it trained doctors for the mining enterprises in Siberia. It taught arithmetic, reading, writing, Latin and medicine. By the late eighteenth century this school had trained about 60 doctors.

Another type of school, in this case intended for general education (*obshcheobrazovatelnaia shkola*), appeared in Siberia at the end of the eighteenth century as a result of Catherine II's educational reform. There were two categories of general education schools established from 1784.

Those of the first category were opened in provincial centres. They were 'main people's schools' (*glavnye narodnye uchilishcha*) and consisted of four grades. In 1804 they were reorganized into secondary schools (*gimnazii*). There were four secondary schools in Siberia in the first half of the nineteenth century: in Irkutsk, Krasnoiarsk, Tomsk and Tobolsk. No more than ten people graduated from each of these schools annually.

Schools of the second category were set up in county centres and were called 'minor people's schools' (*malye narodnye uchilishcha*). In 1804 they were renamed 'county schools' (*uezdnye uchilishcha*). They consisted of two grades. Those who successfully completed the full training course in these schools could go on to secondary schools. There were 20 county schools in Siberia in the first half of the nineteenth century.

In 1804 parish schools (*prikhodskie uchilishcha*) were introduced as general education schools of the third category within large church parishes. These schools had one grade, but in 1822 this was increased to two. Those who had completed these schools could go on to county schools. In the first half of the nineteenth century there were 40 parish schools in Siberia including the Balagansk Buriat School, founded in 1804, which was the first permanent school for Siberian indigenous people.

Educational institutions for women appeared in Siberia in the mid-nineteenth century in the form of the Irkutsk Young Ladies' Institute, women's theological schools in Irkutsk and Tobolsk, and E.I. Medvednikova's Boarding School for Orphaned Girls in Irkutsk.

As a whole, education in Siberia in the eighteenth and first half of the nineteenth centuries was only making its first steps and was poorly developed as yet. The main Siberian towns of Irkutsk and Tobolsk were the chief centres for education. In the late eighteenth century Irkutsk, for example, had five schools with a total of 300 students; Tobolsk had four with 500 students.

In the eighteenth and first half of the nineteenth centuries the Russian Orthodox Church continued to play a significant role in Siberia's cultural development. The Irkutsk Diocese, whose jurisdiction covered east Siberia, was

Figure 18.2 E.I. Medvednikova's orphanage in Irkutsk

Figure 18.3 Institute for daughters of the nobility in Irkutsk

established in 1727. The Tobolsk Diocese (hitherto known as the Diocese of Siberia) covered west Siberia. Two more dioceses were founded in Siberia in the period under review: Tomsk Diocese (1838) and the Diocese of Kamchatka and the Aleutian Islands (1840). As we saw above, the Church made a considerable contribution to the development of Siberian education, especially among the indigenous peoples. As a result of efforts by the Church a certain proportion of the indigenous population began to appreciate Christian culture and consciously embraced the Orthodox faith. The Church often spoke up in defence of the Siberian public against the Administration's unfair treatment and abuses. For instance, it was the clergy who were instrumental in getting the deputy governor of Irkutsk, I. Zholobov, removed from his post in 1736. He was later indicted and executed for 'misappropriation'. The Church made intense efforts to raise moral standards among the Siberian population. The principal tool they used to achieve this was the sermon. The sermons of the first bishop of Irkutsk, **Innokentii Kulchitskii**, for instance, became renowned.

The Orthodox Church undertook construction projects on a large scale, which contributed both to the cultural and economic development of the region. In the early eighteenth century there were slightly more than 200 churches in Siberia, but in the mid-nineteenth century their number had risen to almost 1,000. Many stone churches were built; some of them remain to this day and delight us with their beauty.

The Church made an especially notable contribution to the study of Siberia and its peoples in the period under review. The Orthodox clergy took an active part in exploring remote areas. The missionaries studied the ethnography of the Siberian peoples, their languages, culture, beliefs and Siberia's natural life, geography and climate. The scientific works written by Andrei Argentov, Neil Isakovich and some other clergymen achieved wide renown and recognition in academic circles. **Innokentii Veniaminov**'s works received universal academic recognition.

Innokentii Kulchitskii (year of birth unknown – 1713) was born into a noble family in Volhynia (Ukraine). He graduated from the Kiev Theological Academy and took monastic vows. He taught at the Moscow Slavic-Greek-Latin Academy and later was a synod hieromonk[2] in the Russian Navy where he took part in naval battles. In 1725 by order of Peter I hieromonk Innokentii was ordained bishop in contravention of rules and traditions and appointed as head of the Russian Orthodox Mission to China. In 1722 he arrived in Irkutsk. The mission was denied entry into China, and he lived alternately in Irkutsk and Selenginsk doing missionary work and studying the daily lives and culture of the Buriat people. In 1727 he was appointed head of the newly formed Irkutsk Diocese. He put a lot of effort into getting the new diocese well established. He expanded the curriculum of the Irkutsk Theological School, spent his own money to support it and taught students there. He allowed children of parents other than the clergy to attend this school. He became widely known for his moralizing sermons. He died in Irkutsk and in 1804 he was canonized by the Russian Orthodox Church.

Innokentii (Ivan Evseevich Popov) Veniaminov (1797–1879) was born into the family of a village priest in the village of Anga in Irkutsk Province. He graduated from the Irkutsk Theological Seminary and in 1821–4 was a priest in the Tikhvin church in Irkutsk. In 1824–35 he was a priest in the church on Unalashka Island (one of the Aleutians) and in 1835–40 was a priest in the church at Novoarkhangelsk (New Archangel, Alaska). He devoted a lot of time to teaching the Aleutians different crafts (carpentry, blacksmith's skills and metal work). He opened a school for the Aleutians which had over 600 students. He converted all the Aleutians and some other Alaskan natives to Orthodox Christianity. To this day some native Alaskans profess Orthodox Christianity and revere Innokentii Veniaminov. He sought to learn more about the geography, nature, climate, and the culture and customs of the indigenous peoples. In 1834 he wrote a grammar of Aleutian (*Opyt grammatiki Aleutskogo iazyka*). He also drew up a classification of American native languages. On its publication this work attracted considerable attention from academic circles (it was translated into German, French and English). Veniaminov's works on the languages of American Indians are to this day basic reading for linguistic researchers. In 1840 he published his most significant work *Notes about the Islands of the Unalashka Department*, which brought him world fame. In 1840, after his wife's death, he took monastic vows and was immediately ordained as bishop. In 1840–68 he was head of the Diocese of Kamchatka and the Aleutian Islands. In 1850 he was consecrated as archbishop. He then continued his academic work, translating the Catechism and the Gospels into the Aleut and Yakut languages, and travelled extensively over the diocese; he became a member of the Russian Geographical Society. In 1868 he was ordained metropolitan, and between 1868 and 1879 served as Metropolitan of Moscow.

The development of education and the Church's efforts aimed at the dissemination of knowledge and learning contributed to the cultural development of
Siberia in the eighteenth and first half of the nineteenth century.

In 1789 the first Siberian printing shop was opened in Tobolsk and began
to publish the first Siberian magazine *Irtysh* (though it was only published for
a short time). Libraries began to develop at that time, large examples being
established at Tobolsk and in the seminaries. The library of the Barnaul Mining
School was one of the largest technical libraries in Russia. It had 7,000 books.

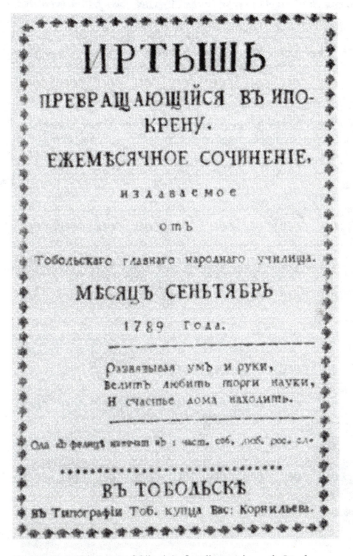

Figure 18.4 Title page of Siberia's first literary journal, *Irtysh*

Amateur theatres began to appear in Siberia (in Irkutsk, Omsk and Tobolsk) where army officers, government officials, merchants and members of the petty bourgeoisie participated in stage productions. Painting and architecture developed. Professional architects began to work in Siberian towns and created many real masterpieces.

In December 1825 a group of people unsuccessfully rebelled against Tsarist authority. Many of the leaders of these 'Decembrists' were exiled and greatly influenced Siberia's cultural development between 1826 and 1859. In 1826, 121 conspirators were exiled to Siberia (including eight princes, four barons, one count, one general and 94 senior officers). After they had served their terms of penal servitude, the Decembrists were sent to live in different places in Siberia, where they created a most favourable impression – they devoted their time to studying local lore, promoting enlightenment and raising the cultural standards of indigenous and Russian Siberians.

> In winter life in the Volkonskii household was active and open. Everyone in Irkutsk society thought it an honour to visit it. This very openness of the Volkonskii house encouraged social rapport and gentler attitudes and tastes.
>
> (N.A. Belogolovii, a citizen of Irkutsk)

Healthcare began to emerge in Siberia during the period under review. The towns began to introduce litter- and waste-disposal practices. In the early eighteenth century garrison infirmaries came into existence, and at the end of the eighteenth century civilian hospitals came into service in the main Siberian towns of Irkutsk and Tobolsk. By the middle of the nineteenth century there were already 30 hospitals in Siberia, including private ones.

Figure 18.5 Chita Ostrog, where the Decembrists were incarcerated

Exploration and research activities continued vigorously in the eighteenth and first half of the nineteenth centuries. A number of large expeditions were formed to explore Siberia in the eighteenth century and in terms of their scope and scientific findings, these expeditions rank alongside some of the most outstanding efforts of world science. Such scientific names as S.U. Remezov, V.I. Bering, G.F. Müller, S.P. Krasheninnikov, P.S. Pallas and others who studied Siberia have gone down in the history of world science.

One of the most significant expeditions was the *Great Northern Expedition* (also known as the Second Kamchatka Expedition) of 1733–43. Its goal was to carry out an extensive study of Siberia, especially of the coastline. Several thousand people participated in its preparation and completion. The organization of the expedition contributed to the development of farming, shipbuilding and education in Siberia and it led to more settlements being built. The expedition was headed by **V.I. Bering**.

The expedition consisted of six groups that conducted research independently of each other. The first group, headed by Malygin, explored the coast from Arkhangelsk to the mouth of the Ob. The second group, under Ovtsin, explored the coast from the Ob to the Taimyr Peninsula. The third group, headed by Cheliuskin and Pronchishchev, explored the coast from the Lena River to the Taimyr. The fourth group, under the Laptev brothers, explored the coast east of the Lena River. The fifth group, headed by Bering himself together with Chirikov, explored the Pacific coast of Siberia. Lastly, the sixth scientific group, under Müller, studied the inland regions of Siberia. The main result of these expeditions was the publication in 1746 of the *General Map of the Russian Empire*, which was kept as a state secret for over 150 years.

Vitus Ionassen Bering (1681–1741) was born in Denmark into the family of a customs officer. In 1703 he graduated from a naval school in Amsterdam (Holland). He was invited to Russia on a recommendation and served in the Baltic Fleet, sailing as captain of a patrol boat. In 1711 he participated in Peter the Great's Pruth campaign as an officer in the Azov Fleet, and later sailed the ships to St Petersburg through the Mediterranean. By the end of the Northern War against Sweden he was captain of the largest Russian frigate. He retired in 1724 and settled in Vyborg. The same year he was called back into service by Peter I, who, in 1725, put Bering in charge of an expedition to search for a sailing route to China. In 1727–30 he led the Kamchatka Expedition with the rank of captain-commander. On its completion he initiated another comprehensive expedition. In 1733–41 he was head of the Great Northern Expedition, during which he discovered Alaska, explored the coasts of Kamchatka and Chukotka and ascertained the existence of a strait between Asia and America. During his expeditions, Bering demonstrated outstanding organizational skills. In 1741 he was shipwrecked off the Commander Islands and died of scurvy.

Research and exploration continued to develop in the first half of the nine-teenth century, so did their scope and variety. A special academic magazine *The Siberian Herald* began to be published in St Petersburg in 1818. In 1845 the Russian Geographical Society was formed and became an important centre for the study of Siberia.

Part VI

Siberia in the second half of the nineteenth and early twentieth centuries

19 Siberia's foreign policy situation

By the mid-nineteenth century the 'Amur question' came back to the fore in Russia's Far East policies. The great world powers – Great Britain, America and France – began to show an active interest in the coastal areas of northern Asia and Alaska as part of their expansionist policies, which posed a threat to Russian territories.

The governor general of eastern Siberia, **N.N. Muraviov**, played a crucial part in the resolution of this issue. He came to believe that the Amur River formed a natural boundary for the defence of Russian interests and said: 'He that owns the left hand bank and the mouth of the Amur owns Siberia.'

In 1848 Muraviov submitted a proposal to Nicholas I to send a comprehensive expedition to the Amur for its exploration and the subsequent resolution of the 'Amur question'. Without waiting for the emperor's response

Nikolai Nikolaevich Muraviov-Amurskii (1808–81) was born into a noble family and went onto graduate from one of the privileged military schools, which were known in Russia as the 'Corps of Pages'. Then he served in the army, taking part in the Russo-Turkish war of 1828–9, the war in the Caucusus and the suppression of the Polish rebellion of 1830–1. In 1844–7 he was governor of Tula Province. He was characterized by liberal views, for instance, supporting the Tula gentry's proposal to abolish serfdom. In 1847–61 he was governor general of east Siberia. He organized the Amur Expedition of 1849–55 which prepared the ground for the Russian annexation of Priamurie (i.e. the territory near the Amur River). He contributed greatly to the exploration and reinforcement of eastern Siberia. In 1851 he initiated the formation of the east Siberian branch of the Russian Geographical Society. During the Crimean War of 1853–5 he directed the defence of Siberia's Pacific coast against the English and the French. In 1858 he signed the *Treaty of Aigun* with China under which the left hand bank of the Amur was handed over to Russia. For this Muraviov was granted the title 'Count of the Amur'. He founded the town of Blagoveshchensk, and he also created the Transbaikal and Amur Cossack armies. He retired in 1861.

he ordered lieutenant-captain **G.I. Nevelskoi** to explore the river mouth, whose suitability for navigation was uncertain.

In 1849 Nicholas I ordered that a special committee be set up on the 'Amur question'; and in 1851 he ordered a comprehensive expedition[1] to be formed to explore the surrounding region (*Priamurie*) and look into the possibility of annexing it to Russia. This expedition was headed by Nevelskoi.

About the same time in 1851 the emperor established a Transbaikal Cossack Army (consisting of about 50,000 men) and gave the order to deploy troops in Transbaikalia according to Muraviov's suggestion.

The necessity for resolving the 'Amur question' was emphasized by the Crimean War of 1853–5. During this war Great Britain and France despatched a naval flotilla to Siberia's Pacific coast. The Russians used the Amur to good effect for defence purposes. In June 1854 Muraviov directed an operation which involved moving 1,500 troops down the Amur from the Transbaikal area. Most of these troops later participated in the defence of the major Russian port of Petropavlovsk-Kamchatskii.

On 18 August 1854 the port was approached by the Anglo-French squadron under Admiral Price. The flotilla consisted of six ships, 236 guns and about 2,000 soldiers and sailors. The Russian garrison under the command of General **V.S. Zavoiko** consisted of about 1,000 soldiers and sailors and 94 guns.

The frigate *Aurora* and a few smaller boats took part in the defence of the town. Seven fortified artillery batteries were set up to defend the settlement. After an artillery bombardment on 20 August an Anglo-French reconnaissance force landed and was repulsed. On 24 August they launched a vigorous attack

Gennadii Ivanovich Nevelskoi (1813–76) was born into a noble family, graduated from a navy school and went on to serve in the navy. In 1847–9 he was captain of the military supply ship *Baikal*, and sailed it from Kronstadt to Petropavlovsk-Kamchatskii. In 1848–9 he explored the mouth of the Amur River and adjacent areas as instructed by the governor general of east Siberia. As a result of his exploration Nevelskoi established that the Amur River entered the sea in a single powerful stream (instead of having a shoal delta as previously thought[2]) and that Sakhalin was an island. These important discoveries were kept as classified secrets and helped the Russians during the Crimean War in 1853–5. In 1849–5 he was in charge of the comprehensive Amur Expedition; in 1853 he founded the first Russian settlement on Sakhalin; and in 1854 he founded a Russian port, Nikolaevsk-on-the-Amur, at the mouth of the river. He participated in the evacuation of the Russian troops and civilian population from Petropavlovsk-Kamchatskii to the Amur in 1855. He was promoted to the rank of rear admiral for his capable leadership of the Amur Expedition and his outstanding geographical discoveries (he was later promoted to vice-admiral and admiral). In 1856–76 he was a member of the Oceanographic Academic Committee in St Petersburg. He wrote many scientific works.

Vasilii Stepanovich Zavoiko (1809–1900) was born into a noble family, graduated from a naval school and went on to serve in the navy. In 1827 he
participated as a warrant officer in the Battle of Navarino against the Turkish
fleet. He took part in two circumnavigations. In 1840–9 he worked for the
Russian-American Company, was in charge of constructing the port of Aian
on the Sea of Okhotsk and later ran the operations of this port. In 1849 he
was appointed military governor of Kamchatka and was promoted to the
rank of major-general. He devoted a lot of effort to protecting sea mammals
from foreign poachers. In 1854 he directed the defence of Petropavlovsk-
Kamchatskii. Fortifications and artillery batteries were built under his leadership.
He personally led the defence operation aimed at repelling the Anglo-French
attacks on the town. In spring 1855 he directed the evacuation of the Petropavlovsk garrison and civilian population to the mouth of the Amur. In 1855 he
was appointed commander of Russian troops on the Pacific coast of Siberia;
he directed the construction and fortification of the naval port in Nikolaevsk-
on-the-Amur. In 1856 he was transferred to St Petersburg and promoted to
vice-admiral; in 1874 he was made admiral.

on Petropavlovsk-Kamchatskii. A 900-man landing party occupied Nikolskii
mountain, which was the key Russian position. But they were defeated in a
fierce hand-to-hand battle. The invaders lost more than half of their landing
force. On 27 August the Anglo-French squadron retreated.

The attack had demonstrated how difficult it was to defend the port which
led to the decision to move the townsfolk and the garrison to the mouth of
the Amur in the spring of 1855. In May 1855 Petropavlovsk was approached
by another Anglo-French squadron of 12 ships only to find the place empty
and evacuated. The squadron went to look for the Russians to the Strait of
Tartary and tried to land a reconnaissance party in De Castries Bay, but without
success.

The Crimean War showed how defenceless the Siberian coast was in the
case of a serious war threat and that only a resolution of the 'Amur question'
would make it possible to defend it successfully.

In May 1858 in the Chinese town of Aigun Muraviov demanded as an ulti-
matum that the Chinese governor of Manchuria, General I Shan, concede the
left-hand bank of the Amur to Russia. The Chinese government acquiesced.
On 16 May 1858 Muraviov and I Shan signed a Russo-Chinese peace treaty,
the *Treaty of Aigun*. This treaty:

- designated the Russo-Chinese border along the Amur River;
- proclaimed the territory east of the Ussuri river to be jointly owned by
  Russia and China pending the completion of demarcation; and
- allowed only Russian and Chinese boats to sail the Amur and its tributaries Ussuri and Sungari.

Two years later in November 1860 the *Treaty of Peking* was concluded which finalized the demarcation of the Russo-Chinese border in Siberia. This treaty:

- re-affirmed the Far Eastern part of Siberia (Primorie) as Russian land – the border ran along the Ussuri River and its tributary the Sungacha, along Lake Khanka, then along the mountain ridge to the Tumanjyang (Tumen) River and along this river to the Sea of Japan;
- designated the border west of the Yenisei to the Irtysh and then to the Tian-Shan Mountains;
- allowed tax-free trade between the Russian and Chinese population along the entire border;

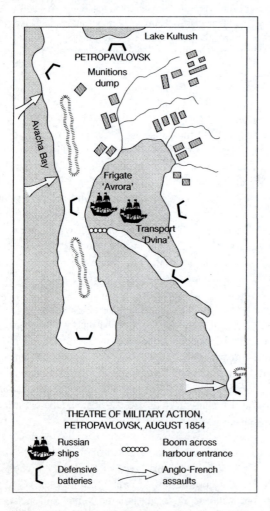

THEATRE OF MILITARY ACTION,
PETROPAVLOVSK, AUGUST 1854

Russian ships		Boom across harbour entrance	
Defensive batteries		Anglo-French assaults	

Figure 19.1 The Anglo-French onslaught on Petropavlovsk, August 1854

- granted Russian merchants free entry into China and the right to trade in Peking (Beijing);
- gave the Russians extra-territorial rights in China; and
- allowed Russia to open consulates in Urga (Mongolia) and in Kashgar (Xinjiang, Chinese Turkestan).

As a result of the successful resolution of the 'Amur question' Russia obtained new Siberian territories which were fit for habitation and began to actively explore them.

The Crimean War had also demonstrated that it was completely impossible to defend Alaska. In the second half of the nineteenth century its fur resource began to diminish, but its minerals had not yet been discovered. However, Russia did not have the means to explore Alaska. By 1867 there were only about 1,000 Russians in Russian America. Therefore the government decided to concede Alaska to the USA, so as not to let Great Britain – Russia's major rival of that time in the Asia-Pacific region – take it. In 1867 Alaska was sold to the USA for US $7.2 million. The sale of Alaska temporarily removed the threat of American expansionism into Siberia.

The annexation of Priamurie and Primorie to Russia brought Russian diplomats face to face with the business of settling territorial issues with Japan, which now became Russia's closest neighbour.

A negotiation process with Japan started in middle of the Crimean War on 26 January 1855 even before the annexation of the Amur, when Russian plenipotentiary representative vice-admiral E.V. Putiatin concluded the *Shimoda Peace Treaty* with Japan. This treaty:

- transferred the northern part of the Kuril Islands to Russia, and the southern part to Japan;
- proclaimed Sakhalin Island 'undivided' between Russia and Japan;
- allowed Russian ships to call at the Japanese ports of Shimoda, Hakodate and Nagasaki; and
- gave Russian merchants most favoured status in trading with Japan.

Some 20 years later, on 25 April 1875, Russia and Japan signed a new peace treaty in St Petersburg, which resolved border demarcation issues with Japan. According to this treaty Russia came into possession of Sakhalin and Japan was given all the Kuril Islands. In addition, Japanese merchants were granted most favoured status in trading with Russia, the right to fish in the Sea of Okhotsk and to use Russian ports including Port Korsakov on Sakhalin.

At the turn of the twentieth century a deterioration took place in Russo-Japanese relations because of a struggle for dominance over Manchuria and Korea. The upshot of this was the Russo-Japanese war of 1904–5 in which many Siberians participated. The war took place mostly on the territory of China and Korea, but some of it also happened in Siberia. In 1904 and 1905 the Japanese conducted naval operations (cruising, laying mines and attempting to shell towns) near Vladivostok. In 1904 they despatched a small reconnaissance party to Kamchatka that was repulsed by soldiers of the Petropavlovsk garrison and local civilian volunteers. In June 1905 the Japanese armed forces conducted a landing operation in Sakhalin. The fleet blockaded the island and the mouth of the Amur and troops (a 14,000-man force with artillery) were landed at several points on Sakhalin. Russian troops (small army units with almost no artillery and groups of poorly armed civilian volunteers and exiles totalling about 4,000) were unable to offer any serious resistance. After a few battles they were forced into the interior of the island and capitulated. As a result of this war and according to the *Russo-Japanese Portsmouth Peace Treaty* signed on 23 August 1905 Russia lost the southern part of Sakhalin.

After the war Russo-Japanese relations were normalized. The reason for this was that both countries were interested in maintaining good relations with each other. Russia sought to secure Siberia from the Japanese threat and Japan did not want Russia to become involved in the growing Japanese-American conflict. The result of this rapprochement was the signing on 17 July 1907 of the *Russo-Japanese St Petersburg Agreement* which normalized relations between the two countries. It contained confidential clauses which dealt with the delimitation of Russian and Japanese interests. The confidential clause of the *St Petersburg Agreement*:

- identified Russia's and Japan's spheres of influence in China (the Chinese border regions adjacent to Siberia – north Manchuria, Outer Mongolia, Tuva and Xinjiang – fell within Russia's orbit);
- recognized Korea to be within the sphere of Japan's 'special interests'; and
- recognized Inner Mongolia to be within the sphere of Russia's 'special interests'.

This agreement guaranteed Siberia's immunity from Japan and enabled Russia to expand Siberian territory.

An anti-Chinese uprising took place in Mongolia in 1911. Russia recognized Mongolia's independence from China and in 1913 obtained recognition of this from the Chinese government. As a result of these developments the province of Tuva (Tyva), hitherto under the control of Beijing, became cut off from China. Russia took advantage of this uncertain situation and made Tuva its protectorate in 1914. Tuva, in effect, became part of Siberia, under the name of the Uriankhai Region. The town of Belotsarsk was founded in Tuva and Russians began to settle in this region. By 1917 there were about 10,000 Russians living in Tuva.

In general, Russia managed to keep and considerably expand the territory of Siberia in the second half of the nineteenth and early twentieth centuries during a period of intense struggle for a division of the world into spheres of influence.

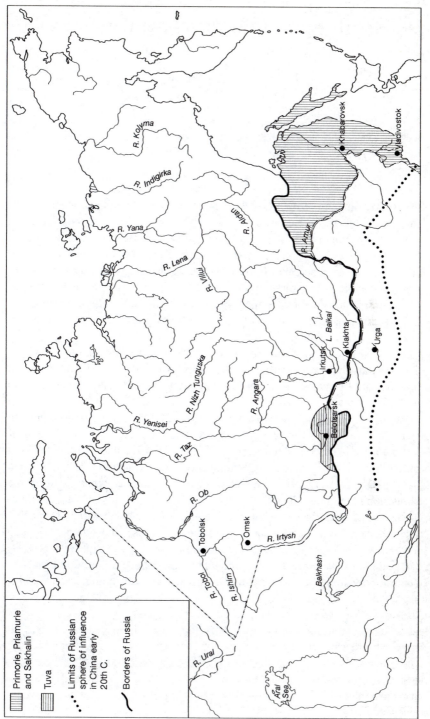

Figure 19.2 Additions to Siberian territory, late nineteenth to early twentieth centuries

R. Kolyma
R. Indigirka
R. Yana
R. Aldan
R. Lena
R. Vilui
R. Nizh Tunguska
R. Yenisei
R. Angara
R. Taz
R. Ob
R. Irtysh
R. Tobol
R. Ishim
R. Ural
Aral Sea
L. Balkhash
L. Baikal
R. Amur
Khabarovsk
Vladivostok
Irkutsk
Kiakhta
Urga
Belotsarsk
Tobolsk
Omsk

Primorie, Priamurie and Sakhalin
Tuva
Limits of Russian sphere of influence in China early 20th C.
Borders of Russia

20 Socio-economic development

Siberia's population growth was the basis of its socio-economic development. The settlement of Siberia intensified during the second half of the nineteenth and early twentieth centuries. This population increase was mainly brought about through settlers from European Russia. Thus, about 1.2 million people came to settle in Siberia in the last decade of the nineteenth century. There were even more new settlers in the early twentieth century: numbers grew to 2.5 million in the course of implementing Stolypin's agricultural reform.

The government's active resettlement policies led to a quick and steady increase in Siberia's population.

Mass resettlement, particularly intense in the south along the railway route, changed the ethnic composition of the Siberian population. The native share dropped to 29 per cent in the nineteenth century and to below 10 per cent in the early twentieth century.

The urban population grew steadily. It was 200,000 in the mid-nineteenth century, but at the end of that century (by the first overall Russian Census of 1897) it already amounted to over 470,000; and by 1917 it had grown to about one million. The populations of Vladivostok, Irkutsk and Omsk had reached the 100,000 mark by 1917. Especially rapid growth was experienced by the towns along the Trans-Siberian Railway: Kurgan, Omsk, Novonikolaevsk (later Novosibirsk), Krasnoiarsk, Irkutsk, Chita and Vladivostok. On the other hand, towns distant from the new railway, Tobolsk, Tomsk and others, began to decline.

Rapid population growth led to frequent modifications of the administrative/ territorial division of Siberia and to the formation of new administrative units.

Table 20.1 Siberian population growth, 1851–1917

Period	Total population	Percentage of Russian total
Mid 19th century	2,700,000	4.5
Late 19th century (1897)	5,700,000	4.5
Early 20th century (1917)	About 9,000,000	6.0

New provinces were formed in the east Siberian Governor Generalship in 1851: Transbaikalia (with its centre in Chita) and Kamchatka (whose centre was Petropavlovsk-Kamchatskii). The Province of Kamchatka was expanded and reorganized into the Province of Primorie in 1856. Its centre was Nikolaevsk-on-the-Amur, though this was changed to Vladivostok in 1856. An Amur Province with its centre in Blagoveshchensk was formed within the same Governor Generalship in 1858.

In 1882 the West Siberian Governor General's territory was abolished. The provinces of Tobolsk and Tomsk began to report directly to the government in St Petersburg, and the Province of Omsk became part of the newly formed Steppe governor generalship (centred in Omsk).

In 1884 the east Siberian Governor Generalship was divided into the Governor Generalships of Irkutsk and Priamurie (the latter centred in Khabarovsk).

In 1903 the Priamurie Governor Generalship was reorganized into a Far Eastern Vicegerency, which included a newly formed Province of Kwangtung (*Kvantun*)[1], centred in Port Arthur. In 1905 the Priamurie Governor Generalship was re-established, and the vicegerency and Kwangtung Province were abolished.

In 1909 the Province of Kamchatka (centred in Petropavlovsk-Kamchatskii) and Province of Sakhalin (centred in Alexandrovsk-Sakhalinskii) were created as entities separate from the Primorie province structure.

The intensive settlement of Siberia in the second half of the nineteenth and early twentieth centuries did not change the social composition of the population as a whole. Generally speaking, it remained the same. Only in a few places did hired workers take the place of craftsmen; and a few other changes occurred within the more numerous social groups, the peasants and Cossacks.

The craftsmen were replaced by workers as a result of a regional economic revolution involving the emergence of industrial production in Siberia. By 1917 the number of hired workers in Siberia was about 700,000. About 300,000 of them formed part of the industrial proletariat, i.e. they worked in large plants, smaller factories, coal mines and transportation. The workers' standard of living depended on their skills and place of work. Skilled workers were paid two to three times what unskilled workers were paid. Siberian workers' wages, as a whole, were higher than those in European Russia. For instance, in the early twentieth century a railway worker's average monthly wage was about 20 roubles, but workers on the Trans-Siberian Railway were making about 45 roubles a month. Most of the workers' working and living conditions were hard (long hours, accommodation in barracks or similar low quality housing, etc.).

During the period under review the peasants continued to be the main population group. As a result of Alexander II's reforms Siberian peasants were no longer divided into state, economic and Cabinet peasants. On the contrary, mass migration to the region in the late nineteenth and early twentieth centuries led to Siberian peasants being divided into 'old timers' (*starozhily*) and 'new comers' (*novosyoly*, i.e. more recent settlers). The 'new comers'' standard of living as a whole was much lower. Because the best farming land had already

Table 20.2 Territorial subdivisions of Siberia, 1851–1917 (all are 'provinces')

	Tobolsk	Tomsk	Omsk	Irkutsk	Yeniseisk	Yakutsk	Transbaikal	Amur	Primorskii	Kamchatka	Sakhalin
1851–6	*West Siberian Governor Generalship*			*East Siberian Governor Generalship*							
	Tobolsk	Tomsk	Omsk	Irkutsk	Yeniseisk	Yakutsk	Transbaikal			Kamchatka	
1856–8	*West Siberian Governor Generalship*			*East Siberian Governor Generalship*							
	Tobolsk	Tomsk	Omsk	Irkutsk	Yeniseisk	Yakutsk	Transbaikal		Primorsk		
1858–82	*West Siberian Governor Generalship*			*East Siberian Governor Generalship*							
	Tobolsk	Tomsk	Omsk	Irkutsk	Yeniseisk	Yakutsk	Transbaikal	Amur	Primorskii		
1884–1903				*Irkutsk Governor Generalship*			*Priamur Governor Generalship*				
	Tobolsk	Tomsk		Irkutsk	Yeniseisk	Yakutsk	Transbaikal	Amur	Primorskii		
1903–5				*Irkutsk Governor Generalship*			*Far Eastern Viceregency*				
	Tobolsk	Tomsk		Irkutsk	Yeniseisk	Yakutsk	Transbaikal	Amur	Primorskii	Kwantung	
1905–9				*Irkutsk Governor Generalship*			*Priamursk Governor Generalship*				
	Tobolsk	Tomsk		Irkutsk	Yeniseisk	Yakutsk	Transbaikal	Amur	Primorskii		
1909–17				*Irkutsk Governor Generalship*				*Priamursk Governor Generalship*			
	Tobolsk	Tomsk		Irkutsk	Yeniseisk	Yakutsk	Transbaikal	Amursk	Primorskii	Kamchatka	Sakhalin

been occupied, the new arrivals were settled in areas that were still available, and they were allocated only 15 *desiatinas* per family (in the past the same size allotments were offered for each male peasant). This resulted in the appearance of poor villages and poor peasants,[2] which gradually led to build up of social tensions among the agricultural population.

The Siberian Cossacks grew considerably in prominence during the latter part of the nineteenth century. As new areas were incorporated into Russian territory during this period, three more Cossack armies were formed in addition to the existing Siberian Cossack Army. They were: the Transbaikal Cossack Army (1851), the Amur Cossack Army (1858) and the Ussurii Cossack Army (1889). Recruits for these armies were drawn from among the peasants. The Cossacks were settled along the border and were allocated better quality land allotments than the ordinary peasants. The average Cossack land allotment in Siberia was 20 *desiatinas*. Social stratification was less pronounced among the Cossacks than among the peasants. By 1917 there were over half a million Cossacks in Siberia (265,000 in the Transbaikal Army, 170,000 in the Siberian Army, 50,000 in the Army of the Amur, and 35,000 in the Army of the Ussurii). The Cossacks served either as border guards or in towns. They participated in the defence of Siberia during the Crimean War in 1853–5, in the conquest of central Asia in 1850–80, in the suppression of the Boxer Uprising in China in 1900, and in the Russo-Japanese and the First World wars.

The intensive settlement of Siberia and its population growth tended to create favourable conditions for the acceleration of Siberia's economic development.

The transport industry played a huge role in the economic development of the region in the second half of the nineteenth and early part of the twentieth centuries. Steam powered river boats came into very widespread use at this time. Vessels and wharves were built on all the large Siberian rivers. In the late nineteenth century, for example, there were 56 steamboats on the River Amur, but by 1917 this figure had risen to over 300. At the outbreak of the February Revolution in 1917, Siberia had 7.5 per cent of all Russian steamboats. Maritime navigation was also developed, especially after the annexation of Primorie and the naval base and port of Vladivostok, whose waters do not freeze. In the early twentieth century there were around 80 Russian ships in the Pacific.

In 1891 the lengthy Trans-Siberian railway began to be built from Cheliabinsk in the Urals to Vladivostok on the Pacific, a distance of about 7,500 kilometres. The sections between Cheliabinsk and Krasnoiarsk and between Vladivostok and Khabarovsk had been built by 1897. The construction of this ambitious undertaking included both a train-carrying ice-breaker to ferry passengers and freight across Lake Baikal and a section of the Chinese Eastern Railway[3] which crossed Manchuria. There was also a line in Transbaikalia, between the station at Karimsk and another at Sretensk on the River Shilka. In 1905 the construction of the most complex section of the Trans-Siberian, a 300-kilometre stretch traversing the extremely difficult terrain to the south of Lake Baikal, was completed. It is a unique monument to Russian

Figure 20.1 The stern wheeler *Columbus* on the Amur

architecture and engineering, with more than 40 tunnels and many other complex constructions: galleries, walls, bridges, etc.

Though the building of the Trans-Siberian Railway had been completed, railway construction continued in Siberia. Lines were built from Ekaterinburg to Omsk[4] and a branch line from a station called Taiga to Tomsk in 1904. In 1911 a line from Novonikolaevsk to Semipalatinsk was built, with a branch line between Barnaul and Biisk. The next year a line was built between Tatarsk and Kulunda. In the same years the main Trans-Siberian Railway between Omsk and Karimsk was double-tracked. In 1916 a line between the station at Kuenga in Transbaikalia and Khabarovsk with a minor line branching off it from Bochkarevo to Vladivostok, as well as a line from Yurga to Kolchugino in the Kuznetsk Basin, were built. With the completion of the line between Kuenga and Khabarovsk trains could make the whole journey through entirely Russian territory, no longer having to take the previous course through Manchuria. The construction of lines between Kolchugino and Kuznetsk and between Achinsk and Abakan began in 1916.

The Trans-Siberian gave a new impetus to the economic development of Siberia. New industries appeared serving the railway and navigation: coal mining, railway workshops, ship building, ship repairing, construction, timber businesses and fishing. Electric power stations were being built in the towns. Of the old mining industries, only the performance of gold mining was stable.

Railway construction depended on the provision of coal. In the late nineteenth century coal mining began in some regions of Siberia. The biggest collieries were in Suchan (Primorie) and in the Kuznetsk coal basin at Anzhero-

Figure 20.2 Arkhipovka Station on the Trans-Siberian Railway

Sudzhensk and Kolchugino. There was a rapid increase in coal production. It grew a hundredfold over 18 years: whereas in 1895, 20,000 tons had been produced, by 1913 the total had already topped two million tons. In 1912, a joint-stock company known as 'Kopi Kuz' (Kuznetsk Collieries) was formed in the most prominent Siberian mining area, the Kuznetsk Basin. Kopi Kuz became a large coal-mining monopoly. Siberia's share in the coal production of the whole Russian Empire was, however, only 8 per cent. Railway work-shops were built at large stations to service the locomotives and rolling stock. The biggest of these were in Omsk, Novonikolaevsk (Novosibirsk), Krasnoiarsk, at Innokentevskaia Station near Irkutsk, in Chita and finally in Vladivostok. During the First World War, a factory producing rolling stock was built in Vladivostok. It was the largest works associated with this industry in Siberia, and employed over 5,000 workers.

Yards to manufacture and repair ships were built on all major Siberian rivers. The biggest of these were situated in Omsk, Krasnoiarsk, in the village of Listvenichnaia (on Lake Baikal) and in Sretensk.

In the late nineteenth century, the Far East Ship Repair Works was built in Vladivostok financed by the state. It was the biggest industrial business in Siberia, and employed well over 5,000 workers. Besides repairing ships, this works also produced machinery.

A fishing industry was developing rapidly in the Far East. In the early twentieth century about 200,000 tons were caught there every year, which comprised 15 per cent of the total catch for the Russian Empire.

The construction of the Trans-Siberian was an extra powerful spur to gold mining. The gold extraction industry became concentrated in two joint-stock companies, the 'Russian Gold Mining Company' and the 'Lena Gold Mining Company (Lenzoto)'. New equipment and up to date technologies were introduced into the process of gold production: draglines, hydraulic sand jets, etc. In 1908 'Lenzoloto', the biggest gold-mining company in Russia, was reconstituted into a joint Russian-English company, in which 70 per cent of the shares belonged to the English company called 'Lena Goldfields'. As a result, there was a consistent growth of gold production in Siberia. By 1910 the average annual production was 35 tons, constituting 75 per cent of Russia's total gold output. It should be noted, however, that the real production of gold was considerably higher since far less than the real total was recorded in official figures.

Nonetheless, despite the intensive growth of some industrial businesses, by 1917 Siberia, on the whole, remained a backward region as far as industry was concerned. Its share in Russia's total industrial production was only 3.5 per cent.

In the late nineteenth and early twentieth centuries agriculture, the leading sector within the Siberian economy, took a further step forward. During this period the sown area used by the peasants increased substantially. During the last decade of the nineteenth century and the first decade of the twentieth century it grew from 20 million to over 46 million *desiatinas* as a result of mass peasant colonization. In addition to this, over a million extra *desiatinas* of Siberian land were in private ownership and these were also mainly brought into agricultural production.

At this time four agricultural regions developed in the region where natural conditions were most favourable. These were the wooded-steppes of west

Figure 20.3 New technology at the Siberian gold diggings

Siberia, contiguous with the Kazakh steppes, the Altai, the Minusinsk Basin on the Yenisei, and territory adjoining Blagoveshchensk. These regions were transformed into Siberian granaries.

The peasants, both the old timers and some of the new settlers, developed their farms by Western farming methods that made it possible to use new agricultural machinery (tractors, steam threshers, multi-share ploughs, etc.) and new technologies, leading to richer harvests. Siberian peasants bought about 25 per cent of all the agricultural machinery sold in Russia.

As a result, agricultural production began to develop rapidly. If in the mid-nineteenth century 1.4 million tons of grain was harvested in Siberia, by the early twentieth century this had risen to over 7 million tons, which amounted to 16 per cent of Russia's total production. About 1.3 million tons of this harvest failed to find a ready sale locally, and was exported to European Russia.

Developments in livestock breeding led to the emergence of a substantial specialized business – butter production. Over 50 per cent of all Russia's butter-producing plants were situated in Siberia, and Siberian butter comprised around 90 per cent of all Russian exports.

> The whole of our butter export to foreign markets is entirely based on the growth of Siberian butter production. Siberian butter-making brings us more than twice as much gold as the whole Siberian gold industry.
>
> (P.A. Stolypin, Russian Prime Minister, 1906–11)

After the construction of the Trans-Siberian Railway, cheap Siberian agricultural products began to provide serious competition for Russian farmers. In 1897 the government had been persuaded to introduce the so-called 'Siberian tariff', an increased rate[5] on transporting grain and butter by rail to European Russia that lasted until 1913. This was done to protect Russian producers from Siberian competitors.

Figure 20.4 A refrigerated butter store, Kurgan, western Siberia

Construction of the Trans-Siberian lowered the cost of freight transportation by five to six times which encouraged the development of Siberian trade. Trade fairs (*yarmarki*) remained the leading method of exchange. The biggest of them was the Irbit Fair which was second in significance in the whole of Russia in the late nineteenth century. In the 1870s–80s annual turnover at the Irbit Fair reached 40–60 million roubles.

On the whole, however, petty, small-scale trade still prevailed in Siberia. Some 75 per cent of Siberian entrepreneurs had a yearly profit of less than 1,000 roubles. The 'Siberian tariff' also prevented trade from developing to some extent. The number of big businesses was not large. At the beginning of the twentieth century only about 70 businessmen had capital over a million roubles.

At the same time, Siberian businessmen were active in charities. The most famous in Irkutsk were I.M. Bazanov, I.N. Makushin, V.P. Sukachov and I.N. Trapeznikov and there were others.

> ... no other Siberian town could boast of such a bright and educated bourgeoisie as Irkutsk. It glorified itself with large financial donations to social establishments and, in later generations, provided a number of intellectual personalities in science, literature, and public affairs.
>
> (G.N. Potanin, a Siberian publicist and scientist)

In the late nineteenth century the cooperative movement became a new form of Siberian business. It was popular among the largest class, the peasantry.

Figure 20.5 A modern clothing store, Pesterov Street, Irkutsk

Cooperatives were formed for various types of economic activities. Consumers' cooperatives were the most widespread form, including 83 per cent of farms in Siberia by 1917. In 1916 all the Siberian cooperatives united into an all-Siberian organization *Zakupsbyt* ('Purchase-Sale'). By that time the share of cooperatives comprised more than 50 per cent of all Siberian commodity circulation.

The late nineteenth century brought quite a few innovations in the lives of Siberia's aboriginal inhabitants; some changes were for the better, others had a negative effect.

On the one hand, the sphere of Siberian aboriginal business and traditional activities broadened (farming, working for wages in the mines, etc.). They began to use new tools: guns, fishing nets, big harpoons, etc.). Their everyday life gradually changed. Russian clothing, houses, steam-baths and household goods became widely used.

On the other hand, assimilation processes began to increase in intensity. With the development of transportation, the places where Siberian Natives lived became easier of access, which strengthened their exploitation. So-called 'social diseases' began to spread among them: venereal diseases, alcoholism, as well as epidemics of smallpox. This led to the reduction of the aboriginal population, especially that of northern minorities.[6] Some peoples seemed almost on the verge of extinction.

21 The development of culture and science

In the late nineteenth and early twentieth centuries education in Siberia made considerable strides. At this time, the main forms of education included primary, secondary and higher education, vocational training, open learning schemes, and women's education.

Primary education was the leading form, since elementary schools comprised over 90 per cent of all Siberian educational institutions. Several types of these had developed, including municipal schools, schools run by government ministries, church schools, and missionary schools. Their curricula and periods of study varied from one to three years. At the beginning of the twentieth century there were about 4,000 elementary schools in Siberia, among which church schools predominated, accounting for around 50 per cent of the total.

The main type of high school was the *gymnasium* (a classical school preparing pupils for entry to university) which had an eight-year curriculum. In 1864 the government established four-year *progymnasiums* as an incomplete form of secondary school. Teaching in these was carried out according to the elementary school curriculum. Its graduates were admitted to the fifth grade of *gymnasiums* without having to take entrance examinations. In 1877 *real schools* were added which taught more advanced classes of science subjects, such as mathematics, physics and chemistry. From the fifth grade onwards *real school* students were able to specialize in different majors (mechanics, chemistry, commerce, etc.). The graduates had the right to continue their studies only at technical educational institutions. In the late nineteenth and early twentieth centuries there were 17 *gymnasiums*, 5 *real schools* and 14 *progymnasiums* in Siberia. During the next 15 years several dozen new educational institutions of these types were opened.

It was during this period that university education appeared in Siberia. In 1888 Tomsk University, the first in Siberia, opened. In 1899, the Institute of Oriental Studies was inaugurated in Vladivostok, becoming the centre for such studies in Siberia. The institute trained specialists in the Chinese, Japanese, Korean, Mongolian and Tibetan languages. In 1900 Tomsk Technological Institute opened. It produced engineers for Siberian industry and transport. In 1916 the Emperor Nicholas II signed an act to set up another university in Irkutsk, but owing to revolutionary events it only opened in 1918.

In the late nineteenth and early twentieth centuries the sphere of vocational training widened considerably. It covered various fields of activity, divided into lower and higher levels.

Vocational schools, providing training for railway workers, miners, metal craftsmen, etc., operated at the lower level. Such schools opened in many Siberian towns: Omsk, Tomsk, Krasnoiarsk, Irkutsk, Chita, Blagoveshchensk, Vladivostok and others.

Trained mechanics, train drivers, teachers, veterinarians, officers, clergymen, etc. were needed. A range of higher vocational training schools, colleges and institutes were opened with specific specialisms in transport, technical subjects, agriculture, teacher training and theology. The largest and most significant vocational training institutions in Siberia in the early twentieth century were the Maritime School in Vladivostok, the Blagoveshchensk River School, the Barnaul and Irkutsk mining schools, the Irkutsk Industrial School, the Irkutsk and Khabarovsk railway colleges, the Irkutsk Military School and the Cadet School in Omsk.[1]

In the late nineteenth and early twentieth centuries open learning received a considerable boost. A variety of Sunday schools, evening classes, social clubs, etc. opened around this time in various towns and villages. They engaged in a range of educational activities, including teaching reading and writing to adults and children.

Women's education was a special type of enterprise. It first appeared in Siberia in the mid-nineteenth century when Institutes for Young Ladies were established in Irkutsk and Tobolsk (1857).[2] Soon after this, women's colleges run by the church, and non-ecclesiastical women's *gymnasiums* and *progymnasiums*, were established. By the early twentieth century a total of some 50 women's educational institutions had been opened, varying in levels and emphases. They educated rather more than 40,000 people[3] which was about 28 per cent of the total student number.

Owing to the development of education, the number of literate people in Siberia was constantly on the increase. The first all-Russian population census in 1897 registered 12.5 per cent of the Siberian population as literate; by 1917 the figure had already risen to 27 per cent. Big cities, especially Tomsk and Irkutsk, remained the largest centres for education. In the early nineteenth and late twentieth centuries they contained 68 and 45 educational institutions respectively.

Despite the positive quantitative improvement in education, however, Siberia was markedly inferior to European Russia, where in 1897 22.5 per cent of population was literate, this figure rising to 47 per cent by 1919. The development of education in Siberia was considerably hindered by the absence of the *zemstvos*.[4]

The late nineteenth – early twentieth centuries added many new things to the cultural life of Siberia. In 1857 there appeared a series of regular news sheets for each province, the *Gubernskie vedomosti*. Soon afterwards a large number of independent and professional newspapers emerged. The most influential and popular papers were the *Eastern Review* (*Vostochnoe obozrenie*), published in Irkutsk,[5] and the *Siberian Herald* (*Sibirskii vestnik*), published in Tomsk. Library affairs achieved considerable development, with public lending libraries appearing in all major Siberian settlements.

Museums came into existence. The first such institution in Siberia was opened in Minusinsk in 1877. At the beginning of the twentieth century museums existed in provincial and regional centres, and some in county (*uezd*) centres such as Troitskosavsk, Nerchinsk, Minusinsk and so on.

Tremendous developments occurred in the arts. The first Siberian professional theatre opened in Irkutsk in 1891. Afterwards, theatres were established in all the major towns of Siberia. Art and architecture were developing. A variety of art exhibitions were regularly held in Siberian towns. **V.P. Sukachov**, a mayor of Irkutsk, founded the first Siberian art museum.

An important role in the cultural development of Siberia was played by various provincial and regional societies for education, medicine, industry and so on. Examples are the Society of Doctors of East Siberia (Irkutsk, 1863), the east Siberian branch of the Russian Technical Society (Irkutsk, 1867) and others. They engaged in a large number of educational activities.

During the second half of the nineteenth century and the early twentieth century intensive research continued into Siberia itself. During this period more detailed and profound investigations were undertaken into its geology, zoology, botany, climate, topography, ethnography, linguistics and ancient history. The centres which carried out this research included the Russian Academy of Sciences and particularly the Russian Geographical Society, with its east Siberian, west Siberian, and Priamur branches founded in Irkutsk, Omsk, and Khabarovsk in 1851, 1877 and 1894 respectively. Other input came from the

Vladimir Platonovich Sukachov (1849–1920) was born into the family of an Irkutsk official. In 1867 he graduated from a *gymnasium* in Irkutsk and entered Kiev University. In the 1870s he graduated from the Science Department at Kiev and the Law Department of St Petersburg University. In 1880 he came back to Irkutsk. Between 1881 and 1885 he was an elected member of the Irkutsk City Council. From 1885 to 1898 he was the mayor. He greatly contributed to the city's development and the organization of public services and amenities. He intiated the establishment of new educational institutions, frequently making financial donations to them. Many public buildings still gracing the city were built on his initiative, including the theatre, the Russian Geographical Society building and others. He developed a sizeable personal art collection and organized the first public art gallery in Siberia. In 1898 he resigned from his post because of his wife's health and left for St Petersburg where he engaged in popularizing Siberia, publishing magazines, albums, postcards, etc. He was elected Freeman of the City of Irkutsk. In 1917 he retired to the Crimea where he died.

Figure 21.1 Irkutsk municipal theatre, 1891

administration of the Siberian governers general, the first Siberian higher educational institutions, the Society for Siberian Research (*Obshchestvo po izucheniiu Sibiri*), the Society for Research into the Amur Region (*Obshchestvo izucheniia Amurskogo kraia*) and from regional professional societies. All these organizations mounted periodic expeditions to investigate Siberia.

World-famous scientists such as V.K. Arsenev, G.N. Potanin, N.M. Przhevalskii, **V.V. Radlov** and many others contributed a great deal to this process.

Polish political exiles **B.I. Dybowski**, I.D. Cherskii and others also played a significant role in studying Siberia.

Vasilii Vasilevich Radlov (1837–1918) was born into the family of a nobleman and went on to study linguistics at German universities. After returning to Russia he worked as a teacher in Barnaul between 1858 and 1871. From 1871 to 1884 he was a regional school inspector. During the years 1858–98 he studied southern Siberia and Turkestan and led a number of research expeditions. He initiated the study of the ancient history of southern Siberia and central Asia and investigated the Turkic-speaking peoples of Siberia – their language, ethnography and history. He is the author of a fundamental scientific work *The Dialects of the Turkic Tribes Living in South Siberia and Dzungar Steppe*. Together with the Danish scientist V. Tomsen he made a discovery of world significance by deciphering the ancient Turkic writings of the Siberian peoples (the 'Orkhon-Yenisei Inscriptions'). In 1884 he was elected academician of the Russian Academy of Sciences. He was the founder of the Museum of Anthropology and Ethnography in St Petersburg and its first director.

Figure 21.2 The Russian Geographical Society building in Irkutsk

Benedict Ivanovich Dybowski (1833–1930) was born into the family of a nobleman in Poland. He graduated from Dorpat University and in 1860 received his Doctor's degree in zoology and was appointed Professor of Zoology in Warsaw Main School. He took part in the Polish movement for national independence and was exiled to Siberia for participation in the Polish Uprising of 1863–4. He served his exile in village of Kultuk on Lake Baikal. Supported by the east Siberian branch of the Russian Geographical Society, he began a comprehensive study of Lake Baikal (its fauna, depth measurements, water temperature and level changes, its chemical composition, etc.). In 1870 he was awarded the gold medal of the Russian Geographical Society for this research. In 1876 he was pardoned and allowed to return to Poland, but voluntarily remained in Siberia. Between 1879 and 1883 he worked as a doctor in Petropavlovsk-Kamchatskii, and was active in exploring Kamchatka. In 1884 he emigrated from Russia to Austria-Hungary where he became a professor at Lvov University (until 1906). He was the author of many scientific works. In 1928 he was elected Associate Member of the Academy of Sciences of the USSR for service to Russian science.

The results of Siberian research of that time have retained their validity to the present-day. It was then that a firm basis for a more profound and comprehensive study of Siberia was created.

22 Siberian social life

Siberia in the Revolution of 1905–7

In the second half of the nineteenth century social life in Siberia became more active. In 1860–70 various professional and educational societies, committees, etc. emerged very quickly. The Siberian independent press, undertaking broad discussions of local and Russia-wide events, played an especially significant role in the development of social life. It began to actively form a public opinion. It was characterized by a critical orientation. The first independent newspaper, the *Amur*, published in Irkutsk from 1860, was closed by the local authorities in 1862 for this very reason. The uncompromising stand of the Siberian independent press ensured it considerable popularity and influence in society. The newspapers *Eastern Review* and *Siberian Herald* were particularly influential. The opposition stance of the press was largely caused by the fact that political exiles, Poles, 1860s radicals, Populists, Liberals and Marxists took an active role in it.

In the late nineteenth century an independent regionalist movement emerged in Siberia (*Sibirskoe oblastnichestvo*). The influence of the political exiles and independent press gave rise to this movement, as did the incomplete implementation of Alexander II's reforms here, such as the refusal to introduce *zemstvos*. The founders of the Siberian Regionalism were **G.N. Potanin**, N.M. Yadrintsev and other Siberian public activists.

The main ideas of the Siberian regionalists were formulated by Yadrintsev in the book *Siberia as a Colony* (*Sibir kak koloniia*), published in 1882. The author argued that a special type of people had developed in Siberia over an extended historical period – active, enterprising people. At the same time, Russia continued to consider Siberia its colony and was artificially hindering its development. Therefore, Siberia needed political autonomy which would create favourable conditions for creative activity of its people and for the development of the region. In Yadrintsev's view, it was also necessary to establish *zemstvos* in Siberia to facilitate its cultural development.

This book had a tremendous effect on the public both in Siberia and in Russia. Its ideas spread among the Siberian intelligentsia, merchants and lower middle class. The independent press also championed the ideas of the Siberian regionalists. This was particularly true of the *Eastern Review*, founded by Yadrintsev himself. It played the role of a real mouthpiece for the members of the society.

Grigori Nikolaevich Potanin (1835–1920) was born into the family of a Cossack officer, in Siberia. He graduated from the Siberian Cadet School in Omsk and then served as an officer in the Siberian Cossack Regiment. In 1858–62 he studied at St Petersburg University. In 1863–4 he took part in an expedition to Lake Zaisan in the Altai organized by the Russian Geographical Society, making a detailed survey and description of the lake. In 1865 he was arrested and imprisoned on a charge of attempting to separate Siberia from Russia. He was then exiled to Vologda Province in northern European Russia where he remained until 1874. After the expiry of his exile, he returned to Siberia. In 1876 he went with an expedition to north-western Mongolia and Tuva, and in 1884–6 and 1892–4 went on expeditions to Mongolia and China. He organized several expeditions in Siberia, during which very valuable material on geography, geology, ethnography, botany, etc. was gathered. He also collected the most detailed herbarium of central Asian flora and discovered many new species of plants. In 1886 he was awarded the gold medal of the Russian Geographical Society. He attracted V.A. Obruchev and I.D. Cherskii to study Siberia; they both subsequently became world-famous scientists. In 1886–90 he was the head of the east Siberian branch of the Russian Geographical Society in Irkutsk. In the 1890s he lived in St Petersburg, after the turn of the century moving to Tomsk where he served in the Tomsk Provincial Council. He was a very active participant in public affairs. He founded the Society for the Study of Siberia, a number of museums and exhibitions, as well as higher educational courses for women in Tomsk. He contributed a number of critical articles on various issues of Siberian life and was one of the founders and leaders of Siberian Regionalism. During the Revolution of 1905–7 he was at the head of the Siberian Regional Union (*Sibirskii oblastnoi soiuz*). In 1917 he was elected Chairman of the Siberian Executive Committee at the First Siberian Regional Congress. The committee was entrusted with organizing elections for a Siberian regional assembly (*Sibirskaia oblastnaia duma*) and with working out a draft constitution for a devolved Siberian government.

In the late nineteenth and early twentieth centuries new political organizations[1] emerged in Siberia. These were small societies of a social-democratic and socialist-revolutionary orientation, formed by political exiles.

In 1901 social-democratic societies in Tomsk, Krasnoiarsk and Irkutsk united to form the Siberian Social Democratic Union which was active until 1908. The union declared itself a regional branch of the Russian Social Democratic Workers' Party (RSDWP). It set itself the task of developing class-consciousness among the Siberian workers and propagandizing for political freedom, as well as uniting the Siberian Marxists into a single unified organization. The union turned out leaflets, distributed illegal Marxist literature, set up Social Democratic groups in Siberian towns and assisted exiled Marxists. Even after the Russian Party's 1903 split into Bolsheviks and Mensheviks, the united organizations and groups of Social Democrats in Siberia continued their activities.

In the early twentieth century underground organizations of the Socialist Revolutionary Party (SRs) began to emerge in Siberia. They were engaged in similar activities from a different ideological perspective.

The people of Siberia were very active in the First Russian Revolution, which took place between 1905 and 1907. Apart from nationwide causes, the movement was protesting against specific local grievances as well. Siberians were displeased with the introduction of a punitive tariff on their exports in 1897, Siberia being kept backward vis-à-vis European Russia (the absence of *zemstvos*, the late and incomplete introduction of the 1864 legal code,[2] etc.), the course of the Russo-Japanese War, and the growing Japanese threat. They were greatly influenced by the independent press, Siberian regionalists and the political exiles who had strong feelings against the government. Apart from this, the political exiles had essential revolutionary experience, which made it easier to fight against the authorities.

As a result, Siberia became one of the hotbeds of the First Russian Revolution and the events proceeded quite vigorously. Various political forces were involved in it across a spectrum beginning with the Anarchists and ending with the Liberals and Regionalists. The forms of their revolutionary activities varied greatly.

Siberian revolutionaries paid a good deal of attention to agitation and the propagation of revolutionary ideas. They published substantial quantities of leaflets and proclamations and later newspapers as well, all of which called for revolutionary struggle. Rallies, demonstrations, meetings, as well as the setting up of trade unions, served the same purposes.

After the emperor's 'October Manifesto' (17 October 1905), which officially allowed political and trade union activities, in October–November of the same year unions of peasants, railway workers, printers, postal workers, etc. were set up in various regions of Siberia. All of them were branches of the appropriate all-Russian Unions and followed their political line of opposition to the government. Somewhat earlier, in August 1905, the Siberian Regionalists formed a Siberian Regional Union headed by G.N. Potanin. The union lobbied for the establishment of *zemstvos* in Siberia, for the region to be granted autonomy and for the convening a Siberian Regional Assembly (*Oblastnaia Duma*).

All of these activities helped spread anti-government sentiments among a considerable part of the population, which enabled the revolutionaries to organize a number of large events in Siberia.

For instance, Siberians took an active part in strikes. During the decade preceding the Revolution (1895–1905), there had been only 321 strikes, in which around 45,000 people were involved. But 347 strikes were registered with more than 70,000 participants in 1905 alone. Siberians were especially active in the nationwide political strike in October 1905 when the whole of the Trans-Siberian Railway workforce, telegraph workers, printers, teachers, students, lawyers, clerks and other workers went on strike.

After the October strike the revolutionaries succeeded in forming soviets of workers' and/or soldiers' deputies in Achinsk, Barnaul, Vladivostok, Irkutsk,

Krasnoiarsk, Novosibirsk, Khabarovsk and Chita. The soviets became the means through which the revolutionary forces organized themselves. It was precisely in the places where the soviets had been formed that the most significant revolutionary actions occurred.

Influenced by revolutionary agitation and propaganda, soldiers began to mutiny in a number of Siberian garrisons: in Tomsk, Khabarovsk, Irkutsk, Sretensk and a few other places. Soviets of soldiers' deputies were formed in some of them at the end of 1905. In Krasnoiarsk and Chita, soldiers took part in seizures of power in December 1905; in Vladivostok and Nikolaevsk-on-the-Amur there were armed uprisings among the military in January 1906.

The biggest mutinies were those that took place in Vladivostok. The first one, on 30–31 October 1905, made the military leaders forbid the soldiers and sailors to attend rallies and other sessions at which the emperor's October Manifesto was being discussed. The uprising was spontaneous. About 15,000 soldiers and sailors from the Vladivostok garrison (25 per cent of its total) were involved in it. It was accompanied by massive pogroms and public disorders. The military leadership managed to suppress it rapidly. The second uprising, between 10 and 16 January 1906, was caused by the military firing at a peaceful demonstration in memory of the victims of 'Bloody Sunday', an event which had taken place in St Petersburg in January 1905. Soldiers of the 32nd Regiment and the Artillery Battery were involved in it. They virtually seized Vladivostok and formed an executive committee to head the uprising. As there were no reliable army units in town, troops had to be transferred from Manchuria to suppress it.

Political terror became one of the leading forms of revolutionary struggle among the Siberians. It was predominantly the Anarchists and Socialist Revolutionaries (SRs) who practised it. Over these revolutionary years, dozens of terrorist acts were committed against governmental personnel. The most infamous acts of terror were the murder of General Litvinov, the Governor of Akmolinsk Oblast in 1906; the killing of the Chief of Police in Irkutsk, Dragomirov, in 1905; and the severe wounding of the Deputy Governor of Irkutsk, Mishin, during the same year.

Overall the revolution caused massive bitterness to develop in Siberia. It was accompanied by terror and mass pogroms from both sides in many Siberian towns. For instance, in October 1905 the Tomsk 'Black Hundred' organization (the so-called *chornosotnye*, who were radical supporters of the monarchy) instigated a massacre, during which around 300 people were killed. The Russian army's revolutionary-minded soldiers, in their turn, committed massacres in railway stations a number of times on the way back from Manchuria. Criminal activity also became very frequent during the revolution.

Gradually, as a result of the revolutionary struggle, the local authorities began to lose control over the political situation in Siberia. This process became especially obvious after the All-Russian Political Strike and the October Manifesto. In December 1905 the so-called 'Krasnoiarsk Republic' and the

'Chita Republic' came into existence when the power in these towns was seized by the soviets of workers' and soldiers' deputies.

In Krasnoiarsk, a united Soviet of Workers' and Soldiers' Deputies was formed on 9 December. SRs, Social Democrats and non-party revolutionaries participated in it. The Soviet aimed for an immediate seizure of power in the city. The rebels seized the provincial printing house and began to issue a newspaper of their own, *Krasnoiarsk Worker* (*Krasnoiarskii rabochii*), through which they informed the people of their actions. The Soviet disarmed the police and the gendarmery, and organized soldiers to keep the peace. It gained control over the railway. The 'Krasnoiarsk Republic' lasted until 3 January 1906 when the uprising was crushed by General Redko's troops on their arrival in the city from European Russia.

In Chita, the revolutionaries also formed a united Soviet of Workers', Soldiers', and Cossacks' Deputies on 28 November 1905. Its party membership was similar to that in Krasnoiarsk. It was headed by the Social Democrats **I.V. Babushkin**, V.K. Kurnatovskii and A.A. Kostushko-Voluiuzhanich.

The Soviet-formed and armed workers' squads, numbering up to 2,000 people, took control over the railway and introduced an eight-hour working day; they began to publish the newspaper *Transbaikal Worker* (*Zabaikalskii rabochii*) to inform the population. On 7 December 1905 the Soviet disarmed the police, seized the arsenal, removed the administration, and virtually seized power in the city. Order in Chita was maintained by the workers' squads

Ivan Vasilevich Babushkin (1873–1906) was born into a peasant family in Vologda Province. Aged ten years, he arrived in St Petersburg and began to work. Between 1891 and 1896 he was a worker at the Semiannikov Factory in St Petersburg. He attended a Sunday school where he met Marxists, including V.I. Lenin. From 1894 he became involved in the revolutionary movement. He was a member of the RSDWP from 1898; after it split up he became a Bolshevik. In 1897 he was exiled to Yekaterinoslav (Dnepropetrovsk) for three years for his revolutionary activities. He became one of the founders of the local RSDWP branch. In 1900–1 he lived in Smolensk acting as a Marxist newspaper agent and in 1901 he was arrested and exiled, but in 1902 he escaped abroad from his place of the exile. In the same year he returned to St Petersburg illegally. In 1903 he was arrested again and exiled for five years to Verkhoiansk in Yakutsk Province. In 1905 he was amnestied and came to Irkutsk where he became a member of the local RSDWP committee and was involved in the revolution. At the end of 1905, he moved to Chita to become a leader of the 'Chita Republic'. In January 1906 he took charge of the transportation of arms to Irkutsk with the aim of spreading the uprising. He was arrested by troops of a punitive expedition in the station at Sliudianka on Lake Baikal, and was shot at Mysovaia (now named Babushkin in his honour).

and soldiers. The Soviet released all political prisoners from the infamous high-security Akatui prison. On 22 January 1906 the 'Chita Republic' was crushed by General P.K. Rennenkampf's troops which arrived in the city from Manchuria.

In early 1906 the authorities succeeded in restoring order in Siberia, with great difficulty, requiring military assistance. However, they had to essentially abolish the Siberian tariff of 1897 which amounted to an important victory by the Siberians in the struggle for their rights. The events in Siberia contributed significantly to Russia becoming a constitutional monarchy. Soon afterwards the revolution in Siberia began to recede noticeably. For example, 131 strikes, involving 22,000 people, occurred in 1906, but throughout the whole of 1907 there were only 75 strikes with 12,000 participants.

The most significant action in the period of revolutionary decline in Siberia was an uprising in Vladivostok on 16–17 October 1907, when revolutionary activity had virtually ended. It had been prepared since the spring of 1907 by an illegal military organization of the Social Democrats (SDs) and SRs. It had not been prepared well enough owing to the arrest of some of the revolutionaries. Soldiers from a sappers' battalion and from the crews of the torpedo-boats 'Skoryi', 'Serdityi' and 'Trevozhnyi' were involved in the uprising. It was soon suppressed.

Russia's transition to a constitutional monarchy as a result of the First Russian Revolution revived the country's socio-political life. Local branches of Russian political parties were established, Siberians playing a significant role in their activities. A noteworthy example was **N.V. Nekrasov**, a professor from Tomsk, who became one of the recognized leaders of the Liberal Constitutional-Democratic ('Cadet') Party.

The most significant of all occurrences in Siberian social life at this time were the Lena Events of 1912 that became infamous in Russia and abroad. A strike began in response to the extremely poor quality of life suffered by the workers at the Bodaibo gold mines. The mines belonged to the Lena Goldfields Company which forced their employees to buy poor quality food at exorbitant rates instead of paying decent wages; private trade was forbidden at the mines. The working day was commonly 13–14 hours long, and day-to-day life was difficult. The strike began on 29 February 1912, and soon it involved nearly all the mines. The strikers demanded an eight-hour working day, a 30 per cent wage increase, and improvements in food supply and living conditions. The authorities arrested members of the Strike Committee, and on 4 April the police opened fire on a protest demonstration. Some 250 people were killed and a further 270 were wounded.

These events became widely known. It was a subject of debate in the State Duma (Parliament) and caused a great deal of social unrest and disturbances all over Russia. The official investigation into the Lena Events revealed the scandalous tyranny under which the workers lived.

Nikolai Vissarionovich Nekrasov (1897–1940) was born into the family of a priest. In 1902 he graduated from the St Petersburg Institute of Railway Engineers. He lived abroad for two years then became a professor at Tomsk Technological Institute. He was a member of the Cadet Party from 1905, and took part in its Constituent Congress. Between 1909 and 1917 he was a member of the party's Central Committee. A freemason since 1910, he was elected a member for Tomsk Province in the new Russian national parliament, the State Duma, during its third and fourth sessions. In 1916 he was elected vice-chairman of the State Duma. Involved in a plot against Nicholas II, he was in favour of establishing a republic. After the February Revolution of 1917 he was appointed minister of railways, then minister of finance and then deputy prime minister in the Provisional Government. During the attempted left-wing insurrection in July 1917 he left the Cadet Party and in August 1917 he was removed from the Provisional Government. After the October Revolution he stayed in Russia, working as a statistician and then taught at Moscow University. In 1921 he was arrested, but released by personal order of Lenin. In 1930 he was arrested again and sentenced to ten years in prison in connection with the so-called 'RSDWP Central Committee Case'. He served his sentence of hard labour building the Moscow–Volga canal. In 1933 he was released, but still kept working on the canal. In 1939 he was arrested again and was shot soon afterwards.

Part VII

The Revolution and Civil War in Siberia (1917–22)

23 1917 in Siberia

The year 1917 entered Russian history as the one that marked the monarchy's downfall and the Bolshevik seizure of power. These events proved to be a turning point for this huge country and its inhabitants including Siberia and the Siberians.

The February Revolution, which resulted in the demise of the monarchy, was caused by the First World War (1914–18). The war had a dual effect on the development of Siberia. On the one hand, there is no doubt that the hostilities accelerated the region's economic development. On the other hand, it led to price rises and inflation. Many thousands of Siberians were drafted into the army, and a large proportion of them perished or ended up in captivity. Many refugees from the occupied territories of western Russia arrived in Siberia. All this gave rise to a certain tension and a mood of protest among the population.

By 1917 Siberians were suffering from war-weariness, but, on the whole, the region remained loyal to the monarchy. The onset of the February Revolution was an unexpected event as far as its people were concerned.

The first news of the revolutionary events in Petrograd (the capital's name had been changed because 'St Petersburg' was rather German-sounding) reached Siberia on 28 February 1917.[1] The governors of Siberia had tried to hide it from the populace. At the same time they forbade any meetings or rallies. These measures gave rise to much rumour and social unrest.

Only between 2 and 5 March, when the victory of the revolution became a fact, did Siberia learn about it. The news caused an explosion of enthusiasm in towns and cities; many demonstrations and rallies were held in support of it.

All the governors general, governors, police chiefs and commanders of the gendarmerie were removed from office. New organs of power, called Committees of Public Safety (CPSs), were formed. These were based on a coalition, established on the basis of the municipal local government councils, socio-political organizations, and the local committees of the various political parties. The CPSs maintained order and organized local political life. Such institutions were formed in all Siberia's provinces and regions and in the major cities as well.

Soviets of Workers' and Soldiers' Deputies began to form in towns alongside the CPSs. They were established by the members of the revolutionary parties, the SRs, Bolsheviks, Mensheviks and Anarchists, of whom there were a significant number in Siberia, particularly after their release from prison and exile. The Socialists envisioned the role of the Soviets as being the establishment of control over the CPSs and other organs of power.

In March 1917 the Russian Provisional Government appointed plenipotentiary commissars, instead of governors, to all Siberian regions. They were, as a rule, outstanding representatives of the Siberian public. All power in the provinces and regions was vested in their hands. They were supported by the former government's administrative bodies. In June 1917 the Provisional Government finally established *zemstvos* in Siberia.

After the February Revolution, a polarizing of political forces and a struggle for influence and power began in Siberia, just as in the rest of Russia. By the autumn of 1917 two political forces had emerged in Siberia, bourgeois-liberal and socialist, both of which on the whole supported the Provisional Government.

The first camp consisted of the Siberian Regionalists, members of the Cadet and Octobrist parties (the latter, founded in support of the 1905 October Manifesto, being somewhat more conservative than the Cadets) and representatives of Siberian commerce and industry. The *Intelligentsia* (an educated, radical socio-political group), officialdom and the bourgeoisie constituted its main support. Its leaders conceived their aim to be support for the Provisional Government and working to prevent the country from degenerating into anarchy, as well as ensuring broader rights and achieving the status of autonomy for Siberia.

This liberal middle-class camp succeeded in having the *zemstvos* established in Siberia, and from summer 1917 played an active part in organizing them. In addition, preparation for the first Siberian Regional Congress began during the summer. The congress was held in Tomsk from 8 to 17 October 1917. Some 169 delegates[2] from towns, public organizations, trade unions and all the political parties, including the Bolsheviks, participated in its deliberations. The congress resolved to convene a Siberian Constituent Regional Congress (*Uchreditelnyi Sibirskii oblastnoi sezd*) in the winter of 1917–18 to adopt a constitution for the future autonomous Siberia. It elected an executive committee entrusted with the task of working out the draft constitution and preparing the congress. The executive committee was headed by G.N. Potanin, the recognized leader of the Siberian Regionalists. However, by the time the October Revolution took place the bourgeois-liberal camp had not become fully organized.

The other camp, the Socialists, comprised members of the SRs, the Bolshevik and Menshevik parties, Soviet delegates with no party affiliation, plus representatives of the Siberian cooperative movement. The socialist camp gained its support from the workers, soldiers and peasants. Originally, its leaders had the following aims: to organize the working people for establishing control over the activities of the authorities and to prevent the restoration of the monarchy. In addition they wished to broaden the workers' socio-economic

Figure 23.1 A revolutionary meeting in Irkutsk, March 1917

rights (an eight-hour working day, democratic labour legislation, etc.). On the whole, the socialist camp supported the Provisional Government's policies, but they also frequently sharply criticized it for inconsistency. The socialists' main aim was to convene an All-Russian Constituent Assembly, whose role would be to devise a constitution for the future democratic Russian state. The socialist camp's representatives were not unanimous on the issue of Siberian autonomy.

To achieve its aims, the socialist camp, as has already been said, intensified the formation of soviets of workers' and soldiers' deputies in the towns, and peasant soviets in the countryside. Whereas there were only 67 soviets in Siberia in March, by the summer there were already more than 150. In the autumn the socialist camp's supporters began active preparation for the elections to the Russian Constituent Assembly.

As the socialist camp contained fairly diverse political forces, it suffered from a lack of inner unity. In the autumn 1917 it was already beginning to fragment politically, owing to the Bolshevik Party's policies. By the time of the October Revolution, several splits had occurred and the camp was in a state of confusion and disorder.

The Bolsheviks played a special role in the events of 1917. It was their party that eventually succeeded in seizing power in Russia.

To start with, the Bolsheviks in Siberia remained in united RSDWP organizations together with the Mensheviks. Yet, as early as late March 1917, exiled Bolsheviks had formed a separate committee, the Central Siberian Bureau of their Central Committee (*Sredne-sibirskoe Biuro RSDRP(b)*) in Krasnoiarsk. Since it was under Bolshevik control, in April the Central Committee approved the bureau as an official organ of its own. The bureau's main task was to set up independent Bolshevik organizations in Siberia and to lead them. However, owing to the weakness of Bolshevik influence, even as late as August they had only been able to set up such an organization in one major city, Krasnoiarsk.

The Sixth Bolshevik Party Congress, held in Petrograd in July–August 1917, adopted a policy of seizing power in the country. The congress demanded that the Siberian Bolsheviks form independent organizations, and entrusted the Central Siberian Bureau of the Central Committee headed by **B.Z. Shumiatskii** with the task. In autumn 1917 the Central Siberian Bureau was renamed the All-Siberian Bureau of the RSDWP Central Committee (*Obshchesibirskoe biuro RSDRP(b)*).

Boris Zakharovich Shumiatskii (1886–1938) was born into the family of a worker in Verkhneudinsk (Ulan-Ude). He worked in Chita from 1899, and later in other Siberian towns. He was involved in the workers' movement, was a member of the RSDWP from 1903 and became a Bolshevik. During the Revolution of 1905–7 he was involved in the 'Krasnoiarsk Republic', and then in the revolutionary events in Cheliabinsk, Kurgan, Irkutsk and other cities and towns of Siberia. After the revolution, he emigrated to South America. In 1913 he returned to Russia and was arrested. In 1915 he was drafted into the army and served as a military clerk in a reserve regiment in Krasnoiarsk. In 1917 he was vice-chairman of the Krasnoiarsk Soviet and the Bolshevik Central Committee's representative in Siberia. He was a delegate at the Sixth RSDWP(b) Congress. He was elected chairman of *Tsentrosibir* at the First All-Siberian Congress of Soviets in October 1917 and was one of the organizers of the Soviet government in Siberia. In 1919–20 he was a member of the Siberian Bureau of the Communist Party's Central Committee and in 1920 became a member of the Far East Bureau of the Communist Party's Central Committee and the deputy chairman of the council of ministers of the Far Eastern Republic (FER). At the beginning of 1921 he was recalled from the Republic for 'attempts to liquidate' the buffer-state. In 1921–2 he was a member of the Revolutionary Military Soviet (*Revvoensovet*) of the Fifth Red Army in Siberia, and became one of the leaders of the struggle against the Siberian peasants. In 1923–5 he was the USSR's ambassador in Iran. From 1926 to 1930 he was engaged in party activities in Leningrad, and was very active in the power struggle within the party in the 1920s. From 1930 to 1937 he worked in the Communist Government's Arts Committee. In 1938 he was arrested and then shot as an 'enemy of the people'.

After the congress, the Siberian Bolsheviks and Mensheviks split under the influence of this bureau. The united Social Democratic organization fell apart, and Bolshevik committees, organizations and cells were gradually formed throughout Siberia. By the October Revolution there was a total of around 10,000 Bolsheviks (out of 350,000 party members) in Siberia.

At the end of the summer and in the autumn of 1917, the Siberian Bolsheviks were very active in setting up their leadership. The main direction of their activities was anti-war and anti-government agitation and propaganda. They distributed the centrally produced Bolshevik newspapers in Siberian cities and towns, issued local newspapers and leaflets, and organized rallies and demonstrations. They severely criticized the Provisional Government and its representatives in Siberia and promised to solve all problems immediately if they seized power. Their slogans were simple and easy to understand: 'Peace to the Peoples', 'Factories for the Workers', 'Land to the Peasants' and 'All Power to the Soviets'. Gradually they succeeded in winning over a section of the workers and soldiers, who dreamt of peace and a home.

The soldiers of the Siberian garrisons were a major object of Bolshevik propaganda and agitation. In 1917 there were over 250,000 soldiers in Siberia, mainly in reserve regiments training to reinforce the front-line units. The Bolsheviks, taking advantage of the unlimited political freedom that existed in 1917, created their own cells in military units and persistently pursued anti-war propaganda among the soldiers. As a result of this work, the Siberian garrison soldiers became the Bolsheviks' main supporting force in the autumn of 1917. It was on them particularly that the Bolsheviks depended when seizing power in Siberia.

At the same time, the Siberian Bolsheviks also tried to establish control over the workers' movement. In addition to agitation and propaganda of their ideas among the workers, they began to form factory committees at large industrial establishments, which served as an alternative to the trade unions that were under the control of the Mensheviks. They succeeded in setting up these committees at some factories. But, by the time of the October Revolution, the Bolsheviks had strong support from workers in a handful of cities: Vladivostok, Krasnoiarsk and a few other places.

The Bolsheviks began to form their own armed forces among the workers with the aim of seizing power. The first Red Guard detachment in Siberia was formed in Krasnoiarsk as early as March 1917. Afterwards, similar detachments emerged in some other urban locations too, especially mining settlements. Most of the Red Guard detachments were small in number. By the October Revolution, there were only 6,000 Red Guards in Siberia (out of a total of more than 200,000 in Russia as a whole).

In the autumn of 1917 the Siberian Bolsheviks succeeded in winning over the Anarchists, who were against any government, as well as the Left SRs by advocating the slogan 'All Power to the Soviets'. A coalition of these political forces developed in Siberia acting as a united front in the Soviets. This coalition gave the Bolsheviks an advantage in many soviets.

The Siberian Bolsheviks had already begun to aim at seizing the leadership of the Soviets in the summer of 1917. The first to fall under their control was the one at Krasnoiarsk. They gradually succeeded in enhancing their influence in some others: in June only the Krasnoiarsk Soviet supported the slogan 'All Power to the Soviets', but by 24 September were in favour of it. On the whole, however, the Bolsheviks had failed to 'bolshevize' the Siberian Soviets by October 1917; the majority remained neutral.

The first All-Siberian Congress of Soviets, which took place in Irkutsk on 16–23 October, was a turning point in this regard. Representatives of 69 soviets from Omsk to Vladivostok were involved in its work. Among its 184 delegates there were 85 SRs, including 35 Left SRs, 64 Bolsheviks, 11 Mensheviks, and 24 members of other parties or without party allegiance. During the course of the congress the Left SRs backed the Bolsheviks. The congress approved the slogan 'All Power to the Soviets' by a majority vote and formed the Central Executive Committee of Siberian Soviets (*Tsentrosibir*). The Bolshevik B.Z. Shumiatskii was elected its chairman.

Soon after this, the Far Eastern Regional Congress was held in Khabarovsk. It elected a Regional Soviet Committee (*Kraevoi komitet sovetov*) with the Bolshevik **A.M. Krasnoshchokov** at its head.

After the October Revolution, the Bolsheviks in Siberia set about seizing power on the order of the new Communist Government, the *Sovnarkom* (SNK – the Council of Peoples' Commissars), but this was a difficult task. The Bolsheviks were not popular in Siberia. In November 1917 they managed to get no more than 10 per cent of the votes[3] at the elections to the Constituent Assembly, while the SRs got 75 per cent. In these circumstances, as has already been said, the Siberian garrison soldiers, as well as the Red Guard detachments, became the Communists' main assault force.

The Krasnoiarsk Soviet was the first to seize power on 29 October 1917. In November, Soviet power was established in Omsk, Irkutsk, Vladivostok and Yeniseisk. In December, it was set up in Tomsk, Barnaul, Novonikolaevsk (Novosibirsk) and Khabarovsk. By the end of February 1918 the Bolsheviks had seized power in almost the whole of Siberia, except Yakutia where Soviet power was only established during the summer of 1918 after the thaw, when navigation on the Lena had begun.

Generally speaking, the Bolsheviks seized power in a peaceful way. Fragmentation and confusion in the ranks of their enemies eased the power seizure. Only in Omsk did they meet with armed resistance. They succeeded in suppressing it with the help of Red Guard units drafted in from European Russia.

In February 1918 the second All-Siberian Congress of Soviets was held in Irkutsk. Some 202 delegates from nearly all the soviets were involved in its deliberations. There were 123 Bolsheviks and 53 Left SRs among them. The congress announced the 'Sovietization of Siberia', approved all the Russian *Sovnarkom*'s decisions, including the armed dispersal of the Constituent Assembly, and re-elected *Tsentrosibir*. It now consisted entirely of Bolsheviks and Left SRs. The Bolshevik, **N.N. Yakovlev**, became its chairman.

Alexander Mikhailovich Krasnoshchokov (1880–1937) was born into a tailoring family and graduated from a *real school*. He was active in the revolutionary movement from 1896. He was a Marxist and a member of the RSDWP from 1898. In 1900–2 he worked as an agent for the revolutionary newspaper *Iskra* (*Spark*) and was arrested several times. In 1902 he emigrated to Germany, and in 1903 he moved to the USA where he worked as a house painter. Between 1903 and 1907 he was involved in the Marxist Movement in the USA and became a member of the American Socialist Workers' Party. In 1912 he graduated from Chicago University as a lawyer. He led court cases for the American labour unions and became famous as a successful defence attorney. After the February Revolution in 1917, he returned to Vladivostok and joined the Bolshevik Party. He became famous as an excellent orator and was elected to the Vladivostok Soviet. In October 1917 he was elected Chairman of the Far Eastern Government and led the struggle for Soviet power in the Far East. After the defeat of the Soviets he went underground. In 1919 he was arrested by the Whites in the Volga region, while attempting to cross the front line, and sent to Irkutsk prison as an unidentified person. During an uprising in Irkutsk in December 1919, he was released. In 1920–1 he was the founder of the FER Government and a member of the Far Eastern Bureau of the Communist Party's Central Committee. In 1921–2 he was deputy finance minister of the Russian Federation and in 1922–3 chairman of the Industrial Bank of the Russian Federation. In 1923 he was arrested, being charged with abuse, and in 1924 sentenced to six years of imprisonment. He was expelled from the party. In 1925 he was amnestied. In 1926–37 he held various leading posts in the USSR Ministry of Agriculture. In 1937 he was arrested and shot as an 'enemy of the people'.

Nikolai Nikolaevich Yakovlev (1886–1918) was born into the family of a jewel maker in Moscow, and was educated at a *gymnasium*. He studied at Moscow University, but did not graduate. He was a member of the Russian Social Democratic Workers' Party (RSDWP) from 1904, supporting the Bolshevik wing. He was active in the Revolution of 1905–7, after which he became a professional revolutionary. He was arrested and exiled a number of times. During the First World War, he was called up and served in a reserve regiment in Siberia. In 1917 he was one of the leaders of the Central Siberian Bureau of the RSDWP Central Committee. In November–December 1917 he led the 'Sovietization' of western Siberia. In February 1918 he was elected chairman of the *Tsentrosibir*. He led the struggle to maintain Soviet power in eastern Siberia in the summer of 1918. After the defeat of the Soviets, he hid in Yakutia where he was arrested in October and shot near Olyokminsk.

In April 1918 the Congress of the Soviets of the Far East was held in Khabarovsk. It elected a Far Eastern Government headed by the Bolshevik Krasnoshchokov. The creation of this government completed the formation of the Soviet power system in Siberia.

24 Reds and Whites in Siberia, 1918–21

After the seizure of power in Siberia, the Bolsheviks set about implementing the Russian Communist Government's policy in the region.

> In 1918 ... we made a mistake when we decided to proceed straight to the Communist method of production and distribution.
>
> (V.I. Lenin, the Bolshevik leader)

The policy was carried out through violence, confiscation, requisitions, etc. The first action towards this end was the introduction of workers' control over food production and distribution. This measure involved worker interference in management, finance, sales and pricing. The workers' decisions became mandatory for the management. Workers' control in Siberia was first introduced in the railway shops in Krasnoiarsk during November 1917. In the first half of 1918 it was disseminated throughout the region.

Control by the workers led to a collapse of production since the proletariat was insufficiantly prepared and did not have enough knowledge for making adequate decisions, apart from which they did not bear any responsibility for their actions. This led to steep pay increases far exceeding factory profits, price rises, the expulsion of qualified specialists and other measures.

Nationalization was the next socio-economic innovation. In late 1917 and early 1918 the Bolsheviks nationalized Siberia's banks, beginning with the largest ones, the Russo-Asiatic Bank, the Bank of Siberia and the Society of Mutual Credit, and then proceeded to take over all the others.

Industry and transport were next in turn. All the more or less significant industries and commercial concerns (coal mines, factories, department stores and so on) were nationalized. In some Siberian towns the local Bolsheviks nationalized everything, down to small craft workshops and corner shops.

An All-Siberian Soviet of the National Economy (*Sovnarkhoz*) was formed in February 1918 to run this nationalized economy. Separate west Siberian and east Siberian *sovnarkhozes* were formed in March, followed by provincial and regional equivalents. However, owing to the absence of qualified professional personnel, these institutions were unable to run the Siberian economy at all adequately. They only contributed to its destruction by their semi-literate decrees.

As regards agriculture, in accordance with the Land Decree issued by the Second All-Russian Congress of Soviets, Siberia's peasants were given all lands owned by the state, the Tsar's Cabinet and the Church. Their taxes were annulled and all debts from previous years were written off. However, the measures did not have a significant effect since there was enough land in Siberia, and peasants had already spontaneously stopped paying their debts in 1917.

> We could not give the peasants in Siberia what the Revolution gave peasants in Russia.
>
> (V.I. Lenin, the Bolshevik leader)

In January 1918, following orders from the Bolshevik leader Vladimir Lenin, the Siberian Bolsheviks began carrying out seizures of food surpluses, the so-called *prodrazverstka*, and imposing trade restrictions. Fixed prices were set for grain, six times lower than market prices, and private trade in grain was prohibited. In some Siberian towns, the local Bolsheviks made an attempt to ban trade in all food products, which had a very painful effect both on urban dwellers and on the suburban farmers whose living depended on marketing their produce. The Bolsheviks formed squads for confiscating grain, the so-called *prodotriady*. During 1918 about 1,040,000 tons of grain was seized by this method in Siberia.

These socio-economic measures caused uncontrolled inflation and price rises, economic anarchy and a collapse of production, as well as shortages of food and household goods. This resulted in the almost total paralysis of Siberia's economic life and aroused bitter feelings in the population including those who had hitherto supported the Bolsheviks.

The usurpation of state power by the Bolsheviks, their socio-economic policy in Siberia (with its negative effects) as well as their weak political influence, made the active involvement of Siberians in the Civil War inevitable. Siberia became one of its epicentres. It was here that it began in May 1918; it was here that it ended in October 1922. The Civil War in Siberia was especially intractable and violent.

As early as late 1917 to early 1918, the first hotbeds of the Civil War began spontaneously developing in Siberia. All of them were caused by a combination of Soviet power and particular local circumstances. The Bolsheviks managed to suppress them with great difficulty, usually by means of compromises. The most serious of them were the uprising in Irkutsk and the activities of Semionov.

The Irkutsk Uprising of 21–30 December 1917[1] was caused by the Bolsheviks' refusal to promote those graduating from military schools to officer rank and to pay for their travel home. The uprising broke out against a background of general resentment caused by Bolshevik policies. Students of the Irkutsk military schools, Cossacks, officers of the Irkutsk Military District Headquarters and students at other educational institutions, were involved, numbering about 1,500 in total. It was led by a so-called 'Committee for the Defence of the Revolution'. Red Guard squads with artillery arrived to help the Bolsheviks. The campaign to quell the uprising was led by **S.G. Lazo**. Fighting in Irkutsk was particularly stubborn and was accompanied by considerable excesses. In the course of fighting over 300 people died and around 700 were wounded.

On 30 December a compromise was reached between the Bolsheviks and the rebels, according to which the power in Irkutsk was transferred to a Coalition Soviet consisting of Bolsheviks, Mensheviks and SRs, plus members of the *zemstvo*, municipal council, and public organizations. The military school graduates were paid for their travel home, but they were not promoted to officer rank. As soon as the students had departed for their homes, the Bolsheviks reneged on the compromise and eliminated the Coalition Soviet on 4 January 1918.

In late 1918 a Cossack officer, **G.M. Semionov**, formed a so-called 'Special Manchurian Detachment' at a railway station in Chinese Manchuria. The detachment consisted of Cossacks, officers, cadets from military schools, and other volunteers and numbered around 500.

In January 1918 the Semionov Detachment crossed the Russian border and occupied the Dauria railway station in Transbaikalia. Soon afterwards they

Sergei Georgievich Lazo (1894–1920) was born into the family of a nobleman in Bessarabia (Moldova). After graduating from a *gymnasium* he studied at St Petersburg Technological Institute and Moscow University. In 1915 he was called up and trained to be an ensign. He served in a reserve regiment in Krasnoiarsk and was active in the revolutionary events in 1917, becoming chairman of the Soldiers' Section of the local Soviet. In 1917 he joined the left wing of the SR Party. In December 1917, he arrived in Irkutsk as the head of the Krasnoiarsk Red Guard detachment and led the struggle against the Irkutsk Uprising. From February 1918 he was a member of *Tsentrosibir*. In April–July 1918 he took command of the Red Forces on the Dauria (Transbaikal) front against Semionov's soldiers. He defeated them. After the defeat of the Soviets in Siberia he left for Primorie and became one of the leaders of the guerrilla movement in the region. In late 1918 he resigned from the Left SRs and joined the Communist Party. In early 1920 he was one of the organizers of the Anti-Kolchak Uprising in Primorie, then of the Revolutionary Army formed from former Kolchak soldiers and guerrillas. He was in favour of immediate Sovietization in Primorie. During the events of 4–5 April 1920, he was arrested by the Japanese who passed him on to the Whites. He was burnt alive in a locomotive furnace. After the Civil War the Communists made Lazo an official hero.

Grigori Mikhailovich Semionov (1890–1946) was born into a Cossack family. He graduated from Orenburg Military Cossack School and was involved in the First World War as a Cossack Officer. After the October Revolution he was active in organizing a struggle against the Bolsheviks in east Siberia. In September 1918, supported by Czechoslovak troops, he seized power in Transbaikalia where he set up a personal dictatorship. He was *ataman* (a Cossack term for commander) of the Transbaikal Cossack Armed Forces and involved with the Japanese. At the end of 1918 he refused to accept the power of the 'Supreme Governor of Russia', Admiral Kolchak, however, the conflict between these two White forces was extinguished with the help of, and under pressure from, the Allied intervention forces. In the spring of 1919, backed up by the Japanese, he sought to create a so-called 'Pan-Mongolian State' which was to comprise western Transbaikalia (Buriatia), Mongolia and Tibet. In 1919 he was promoted to major-general, then lieutenant-general. In January 1920 Admiral Kolchak appointed Semionov commander-in-chief of the White forces in the east of Russia. In 1920 he made an unsuccessful attempt to create a buffer state in Transbaikalia, as an alternative to the FER, hoping for help from the Japanese. Having lived as an émigré since 1920 he was arrested by Soviet troops in Manchuria in 1945. In 1946 he was sentenced to be hanged.

were defeated and retreated into China where the formation of the force continued. By April 1918 there were already 1,800 people in Semionov's Detachment. They were armed with help from the Japanese.

On 5 April 1918 they marched into Transbaikalia again. Semionov's action was backed up by the well-to-do Transbaikal Cossacks. His forces increased to 5,000 and succeeded in advancing as far as the River Onon. In reply *Tsentrosibir* brought armed forces from the whole of Siberia to the region and mobilized the Transbaikal Cossacks. A Dauria (Transbaikal) Regiment was formed numbering over 10,000 people with S.G. Lazo in command. After a number of clashes, by the end of June, Semionov's troops had been defeated and were driven back into China.

In the second half of 1918, as social and economic conditions worsened, political conflicts in Siberia continued to grow in intensity. The dispersal of the Russian Constituent Assembly in Petrograd and of the Siberian Regional Duma[2] stimulated organized resistance to the Bolsheviks. These events showed anti-Bolshevik-minded Siberians once and for all that no compromise was possible with the new authorities.

Those deputies to the Siberian Regional Duma who managed to avoid being arrested formed a 'Provisional Government of Autonomous Siberia' with the Socialist Revolutionary P.Y. Deriabin at its head (though he departed for the Chinese city of Harbin soon afterwards). The deputies made a decision to set up an anti-Bolshevik military underground. Underground military organizations were formed in many towns and were supplied by the Siberian cooperative movement. The largest of them were in Omsk (about 2,000 members), Tomsk and Irkutsk (about 1,000). The total number of people involved in the anti-Communist Siberian underground was around 8,000.

The Siberian Bolsheviks were also getting ready to fight, hastily setting up armed forces. These included Red Guard detachments, Red Army units and squads formed by Socialists from the armed forces of the Central Powers who had become prisoners of war during the First World War and had been sent to Siberia.[3]

The Red Guard detachments were the largest in number. They were formed in factories, coal mines and transport depots. The total numerical strength of these detachments was over 10,000. However, their fighting efficiency left much to be desired owing to lack of training, poor discipline and a mixed volunteer-compulsory principle of recruiting.

The Red Army units were initially formed on a voluntary basis, mainly from former soldiers of the Tsarist Russian Army. They amounted to no more than 2,000 in total.

Tsentrosibir also set up 'Internationalist' detachments from 5,000 ex-prisoners of war. They became the Bolsheviks' main military force in Siberia after the former Russian Army ceased to exist and the soldiers in the Siberian garrisons left for their homes.

> ... international detachments formed from Hungarian, German, and Czechoslovakian prisoners of war were the most substantial and positive support for the Soviets ... They obeyed the officers' orders without question and flawlessly fulfilled their duties, be it guard duty, round-ups [of suspects] or fights against the enemies of Soviet Power.
>
> (V.D. Vegman, a Siberian Bolshevik historian and veteran of the Civil War)

All told, there were about 20,000 people in the Bolsheviks' Siberian armed forces. By the end of May 1918, most of them were in Transbaikalia where hostilities were under way against Semionov's detachments.

In the spring of 1918 the political situation in Siberia was strained to breaking point. Large-scale civil war broke out on 25 May with the mutiny of the Czechoslovak Legion. This legion, numbering about 40,000, had been formed by the Provisional Government in 1917 from Czech and Slovak prisoners of war who were willing to fight for independence within the old Austro-Hungarian Empire. After the October Revolution, it was decided to transfer the legion from Russia to Europe by rail and sea via Vladivostok to fight against the Central Forces on the Western front. Relations between the Bolsheviks and the leadership of the legion gradually worsened. Neither side trusted the other, both suffering from suspicion of the other's intentions. The mutiny was triggered by a secret order from L.D. Trotskii, the Communist Government's People's Commissar of the armed Forces, to disarm all the Czechoslovak units forthwith. This order was intercepted by the legion.

By the beginning of the mutiny there were over 30,000 Czech and Slovak troops in Siberia disposed in the following locations: 14,000 in Vladivostok, roughly 2,000 around Irkutsk, about 1,000 in the Nizhneudinsk area, approximately 4,500 in the Novonikolaevsk-Mariinsk area, and finally 9,000 in Cheliabinsk in the Urals. During the last few days of May, the Legionaries seized control of the Nikolaevsk-Tomsk-Mariinsk area and the Kansk-Nizhneudinsk area.

This 'mutiny' initiated an almost universal uprising against the Bolsheviks in western Siberia, as a result of which they were easily overthrown. On 7 June, Czechoslovak units of the White Siberian Army[4] took Omsk and made contact with their counterparts in Cheliabinsk. On 15 June they took Barnaul in the Altai region with the Whites, and on 20 June they occupied Krasnoiarsk. On 22 June they had seized Vladivostok.[5] On 11 July, after stubborn fighting at Nizhneudinsk and on the River Belaia, Irkutsk was taken.

The Bolsheviks are running for their lives without stopping even in stations. Panic in their midst is catastrophic.

(The newspaper *People's Siberia* (*Narodnaia Sibir*))

The panic retreat was caused by our army being poorly prepared, lacking a command staff, and a supreme command centre.

(P.K. Golikov, Commander of the *Tsentrosibir* troops)

Only at Tiumen, around Lake Baikal, and in Primorie did the Bolsheviks succeed in mounting serious resistance, but, eventually, this was also broken, and by the end of September 1918, the whole of Siberia was in the hands of the Czechoslovaks and the Whites.

In the summer of 1918 Siberia became the object of open military intervention by the Atlantic pact countries. Even at the beginning of the year, worried by Russia's withdrawal from the First World War and its refusal to pay back debts owed to them, the Allies had begun offering financial support to the anti-Bolshevik underground in Siberia, and had also begun to prepare the ground for direct intervention. In August 1918 allied forces were sent to Siberia on the pretext of 'defending the Czechoslovak troops'. Military forces from Japan, the USA, and other countries were involved in the intervention. A total of 100,000 foreign soldiers came to Siberia including 80,000 Japanese, 12,000 Americans, 6,000 from the British Empire, 5,000 Chinese, 1,000 French, and small units of Italian, Yugoslav and Romanian troops. Formally, all these forces were united by one single headquarters, but in reality each country's troops acted independently.

The interventionists set up control over the section of the Trans-Siberian Railway between Omsk and Vladivostok. They also provided considerable aid to the White movement.

At the same time, each of the powers involved, Japan, the USA, and to some extent Great Britain, pursued its own objectives in the Siberian intervention, in addition to combating the Bolsheviks. Japan, in particular, sought territorial expansion in the Far East; the USA sought control over the Trans-Siberian and Siberia's economy. This gave rise to mistrust and rivalry. The Japanese even encouraged *Ataman* Semionov's Cossacks to rob trains containing weapons, ammunition and uniforms intended to help the Kolchak army. Likewise, the Americans secretly armed the Red guerrillas who were at war with the Japanese and the Whites. In the end, the interventionists refused to send their troops to the front or to give the necessary military help to the White movement.

Eventually, owing to disagreements among the Great Powers, the organizers of the intervention, and its unpopularity in the home countries, the intervention failed. As early as December 1919 the Allies, apart from Japan, were forced to announce the end of their involvement and to withdraw their troops. Japan virtually occupied the Russian Far East on the pretext of guarding the property of, and ensuring security for, its citizens.

In the summer of 1918, after the defeat of Bolsheviks, disagreements among the various political groups increased. The groups in question included members of the Siberian Regionalist organizations, the SRs, the Mensheviks and sections of the right-wing troops. The Provisional Siberian Government, under the leadership of **P.V. Vologodskii**, won a victory in the struggle. The

Piotr Vasilevich Vologodskii (1863–1928) was born into the family of a priest in Yenisei Province. He studied at St Petersburg University, but was expelled in 1887 for being involved in student disturbances and was exiled from the city. In 1892 he graduated from Kharkov University in the Ukraine. He became a lawyer, and served in government bodies in Omsk, Vernyi (Alma-Ata, now Almaty) and Semipalatinsk. He went on to be a barrister in Tomsk. He was involved in the Regionalist movement and cooperated actively with their newspaper *Vostochnoe obozrenie*. Between 1903 and 1907 he was a member of the SR Party. He was involved in the Revolution of 1905–7 and defended Siberian revolutionaries in court. He was a delegate from Tomsk to the All-Russian Convention of Zemstvos and Municipalities and a member of the State Duma. After the revolution he practised as a barrister in Tomsk. In 1917–18 he was involved with the anti-Soviet underground in Omsk. From June 1918 he became chairman of the Provisional Siberian Government in Omsk and from September 1918, he was a member of the All-Russian Provisional Government (Directory), being appointed chairman of its ministerial council in November. He was one of the organizers of the Omsk putsch of 17–18 November 1918. After this event he became chairman of the Kolchak government's council of ministers, hence emerging as one of the leaders of White Power in Siberia. In November 1919 he retired and emigrated from Russia to China.

government was formed in Omsk in late June by the Siberian Regionalists. This government annulled all decrees issued by the Bolsheviks and formed the White Siberian Army. In September 1918, after the founding of the All-Russian Provisional Government (Directory) in Ufa, the Provisional Government dispersed.

In October 1918, owing to an advance by the Red Army, the Directory moved eastwards from Ufa in the Urals to Omsk. Once they had reached the city a military-political plot was devised against them. The conspirators were aiming at the establishment of a military dictatorship to oppose Bolshevism effectively. As a result of the resulting military coup on 17–18 November 1918, the Directory was overthrown and power passed to Admiral **A.V. Kolchak** who was created 'Supreme Ruler of Russia' with unlimited powers on paper.

The programme of the Kolchak Government involved:

*   putting an end to Bolshevism and restoring law and order;
*   re-creating the Russian armed forces;
*   convoking a new Constituent Assembly[6] to resolve the issue of Russia's socio-economic system;

Figure 24.1 Admiral A.V. Kolchak

Alexander Vasilevich Kolchak (1874–1920) was born into the family of a military officer. After graduating from the Naval Cadets Academy, he served in the Russian Navy. He became famous as an explorer of the Siberian Arctic. He was involved in the Russo-Japanese War of 1904–5, during which he first commanded the torpedo-boat *Serdityi*, then an artillery battery in Port-Arthur. He was awarded the Golden Weapon 'For Bravery'. After the war he undertook an analysis of the experience and further scientific explorations in the Arctic. At the beginning of the First World War he served in the headquarters of the Baltic Fleet and organized successful mine warfare. In 1916 he was promoted to rear admiral and then vice-admiral and appointed commander-in-chief of the Black Sea Fleet. He supported the February Revolution. In June 1917 he retired in protest against the deterioration of the Russian Fleet – he made an angry speech in front of the sailors and threw his Golden Weapon into the sea. This deed made him extremely popular in liberal and bourgeois circles. In August–October 1917 he was a consultant with the US Navy. In December 1917 he joined British Navy, but did not take up his duties. In April–May 1918 he was forming White troop units in Manchuria. In November 1918 he arrived in Omsk and was appointed minister of war within the directory. After the military coup of 17–18 November, he became 'Supreme Ruler of Russia' with dictatorial powers. After the collapse of the Kolchak regime he was arrested by Czechoslovaks in the environs of Irkutsk and handed over to the SR-Menshevik Polittsentr, and then to Bolsheviks. He was shot in February 1920 in Irkutsk on the personal order of V.I. Lenin.

- introducing necessary economic reforms (to continue Stolypin's agricultural reforms without the landed gentry retaining ownership of the land; to denationalize industry, banks and transport; to retain democratic labour legislation, and to develop labour productivity in every possible way); and
- maintaining the territorial integrity and sovereignty of Russia.

However, this programme could only remain a statement of good intentions, given the prevailing civil war situation. Moreover, the White government managed to increase the irritation and alienation of the peoples of Siberia by its actions.

During the course of the Civil War, a specific phenomenon called the 'rule of the Siberian *atamany*' (*sibirskaia atamanovshchina*) came into being. It was characterized by the almost unlimited power wielded by the commanders of the various levels of military forces. The phenomenon was most widespread in the Cossack regions, hence the name. Separatism of the 'Siberian *ataman*' type was actively encouraged by the Japanese interventionists, who saw it as a means for the realization of their territorial expansionism in Siberia. The period was accompanied by unrestrained tyranny and violence over the civilian population. It completely frustrated all the Kolchak authorities' attempts to restore order and normal everyday life.

> The 'Atamanovshchina' works for Bolshevism more effectively than any
> of the propaganda or preaching by Lenin and Trotsky's comrades.
>   (A. Budberg, minister of war in the Kolchak Government)

The popular response to White policy and the rule of the *atamany* was a
massive guerrilla movement. It was caused by the authorities' inability to overcome chaos in the Siberian economy, by tyranny and violence, as well as by
a forced mobilization of the peasantry into the White army. The inadequate
influx of volunteers into the army forced the authorities to resort to mobilization. It enabled them to form a 300,000-strong White army in Siberia, though
with great difficulty. At the same time, this caused acute resentment among
the population, who were unwilling to be involved in the Civil War.

> A year ago the population saw us as saviours from their harsh captivity
> under the commissars, but now it hates us as much as it hated the commis-
> sars, if not more. And what is worse than hate, it does not trust us
> anymore, does not expect anything good from us.
>   (A. Budberg, minister of war in the Kolchak Government)

The guerrilla movement involved the whole of Siberia. Over 100,000
peasants, workers and members of the intelligentsia were active in it. Its
slogan was the overthrow of the Kolchak regime. The guerrilla movement

Figure 24.2 Siberian partisans with a home-made field gun

disorganized virtually the whole of the White army's rear and contributed in many ways to the defeat of the White movement in Siberia.

In August 1919 the advancing Red Army marched into Siberia. Before this the Bolshevik Government had issued a special proclamation 'To the Population of Siberia', in which it promised to put an end to the Civil War as soon as possible, to restore normal life and to retain the social status and mode of living of all the working people of Siberia. The appeal had a great effect on the sentiment of the Siberian population, particularly the Cossacks and the White troops.

However, the Red Army took Tiumen on 8 August and on 15 August was in Kurgan. Shortly afterwards a decisive action between the Reds and the Whites took place. Called the Battle of Tobolsk-Petropavlovsk, it lasted over two months and was distinguished by great tenacity on both sides.

Fighting began on 20 August, when the Red troops of the Eastern Front under V.A. Olderogge[7] (around 70,000-strong) advanced on Petropavlovsk from Kurgan, reaching their objective ten days later. In response, the White forces under General M.K. Diterikhs (around 58,000-strong) counter-attacked on 1 September driving the Reds westwards beyond the Tobol River, retaking Tobolsk. On 14 October the Red troops (now numbering some 75,000) launched a new offensive, which resulted in the defeat of the 56,000-strong White Army, and on 29 October it retreated from Petropavlovsk. In the course of the fighting the White troops lost about 5,000 dead with 8,000 taken prisoner. They also lost the ability to fight.

Figure 24.3 The Fifth Red Army marching into Irkutsk, March 1920

After the end of the Battle of Tobolsk-Petropavlovsk an unceasing advance of the Red Army into Siberia began. On 14 November 1919 they took Kolchak's capital city of Omsk; exactly a month later they were in Novoniko-laevsk (Novosibirsk). The latter having been taken, the Eastern Front was eliminated, and the Fifth Red Army under G.H. Eikhe pursued the Whites further. On 20 December the Reds took Tomsk, on 6 January 1920 they took Krasnoiarsk and on 7 March the Red Army marched into Irkutsk. In the course of the advance around 100,000 White soldiers were taken captive and vast amounts of booty were seized. The Siberian guerrillas rendered a great deal of assistance to the Red Army, independently seizing many regions and towns.

An uprising by the 'Political Centre' (*Polittsentr*) in Irkutsk in late December 1919 and early January 1920 drew the final line under the history of the Kolchak regime. After the Omsk putsch of 17–18 November 1918, Irkutsk had become the centre of an anti-Kolchak opposition, uniting all supporters of democracy (SRs, Mensheviks, Siberian Cooperators, Regionalists, and munici-pal and rural councils). In December 1919 the democratic opposition had set up the *Polittsentr* in Irkutsk. It had the following tasks: to overthrow the Kolchak regime, to negotiate the cessation of the Civil War with the Bolsheviks and to lobby for the creation of a democratic buffer state in eastern Siberia. This *Polittsentr* prepared an uprising in Irkutsk, which began on 24 December 1919 and ended on 5 January 1920; the uprising was crowned with success. After the victory, A.V. Kolchak was arrested and on 19 January in Irkutsk the Bolshevik Siberian Revolutionary Committee (*Sibrevkom*) and the *Polittsentr* reached an agreement on the creation of a buffer state. Power in Irkutsk was handed over to the Bolsheviks.

In early February 1920, 25,000 troops (remnants of the White forces who had been retreating along the railway) approached Irkutsk from the west. After negotiations the White troops bypassed the city and left for Transbaikalia. During these events Kolchak was shot.

Sibrevkom became the chief instrument of state power in the part of Siberia occupied by the Reds. It had been established in August 1919 on the eve of the Red Army's entry into Siberia by a decree of the Soviet Supreme Central Executive Committee (*VTsIK*). **I.N. Smirnov** was appointed chairman of *Sibrevkom*, which had both civil and military powers. General supervision of its work was undertaken by the Siberian Bureau (*Sibbiuro*) of the Communist Party's Central Committee, which was also headed by Smirnov.

While the Red Army was advancing on Siberia, revolutionary committees (*revkomy*) were set up in provinces, districts and counties. In 1920–1 soviets were elected in rural and urban areas, but the real power belonged to the *revkomy* and other Communist Party bodies.

In Siberia the Bolsheviks established a regime of 'War Communism'[8] and 'Red Terror'[9] which enabled them to begin to overcome the devastation caused by the war. Any political activities outside the Communist Party were banned.

In 1920–1, at the end of the Civil War, there was a new tide of powerful

Ivan Nikolaevich Smirnov (1881–1936) was born into the family of a peasant in Riazan Province. The family moved to Moscow shortly afterwards and Smirnov graduated from a Moscow municipal school. He worked on the railways and then in a factory. From 1898 he was involved in the revolutionary movement as a member of the RSDWP. After the party split he became a Bolshevik. In 1899 he was arrested and after two years in prison was exiled to Irkutsk Province for five years, but he soon escaped. He was engaged in revolutionary activities in Tver Province in European Russia. In 1902 he was arrested again and in 1905 exiled to Vologda Province in the European north. He was, however, amnestied in the autumn of the same year. He was active in the Revolution in 1905–7, becoming one of the organizers of the December 1905 Uprising in Moscow. After the revolution he was engaged in revolutionary activities in Moscow, St Petersburg and Kharkov. He was arrested three times and exiled to Siberia, escaping every time. In 1916 he was drafted into the army and served in a reserve regiment in Tomsk. After the February Revolution he left for Moscow. In Moscow he was involved in the October Revolution. During the Civil War he was a member of the Revolutionary Military Soviet (*Revvoensovet*) of the Eastern Front. In 1919–21 he was chairman of *Sibrevkom* and headed the Siberian Bureau of the Communist Party's Central Committee. He led the restoration of Soviet power in Siberia and the struggle against peasant uprisings. He was one of the founders of the FER. In 1919–20 he was a candidate member of the Communist Party's Central Committee. In 1920–7 as a full member of the Central Committee he was very active in the inner-party power struggle. In 1927 he was expelled from the Communist Party. In 1929 he was rehabilitated, but in 1930 he was again expelled and arrested in 1933. He was one of the main accused during the first Moscow trial of 'enemies of the people' in 1936 and was the only one not to plead guilty in public. He was shot.

peasant uprisings in Siberia. All of these were caused by the forced procurement of agricultural products and a lack of manufactured goods, as well as by violations of the principles of peasant democracy.

In July 1920 the Council of People's Commissars (*Sovnarkom*) approved a decree 'On the Confiscation of Grain Surpluses in Siberia'. The government forced the Siberian peasants to surrender the appropriations for the previous years too. The Siberian *prodrazverstka*, 1,660,000 tons, was 25 per cent of the total demanded from Russia as a whole. In Siberia the authorities dramatically curtailed the norms of consumption. Armed groups (*prodotriady*) arrived from European Russia to enforce the appropriations; they numbered 35,000 in total. This caused a burst of resentment among the Siberian peasants who began an armed defence of the fruits of their labour.

The election of soviets in small rural districts (*volosty*) and villages also caused peasant protests. The Communists widely deprived the peasants of the right to vote and blatantly falsified the results.

The peasant uprisings covered the territory of Siberia from Kurgan to Irkutsk. Nearly 150,000 people were involved in them. The uprisings proceeded under the slogans 'For Soviets without Communists!' and 'Down with Appropriations and the Communists!' Despite severe punitive measures, the Bolsheviks succeeded in overcoming them only after *prodrazverstka* was cancelled.

These active protests by the Siberian peasantry made a substantial contribution to the Bolsheviks giving up the adventurous, hazardous experiments of War Communism and introducing the New Economic Policy (NEP).

25 The Far Eastern Republic of 1920–2

In early 1920 there emerged an extremely unusual political entity, the Far Eastern Republic (FER). Its emergence was caused by the general military, political and international situation of Soviet Russia, as well as by Japan's expansionist policies.

At that time Soviet Russia found itself in an extremely complicated situation. The Civil War had not ended yet, and it was already on the brink of a military conflict with Poland, which could lead to a new intervention in Russia. Lenin considered it dangerous for the Red Army to advance too far into the depths of Siberia, since it could lead to a face-to-face war with Japan, which was beyond their strength. In January 1920 he approved a proposal by the Irkutsk *Polittsentr*, which was dominated by the SRs and Mensheviks, to create a buffer state in Siberia. The Japanese government, for its part, declared in December 1919, when the European *entente* countries adopted a declaration on the cessation of military intervention in Russia, that Japan and its citizens had special interests in eastern Siberia, and that the Japanese troops would remain there[1] to guard its citizens' life and property until the Civil War in the region was ended and a stable democratic government had been established. At the same time Japan flatly refused to have any official contacts with Soviet Russia, but supported the *Polittsentr*'s idea about the creation of a democratic state in the east. It cherished hopes for territorial expansion.

Under these circumstances, the Bolsheviks opted for the creation of the buffer state in Siberia. This tactical *démarche* was in pursuit of two basic interconnected aims: to avoid open war between Soviet Russia and Japan, and to bring about the end of Japanese intervention by peaceful means. As mentioned above, on 19 January 1920 *Sibrevkom* and the Irkutsk *Polittsentr* had concluded a preliminary agreement on the creation of a buffer state, which was approved by Lenin. A month later, on 18 February the Communist Party's *Politbureau* adopted a final resolution on the creation of the 'buffer'. However, the Siberian Bolsheviks took their time over putting this into practice, waiting to see how the military and political situation in Siberia would develop.

In the spring of 1920, the Japanese interventionists sharply aggravated the situation in the Far East. They organized the so-called 'Nikolaevsk incident' and the 'events of 4–5 April 1920'.

In early March 1920, a guerrilla army of approximately 5,000 in number marched into the city of Nikolaevsk-on-the-Amur. Meanwhile, the Japanese garrison (800-strong) declared its neutrality. On 12 March the Japanese suddenly attacked the guerrillas, but in the course of three days' severe fighting they were totally annihilated (the remaining few killed themselves by *harakiri*). The Japanese interventionists used this incident to create tension and the 'events of 4–5 April 1920'.

During the night of 4–5 April, Japanese forces suddenly attacked the so-called Primorie Revolutionary Army, composed of former Kolchak units and guerrilla detachments numbering around 19,000 in total.

In the course of the fighting, over 4,000 people perished and the Revolutionary Army ceased to exist. The Primorie region was virtually occupied by the Japanese. They also occupied Kamchatka and the northern part of Sakhalin Island.

The Japanese, however, failed to profit from their actions: they were unable to create any puppet government in Primorie. On the contrary, the events aroused resentment among all strata of the population, including supporters of the White movement. The Japanese interventionists found themselves politically isolated.

These aggressive actions by the Japanese interventionists accelerated the creation of the buffer state. On 6 April 1920, in accordance with a decision by *Sibrevkom*, a Constituent Convention held under Bolshevik auspices proclaimed the creation of the FER. This convention also determined its borders:

Figure 25.1 Japanese interventionists by the bodies of inhabitants executed in Primorie

the FER's western border would run along the River Selenga and Lake Baikal. The convention declared that the FER would be a democratic state, but that a constitution would be approved by the Constituent Convention after all the regions of the Far East regions had become united in actual fact. The convention elected a FER Government under the head of A.M. Krasnoshchokov, and a council of ministers. Verkhneudinsk became its first capital.

The announcement of the FER did not imply that the Republic had in fact been created as yet. In actual fact, after the downfall of the Kolchak regime, there were four other governments on the territory of the FER, all independent of each other. The FER Government only had control over western Transbaikalia. In the Primorie zone, occupied by the Japanese, there was a *zemstvo* coalition government, which also laid a claim to become the centre of the FER. In the Amur region, after the Japanese troops left, the local Bolsheviks restored Soviet rule and considered the area an inseparable part of Soviet Russia. In eastern Transbaikalia *Ataman* Semionov's regime remained, supported by the Japanese. Since it blocked any advance it was given a nickname, the 'Chita Cork'. In 1920 it was the only White authority in the whole territory of Siberia. The Japanese tried to create their own buffer state on the basis of the Semionov regime, but the Siberian public did not wish to cooperate with it, and they failed in their attempts.

To bring about a real unification of all the Far Eastern territories under the power of the FER Government, it was above all necessary to deal a death blow to the 'Chita Cork'. In April–May 1920, the FER troops tried to do this twice, but were beaten off both times with the help of Japanese military.

Figure 25.2 Partisan tanks before the liberation of the 'Chita Cork'

After their failures during the spring, the leadership of *Sibrevkom* and the FER realized that it would only be possible to eliminate the 'Chita Cork' if the Japanese troops were withdrawn from Transbaikalia. Delegations from the FER Government and the Japanese military leaders began negotiations over this issue in a railway station at Gongotta in Transbaikalia. As a result of complex and lengthy negotiations, the Gongotta Agreement (*Gongottskoe soglashenie*) was concluded on 15 July 1920. It stipulated:

* the declaration of the Transbaikal region as a 'neutral zone', which troops would not have the right to enter; and
* the withdrawal of the Japanese forces from Transbaikalia within a three-month period.

On 15 October 1920 the Japanese troops left Transbaikalia. In October they also left the Khabarovsk area, having departed from Kamchatka even earlier.

The FER Government began preparations for a military operation to eradicate the 'Chita Cork' even before the Japanese troops had completed their withdrawal. Since the Gongotta Agreement had declared Transbaikalia to be a neutral zone, it was decided to carry out the operation as if on behalf of the local population, rising up against the Semionov regime.

> Convince the whole guerrilla detachment that they are acting on behalf of a rising population. The Party detachments ... have nothing to do with the People's Revolutionary Army (PRA).
>
> (G.K. Eikhe, chief commissar of the PRA of the FER, from the order to prepare a military advance)

The main blow was delivered from the east purportedly by guerrillas, but in reality by disguised troops from the Amur and Pribaikalie. The number of forces was roughly equal, with around 30,000 on either side, but the Whites were unable to offer serious resistance owing to disagreements between their leaders and low morale within the ranks. The operation began as soon as the last Japanese soldiers had left Transbaikalia and ended up forcing the Whites out into Manchuria. On 22 October 1920 the FER's forces occupied Chita, and hostilities ceased on 31 October. The overall leadership of the operation was carried out by the commander-in-chief of the People's Revolutionary Army (PRA) of the FER **G.K. Eikhe**.

After the Whites had been driven out of Transbaikalia, a unification conference was held in Chita, in which the FER Government and the governments of the Amur and Primorie regions participated.

The Communists' stance at the conference was set out in the *Brief Theses on the FER*, approved by the Communist Party's Central Committee on the initiative of Lenin and Krasnoshchokov as far back as 13 August 1920. This document listed the reasons for the establishment of the FER, emphasizing

Genrikh Khristoforovich Eikhe (1893–1968) was born into the family of a worker in Latvia. He graduated from Riga Commercial College and the Peterhof Ensign School. He fought in the First World War as a junior captain. He was involved in the revolutionary events of 1917 on the front, was chairman of the regimental committee and a member of the Soviet of Soldiers' Deputies of the Tenth Army. He became a Bolshevik in 1917. In March 1918 he joined the Red Army voluntarily and commanded a regiment, then a brigade, then a division on the Eastern Front. He was involved in the Tobolsk–Petropavlovsk Battle for Siberia. From November 1919 he was the commander of the Fifth Red Army during its attack on Siberia. Between March and April 1920 he was commander-in-chief of the PRA of the FER and commanded the campaign against the 'Chita Cork'. In 1921–3 he was commander of the Minsk Army Group. From 1927 he worked in the Ministry of Foreign Trade. In 1937 he was subjected to repression, and remained in prison until 1954. After his discharge he was engaged in scientific research and literary activities. He is the author of a number of works on the history of the Civil War in Siberia.

that all its foreign and internal policies would be controlled by the Central Committee of the Communist Party through a Far Eastern Bureau (*Dalbiuro*), created specifically for this purpose, and that Communists should hold all the key government posts. The *Theses* also stated that the FER's PRA was one of the Red Armies, subject to the Soviet Russian Revolutionary Military Soviet (*Revvoensovet*). The document was particularly clear in stating that democracy in the FER was purely formal.

The Unification Conference met from 28 October to 10 November 1920. It adopted a 'Declaration of Independence' which declared the FER an independent, democratic, sovereign state. This 'declaration' was designed to gain a favourable international response. The conference also resolved to convene an FER Constituent Assembly in February 1921 to adopt the constitution, and set up a reshuffled FER Government, again headed by Krasnoshchokov.

Elections to the constituent assembly of the FER were held in early 1921. Given the hostility towards the Japanese intervention, the Communists and their supporters received about 80 per cent of the votes. The constituent assembly (12 February–27 April 1921) adopted a constitution which:

- declared the FER a democratic republic;
- proclaimed equality for all peoples and classes;
- established universal, direct and equal suffrage;
- proclaimed equality for all forms of ownership; and
- determined the structure of the FER.

The constitution was a disguise intended to conceal the fact of Communist control from the eyes of the international public, particularly America and Japan.

> "Sometimes people prefer to be deceived."
>   A.M. Krasnoshchokov, chairman of the FER Government,
>   about the international reaction to its establishment

The real nature of the FER was defined by the Communist Party Central Committee's previously mentioned *Brief Theses on the FER*. Even though the supreme institution in the FER, the People's Assembly (*Narodnoe sobranie*) had been elected by universal, direct and secret ballot, the Communists had quite a few means of forming a balance of parties favourable to them. This was vividly demonstrated in the summer 1922 elections when the Communists deprived so-called 'enemies of the people' of the right to vote, staged elections twice or even three times, and used direct vote-rigging which allowed them to win a victory. The Communists and their supporters 'collected' 66 per cent of the votes. Moreover, the powers permitted to the People's Assembly were extremely limited. It met for brief sessions to pass laws, elect a government,[2] and approve the prime minister.

The real boss in this buffer state was the FER Government, a collective power body with presidential powers. It appointed the Council of Ministers (*Sovmin DVR*) and directed all activities of the executive. Its decrees had legal status. The membership of the FER Government was actually determined by the Central Committee of the Communist Party, and it consisted entirely of Communists. It was headed by a chairman who was also 'recommended' by the Communists.

The executive body in the FER was the Council of Ministers. It was formed on a coalition basis, presenting a democratic front. The first council contained 11 Communists, three Mensheviks, one SR and one NS (Popular Socialist).

A special body within the state hierarchy was the FER State Political Guard (*Gospolitokhrana DVR*). Structurally, it was a subsection of the Soviet Cheka or GPU (forerunners of the KGB). The State Political Guard was directly

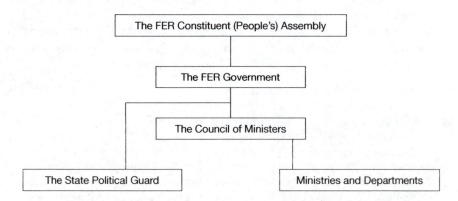

Figure 25.3 The state structure of the FER

subordinate to the FER Government and the Cheka (GPU) leadership in Moscow, and consisted entirely of Communists. Through it the Communists ensured their control of the FER.

In the spring of 1921 the Japanese interventionists made one last attempt to create a buffer state of their own. On 26 May 1921 a military mutiny took place in Vladivostok. Power was seized by remnants of the White forces brought from Manchuria to Primorie by the Japanese. A 'Provisional Government of the Amur' was formed, headed by **S.D. Merkulov**. It received the nickname 'Black Buffer' or 'Merkulovshchina'.

With Japanese assistance, S.D. Merkulov's government began to form a White Insurgents' Army[3] to advance on the FER.

At the same time, Japan proposed holding negotiations regarding the cessation of intervention. The negotiations were held in the city of Dairen (Dal'nyi or Dalian, China) from 26 August 1921 to 16 April 1922 and received the name 'the Dairen Conference'. By acting as the initiator of negotiations on the intervention, Japan was aiming at avoidance of the discussion of the issue at the International Washington Conference.[4] The Dairen Conference ended without any results, but drew international attention to the Japanese intervention issue. Under pressure from America and other countries unhappy about its expansion in Siberia, Japan was forced to announce the withdrawal of its forces at the Washington Conference.

During the Dairen negotiations in November 1921, the White Insurgent Army (about 1,200 in number) began to advance aiming to take over the whole of the FER's territory and to drive the Communists away. In December the Whites took Khabarovsk and advanced as far as the railway station at In, where they were halted by the PRA.

Between 5 and 14 February a decisive battle between PRA troops and the White Insurgent Army occurred at Volochaevka station. The Red forces (around 8,000 people), led by **V.K. Bliukher**, had to attack heavily fortified White positions (defended by around 5,000 people) in a temperature of 35 degrees below zero. After tough fighting and a flanking movement, the

Spiridon Dionisevich Merkulov was born into the family of an entrepreneur. He graduated from St Petersburg University and became a lawyer. He worked as a barrister in Vladivostok, specializing in labour and agriculture in the Far East. During the Civil War he lived in Vladivostok. After the FER was founded, he created and led a public anti-socialist organization, the 'National-Democratic Union'. In 1921 he was one of the organizers of a military coup in Primorie. He headed the so-called 'Provisional Government of the Amur' and was in favour of the Japanese intervention. He was one of the initiators of an armed insurrection against the FER. In August 1922 he transferred power to General M.K. Diterikhs, and subsequently emigrated to Canada.

Vasilii Konstantinovich Bliukher (1889–1938) was born into a peasant family in Yaroslavl Province and educated in a Sunday school. From 1904 he lived and worked in St Petersburg and was involved in the workers' movement. In 1910 he was convicted of organizing a strike in Moscow and sentenced to three years in prison. In 1914–15 he served in the army and fought in the war as a junior officer, ending up badly wounded and demoralized. In 1916–17 he worked in factories in Nizhnii Novgorod, Kazan and Samara. He became a member of the RSDWP in 1916, supporting the Bolsheviks. In 1917–18 he commanded a Red Guard detachment. In 1918 as chairman of the Cheliabinsk Soviet he led the South Urals Red Guard in an escape from encirclement. He directed a 1,500-kilometre raid deep in the enemy's rear, for which he was awarded the Order of the Red Banner No 1. In 1918–20 he took command of a Red Army rifle division and took part in the Tobolsk-Petropavlovsk Battle for Siberia and in the famous Perekop Assault in the Crimea. In 1921–2 he was the war minister of the FER and commander-in-chief of the PRA. He restructured the PRA, improving its combat readiness and led the Battle of Volochaevka. In 1922–8 he was in command of a corps in Petrograd (Leningrad) and in 1924–8 he was the main military adviser in China. In 1928–9 he was commander of troops in the Ukrainian Military District and in 1929–38 he commanded the Special Far Eastern Army, and also commanded military action in the conflict over the Chinese Eastern Railway (1929) and at Lake Khasan (1938). In 1934–8 he was an alternate member of the Communist Party's Central Committee. In 1935 he was created Marshal of the Soviet Union (one of the first five such marshals). In August 1938 he was recalled from Siberia and arrested, and in November was shot.

Whites were defeated and deserted the fortifications. On 14 February the Reds took Khabarovsk. The White insurgents retreated to southern Primorie under the protection of Japanese troops, and a break in the fighting occurred until October 1922.

In summer 1922 the so-called 'Assembly of the Land' (*Zemskii sobor*) met in southern Primorie, in the election of which only supporters of the White movement took part. It delegated power to General **M.K. Diterikhs** and proclaimed the establishment of the 'Priamur Monarchy'. This step was made in the hope of attracting international support with the help of the Romanov Dynasty.

In September 1922, on the eve of the withdrawal of Japanese troops from Siberia, negotiations between delegations from Japan, the FER and Soviet Russia were held in the Chinese city of Chanchung. Japan tried to retain its 'special rights' in the Russian Far East, but without success. On 25 October 1922 the Japanese troops left the territory of the FER except the northern part of Sakhalin Island.

In October 1922 the PRA of the FER defeated the White troops at Spassk and Monastyrishche and eliminated the 'Black Buffer'. On 25 October 1922 the Red forcers took Vladivostok, and with this the Civil War in Siberia ended.

Mikhail Konstantinovich Diterikhs (1874–1937) was born into the family of a nobleman. He graduated from the Corps des pages[5] and the General Staff Academy and served in the army. He was involved in the Russo-Japanese War (1904–5) and the First World War. In 1915 he was promoted to major-general. In the autumn of 1917 he became quartermaster general within the Staff of the Supreme Commander in Chief of the Russian Army General Headquarters, then chief of staff of the Czech Legion. He was one of the organizers and leaders of its 'mutiny'. In 1918–19 he commanded the White Siberian Army. From July 1919 he became the minister of war in the Kolchak Government and he led the White forces in the Tobolsk-Petropavlovsk Battle for Siberia. In 1920–1 he lived in emigration in Manchuria. He supported the restoration of the Russian Monarchy. In 1922 he came to south Primorie, removed Merkulov from power and seized it himself. He declared himself Dictator, and established the 'Priamur Monarchy'. After the Japanese intervention ended and the Whites were defeated, he emigrated.

> The eighteen-month rule of S. Merkulov and his successor General Diterikhs in Primorie is a curious epilogue to the White movement in Siberia. This epilogue lasted as long as the end of 1922 only because the Japanese occupation of Vladivostok lasted that long.
>
> (P.N. Milukov, a Russian historian and politician)

The end of Japanese intervention, the defeat of the White movement, and the elimination of the 'Black Buffer' rendered the existence of the FER superfluous. On 14 November 1922 the People's Assembly of the FER, in accordance with a decision by the Communist Party's *Dalbiuro*, appealed to the Russian Government, requesting that the FER be included in Soviet Russia. On 15 November the Soviet Supreme Central Executive Committee (VtsIK) declared the FER a constituent part of Russian Federation and abolished it. The buffer state ceased to exist.

Part VIII

Siberia in the 1920s–90s and beyond

26 Siberia's foreign policy situation

In the 1920s the party-state leadership of the USSR and the Communist International (*Comintern*)[1] made an attempt to spread Communist influence in Asia. China became the main target of this activity and Siberia acted as its base.

In 1920, the Far Eastern branch of *Comintern* was founded in Irkutsk to spread Communist ideas and to organize revolutionary activities in China and other countries of eastern Asia.

In the early 1920s the USSR established direct control from Siberia over Mongolia and Tuva, formerly parts of China.[2] In 1921 the Red Army, under the pretext of fighting against the White movement, seized Mongolia and Tuva, driving out the Chinese troops and administration. The creation of two independent states, the Mongolian and the Tuvan people's republics, was proclaimed,[3] and power was handed to local pro-Communist elements. In actual fact, both states were in total political, economic and ideological subjection to the USSR.

During the 1920s–40s the Soviet Union succeeded in regaining almost all the Siberian territories lost earlier, using diplomatic and military action. These territories included the island of Sakhalin, Tuva and the Kuril Islands.

In January 1925, in Beijing a Soviet-Japanese Convention was concluded which involved:

- the withdrawal of Japanese troops from northern Sakhalin;
- the establishment of diplomatic relations between the USSR and Japan;
- the granting of a concession to Japan for oil and coal exploitation in northern Sakhalin; and
- the recognition of the 1905 *Portsmouth Peace Treaty* between Russia and Japan, which mirrored the results of the Russo-Japanese War.

However, the USSR declared that it did not bear any political responsibility for this treaty.

In 1944, at the height of the Second World War, the USSR's party-state leadership liquidated the Tuvan People's Republic (TPR). This action was undertaken 'at the request' of Tuva's leadership, who were 'prompted' to act in this way by Moscow. On 17 August an extraordinary session of the Minor People's Khural (Assembly) of the TPR adopted a declaration requesting admission to the USSR. In October 1944 the USSR Supreme Soviet 'granted' this request and admitted Tuva to the Soviet Union as an autonomous region.

In 1945, in accordance with decisions adopted at the Yalta Conference,[4] the USSR regained the southern half of Sakhalin and the Kurils after the defeat of Japan. The territories were physically regained during the course of Sakhalin and Kuril operations by the Red Army during the Soviet–Japanese War of August 1945. Both operations were carried out by troops of the second Far Eastern Front under the command of General M.A. Purkaev in conjunction with sailors of the Pacific Fleet.

The Sakhalin operation took place between 11 and 25 August 1945. At first the Red Army had the advantage of practically double the number of troops and an overwhelming technical superiority. The Japanese on the island had not a single aircraft to face over 100 Soviet tanks and almost 200 military aircraft. However, their troops were occupying well-defended positions along the front line, including 17 reinforced concrete pill-boxes and many other military engineers' constructions and defences. The approaches to these positions were protected by almost impassable swamps. For a whole week Red Army units launched fierce attacks to break through the Japanese defences. By 18 August the Japanese opposition had been overcome and the Red Army detachments advanced southwards. A short time earlier, on 16 August, amphibious landings had begun on the western shoreline of Sakhalin behind the Japanese troops. On 19 August the Japanese Command announced its capitulation. Nonetheless, fighting continued until the 25 August, when Red Army units occupied the main towns in southern Sakhalin, Toiokhara (Yuzhno-Sakhalinsk) and Otomari (Korsakov). During the operation 18,000 Japanese officers and other ranks were captured.

The Soviet armed forces faced a far more complex situation in the Kuril Islands. In contrast to Sakhalin and other theatres of the Soviet–Japanese War, the advantage belonged to the Japanese here. They had more troops and armaments. For instance, there were 60 tanks on the northernmost island of the Kuril Archipelago, Siumsiu (Shumshu), whereas the Soviet marines had no tanks at their disposal. In addition, the Japanese troops could rely on a formidable system of defences including reinforced concrete pill-boxes, complex underground defences up to 50 metres in depth, plus other defence installations. Therefore, the decision to initiate the Kuril operation was taken only when Japan's complete and total military defeat had become obvious. The operation began on 18 August 1945 by an amphibious landing on the Island of Shumshu. The landing force occupied a small bridgehead, but they soon faced a difficult situation. The Japanese utilized their superior manpower to go over onto the offensive, supported by tanks and artillery. The landing party bravely resisted all the enemy onslaughts and managed to inflict heavy losses, destroying 32 of the 38 tanks that had taken part in the attack. Fierce fighting continued until late that night. On the morning of 19 August the Japanese announced their capitulation. After this, amphibious landings led to the seizure of all the Kuril Islands by 1 September 1945 and the capture of around 60,000 Japanese officers and other ranks.

During the Sakhalin and Kuril campaigns the Red Army soldiers and sailors of the Pacific Fleet demonstrated enormous heroism, mutual assistance and self-sacrifice. Thousands of participants were awarded medals for heroic feats and excellence in combat. Five participants in the Sakhalin campaign and nine in the Shumshu events received the high military honour of Hero of the Soviet Union. Among them were Sergeant Anton Buiukly (Sakhalin) and two sailors, Nikolai Vilkov and Pyotr Il'ichov (Shumshu), who repeated A. Matrosov's immortal feat by blocking the embrasures of pill-boxes with their own bodies, saving their comrades in arms at the expense of their own lives.

From the end of the Civil War to the late twentieth century, Siberia's security was ensured by international agreements between the USSR (later the Russian Federation) and neighbouring countries: China, Mongolia, Japan, North and South Korea, the USA and other countries as well.

However, Siberia's borders became the object of aggressive actions on the part of neighbouring states several times; three times these developed into serious armed conflicts.

The first of them, in October 1929, came to be known as the 'Conflict on the CER'. It was caused by the worsening of Soviet–Chinese relations. In July 1929 the Chinese government, in response to an uprising in the city of Guanchow (Canton), organized by the *Comintern*, took control over the CER, which belonged to the USSR. Chinese troops attacked the borders of Siberia. To defend the Siberian frontiers, the USSR formed a Special Far Eastern Army of around 20,000 under the command of V.K. Bliukher. The Soviet troops, far superior technically to the numerically superior Chinese forces (in aviation, warships and tanks), defeated the 130,000 Chinese in three operations and took the cities of Fujin, Mishan, Manchuria and Hailar. After this, negotiations began to put an end to the conflict. On 27 December 1929, in Khabarovsk, the USSR and China concluded an agreement in accordance with which the CER was returned to the USSR.

Almost ten years later, Japanese militarists waged a military conflict at Lake Khasan. Its aim was to probe the Red Army's fighting capability in case of a possible war. On 29 July 1938 a Japanese battalion violated the Soviet border, but were beaten back after a fight. On 31 July, two Japanese regiments supported by artillery made a new attack, occupied several hills by Lake Khasan and began to fortify them. Red Army units made several attempts to expel the Japanese from their positions between 31 July and 2 August, but failed. Following this the Soviet leadership decided to carry out a massive attack against the Japanese troops. The overall leadership of the operation was carried out by Marshal Bliukher. An attack group was formed, consisting of about 23,000 men, 237 guns, 285 tanks and 250 aircraft. Between 6 and 9 August this group was able to push the Japanese troops (around 10,000 men with artillery) out of the occupied heights in a tough action, restoring the integrity of the USSR's borders. On 11 August 1938 the battle at Lake Khasan was concluded after talks in Moscow between the Japanese ambassador to the USSR and Soviet diplomats.

The third substantial conflict occurred between 2 and 21 March 1969 at Damanskii Island on the River Ussuri. It was organized by the Chinese government who were displeased with the borders along on the rivers Amur, Argun and Ussuri.[5] The conflict happened at a time of general deterioration in Soviet–Chinese relations. On 2 March a battalion of Chinese troops, supported by mortars, suddenly attacked the Soviet frontier-guards and seized Damanskii Island, but it was beaten off in the course of fighting between 2 and 3 March. On subsequent days both sides built up their forces in the region of conflict and carried out reconnaissance. On 14–16 March decisive fighting for Damanskii Island took place, involving infantry, tanks and artillery, in the course of which it changed hands several times. The Soviet troops finally succeeded in driving the Chinese off the island. By 21 March military action in the Damanskii area had ceased.

Thus, during the period under consideration, the leadership of the USSR, and later Russia, succeeded in maintaining the territorial integrity of Siberia and ensuring its security. Nonetheless, there were still threats to some Siberian territories. The islands in the rivers Amur and Ussuri, which form the border between China and Russia, remained a subject of diplomatic dispute. The Kuril Islands[6] also became a cause of tension, but this time between the USSR, subsequently Russia, and Japan. This has prevented Russia from a complete normalization of relations with Japan and the conclusion of a post Second World War peace treaty.

27 The administration of Siberia

In Siberia, as well as throughout the rest of the country, a party-state system of government functioned between the 1920s and 1991. All important decisions were made by Communist Party bodies. Government bodies were entrusted with the execution of these decisions under the supervision of party institutions. The system represented an extremely rigid and centralized power structure.

Between 1922 and 1925 the majority of Siberia was governed by the Siberian Bureau of the Communist Party's Central Committee (*Sibbiuro*) and the Siberian Revolutionary Committee (*Sibrevkom*). The territory of the former FER was run by the Far Eastern Bureau of the Communist Party's Central Committee (*Dalbiuro*) and the Far Eastern Revolutionary Committee (*Dalrevkom*). After 1925 regional committees of the party and regional Soviets began to govern Siberia. They controlled provincial, republican, district and county party bodies and Soviets. Party committees within the autonomous republics had the fairly minor status of a district.

After a new constitution was adopted for the USSR in 1936 the structure of government in Siberia changed somewhat. Regional and district party committees and regional, republican and district Soviets were given equal rights. The All-Union and Russian Republic Soviet Central Executive Committees (VTsIK SSSR and VtsIK RSFSR) were replaced by the corresponding Supreme Soviets.

After the break-up of the USSR and the collapse of the Communist System in 1991, Siberian republics, regions, districts and autonomous counties were given equal rights as subjects (*subekty*) of the Russian Federation (RF). They all reported directly to the president and government of the RF.

The collapse of the Communist system, the fragmentation of the USSR and the formation of a new state structure in Russia gave rise to a negative phenomenon, which threatened Russia's integrity, the so-called 'parade of sovereignties'. During this period individual parts of the RF attempted to secure exclusive rights, deeming regional legislation superior to federal laws. The 'parade of sovereignties' became widespread in Siberia too, particularly in the national minority republics. In some of them, for instance Yakutia (Sakha), the rights of the ethnic Russian population began to be infringed, and in Tuva

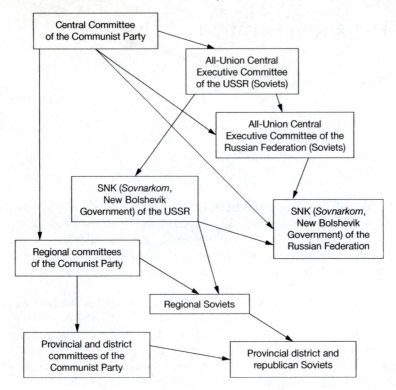

Figure 27.1 The administration of Siberia between 1925 and 1936

(Tyva) there were anti-Russian pogroms in the early 1990s, which put part of the population to flight.

The federal authorities appeared unable to combat the 'parade of sovereignties' directly from the centre. In an attempt to overcome the problem federal districts (*okrugs*) were formed throughout Russia in 2000, headed by the president's plenipotentiaries.

They began to take control of all areas within the federation and succeeded in putting an end to the 'parade of sovereignties'. The territory of Siberia was divided between three federal districts: the Far East, Siberia and the Urals, headed by K.B. Pulikovskii, L.V. Drachevskii and P.M. Latyshev respectively.

Between 1920 and 1990 the administrative-territorial division of Siberia was changed a number of times, the boundaries of territorial formations changing relatively frequently.

In 1922 the following were created:

- the Far Eastern Oblast (centre Chita, replacing the FER);
- the Yakut Autonomous Soviet Socialist Republic (replacing the Yakutsk Oblast);

- the Oirot Autonomous Oblast (centre Oirot-Tura; renamed Gorno-Altai Autonomous Oblast in 1948);
- the Buriat-Mongol Autonomous Oblast; and
- the Kirghiz Autonomous Soviet Socialist Republic (which included several previously Siberian areas, namely the right bank of the River Irtysh and the cities of Pavlodar, Semipalatinsk, Ust-Kamenogorsk and the region around Petropavlovsk).

In 1923 a new Buriat-Mongol Autonomous Soviet Socialist Republic was formed by uniting two formerly separate Buriat regions. The centre of the Republic was Verkhneudinsk (renamed Ulan-Ude in 1934).

In 1925 the territory of Siberia was again divided, this time between the Siberian Krai and the Far Eastern Krai. Their centres were Novonikolaevsk (renamed Novosibirsk in 1926) and Chita, later transferred to Vladivostok.

In 1930 the Siberian Krai was subdivided into the west Siberian Krai (centre Novosibirsk) and the east Siberian Krai (centre Irkutsk). Transbaikalia was transferred to the latter from the Far Eastern Krai. Apart from this, new national minority subdivisions were created: the Khakass Autonomous Oblast (centre Abakan), and the Koriak, Ostiako-Vogul, Taimyr, Chukotsk, Evenk and Yamalo-Nenetsk autonomus *okrugs*.

In 1934 a new Krasnoiarsk Krai was set up from within eastern Siberia and Omsk Krai from its west Siberian counterpart. A special new administrative entity established within Far East was the Jewish Autonomous Oblast (centre Birobidzhan).

In 1937 another major reorganization occurred. The west and east Siberian regions were divided between the Altai Krai (centre Barnaul), the Irkutsk, Novosibirsk and Chita *oblasts* and the Aginsk and Ust-Ordynsk Buriat autonomous *okrugs*. A year later the Far Eastern Krai was subdivided between the Primorsk (centre Vladivostok) and Khabarovsk *krais*.

In the mid-1940s parts of the Urals became the Kurgan Oblast, parts of Novosibirsk Oblast became Kemerovo and Tomsk *oblasts*, and the Tiumen Oblast was set up from part of Omsk Oblast. The incorporation of Tuva led to its inclusion as the Tuva Autonomous Oblast (centre Kyzyl; raised to Autonomous Republic status in 1961). In 1947 Sakhalin Oblast was established with its centre in Yuzhno-sakhalinsk. A year later parts of the Khabarovsk Krai became the Amur Oblast, and in 1953 a further subdivision led to the formation of the Kamchatka Oblast (centre Petropavlovsk-Kamchatskii) and Magadan Oblast.

In 1992 the Yakut, Buriat and Tuva Autonomous Soviet Socialist republics were transformed into republics of the Russian Federation, as were the Gorno-Altai and Khakass autonomous *oblasts*.

In 2000 the whole area was redivided into three: the Urals, Siberian and Far Eastern Federal *okrugs*.

28 Socio-economic and cultural development from the 1920s to the 1940s

Having won the Civil War, the Communists were forced to retreat from the policy of War Communism by popular pressure and introduced a compromise known as the New Economic Policy (NEP) which involved:

- abolition of *prodrazverstka* (surplus expropriation) and the introduction of a tax in kind;
- restoration of freedom to trade;
- restoration of money circulation and a banking system;
- relegalization of entrepreneurship;
- reintroduction of market methods in economics; and
- renewed permission for economic concessions and the restoration of foreign trade.

The NEP made it possible to overcome the surge of popular anger and to start restoring the country's economy, destroyed as it had been by war and revolution.

In Siberia, as well as throughout the whole of Russia, the transition to the NEP began with the replacement of *prodrazverstka* by a tax in kind, which was calculated as a percentage of crops fixed in advance. The tax in kind averaged 50 per cent of the previous surplus expropriation. However, in Siberia the proportion was bigger than in European Russia. It amounted to 20 per cent of the grain crops, while it averaged only 12 per cent throughout the rest of the country. Nonetheless the tax in kind stimulated the growth of agricultural production in the region, in particular cattle breeding.

Table 28.1 The growth of livestock production in Siberia*

Livestock species	1917	1922	1927
Cows	2,600,000	1,800,000	2,900,000
Horses	3,900,000	3,400,000	3,800,000

*Not including the Far Eastern region.

The growth of livestock production made a sharp increase in the production of the famous Siberian butter possible. Whereas in 1922 only 6,000 tons of butter was produced in Siberia, as much as 37,000 tons was churned in 1927. Siberian butter became an important item of export again.

During the NEP Siberian agriculture fully and sufficiently provided for the region's food needs. However, it never fully recovered from the consequences of the Bolshevik Revolution and the Civil War, nor did it attain its pre-revolutionary level of production.

The complete restoration and development of agriculture was hindered by the Communists' agricultural policy, which aimed at limiting the activities of the so-called *kulaki* – the most active and economically significant stratum of farmers. This, in its turn, gradually made a significant number of Siberian farmers dissatisfied with both the NEP and its results.

From 1922, private entrepreneurial activity in trade and minor industries was allowed in Siberia, which encouraged their development. As early as 1925 there were over 80,000 small private businesses in Siberia (making and repairing footwear, clothing, kitchen utensils, tools and so on). Some businesses were de-nationalized: out of more than 1,500 once nationalized firms about 50 per cent were returned to their former owners.

Entrepreneurship in the retail trade was particularly well-developed. In 1920s over 90 per cent of retail commodity circulation in Siberia was in private hands. The Russia-wide market was rebuilt. The Irbit Fair once again became one of the largest in the world. All these made it possible to overcome the acute dearth of goods in Siberia in many sectors.

The use of market methods of economic management helped to rebuild Siberia's weak industry. By 1927 industrial production had once more reached the 1913 level. Foreign concessions played an important role in this process.[1] The largest concessions were in fishing, oil (Primorie and northern Sakhalin) and the gold industry (for example, the concession operated by the British Lena Gold fields Company in Bodaibo).

Generally, however, the NEP economic system turned out to be less efficient than that prevailing in pre-revolutionary times. In the second half of the 1920s, once people had recovered from the disasters of the Civil War and War Communism, most Siberians became dissatisfied with the NEP to one degree or another. The farmers were not happy about the existing restrictions on the development of their farms, the *nepmany* (entrepreneurs) were displeased with the tax burden and the absence of legal guarantees for their economic activities, the intelligentsia was dissatisfied with the absence of political freedom and the workers were displeased with their low standard of living[2] and unemployment (in 1927 the number out of work in Siberia was over 60,000). On the other hand, many Communist Party members were convinced that the NEP was a capitulation to the bourgeoisie.

In the late 1920s the NEP was abolished and the USSR Party leadership made a new attempt at an accelerated transition to a socialist society. Siberia and Siberians had to take a most active part in this. As is well known, the accelerated building of socialism in the USSR proceeded along three main lines: the industrialization of the economy, the collectivization of agriculture, and a Cultural Revolution.[3] All these elements were put into practice in extreme form in Siberia.

During the industrialization many industrial enterprises were built in various regions of Siberia. Mining and metallurgical complexes, to serve the needs of the defence industry, predominated among them. More than a hundred new coal mines were constructed. Electric power stations, machine building plants and railway transport were developed particularly intensively. Power stations were put up in many Siberian towns, especially those near large industrial plants. Particularly noteworthy because of their size were an agricultural machinery plant in Novosibirsk (*Sibselmash*) and a heavy engineering works in Irkutsk. New railway lines were built: Volochaevka to Komsomolsk-on-the-Amur, Leninsk-Kuznetsk (Kolchugino) to Novosibirsk, Leninsk-Kuznetsk to Stalinsk (Kuznetsk) and Mundybash, Norilsk to Dudinka (within the Arctic Circle) and Partizansk (Suchan) to Nakhodka in the Far East. In total these line added over a thousand kilometres to the existing network.[4]

Totally new branches of industry also made their appearance. Examples include the aviation industry represented by factories in Novosibirsk and Irkutsk, the oil refining industry represented by the Khabarovsk Refinery, which used oil from Sakhalin, and a series of other sectors.

The Kuzbass (the Kuznetsk coal-mining region) was developed particularly rapidly. Large-scale coal mines, coking plants and one of the largest industrial undertakings in the world, the Kuznetsk Metallurgical Combine, were constructed here. In the late 1930s the USSR's second military-industrial complex was created in the Urals and western Siberia.

Apart from the construction of new industrial projects, older pre-revolutionary enterprises were reconstructed. As part of this process one of the oldest factories in Siberia, the Petrovsk-Transbaikal Metallurgical Works,

Figure 28.1 The Kutnetsk metallurgical combine

which had begun its existence in the eighteenth century, was modernized. This also applied to the first machine building works, 'Dalzavod' in Vladivostok.

Industrialization generated a tremendous enthusiasm for work in Siberia as it did in the rest of the country. As early as the end of the first five-year plan (1932) about 70 per cent of the workers were involved in 'socialist competition' to increase production and productivity. Famous in this respect was the 'Stakhanovite Movement'. It had a tremendous influence in Siberia, and the names of some Kuzbass miners became household words because of their amazing feats of production.

As a result of this process Siberia made significant strides towards industrial development. Before the revolutionary events of 1917–21 the region's share in the country's industrial production amounted to no more than 3.5 per cent; on the eve of the Second World War this had exceeded 10 per cent. Even more startling were the growth figures for individual sectors. For instance, before 1917 Siberia had produced no more than two million tons of coal (8 per cent of the total Russian production). In 1940 39 million tons were mined (20 per cent of the total). A huge leap forward was made in electricity generation. In 1928 before rapid industrialization began Siberia produced 15 million kilowatt/hours of electricity. By 1940 this had risen to 320 million kw/h.

Overall, this period laid a firm basis for the further steady development of Siberian industry.

The collectivization of agriculture affected the lives of Siberians, especially the farmers, particularly badly. Supporters of the collectivization movement were considerably rarer in Siberia than in European Russia. Therefore, the local authorities had to act harshly when carrying it out. The well-to-do Siberian farmers had suffered a first attack well before the beginning of collectivization, during the famous Communist leader Stalin's tour of Siberia for grain requisitioning in early 1928. Stalin accused the Siberian farmers of 'kulak sabotage', and the local authorities of 'assisting them'. During these requisitioning forays exceptional measures similar to *prodrazverstka* were frequently undertaken. Their victims were thousands of farmers accused of the 'kulak sabotage' and sentenced to various terms of imprisonment. The Communists had to actually ruin agriculture in Siberia to carry out collectivization here. At this time, in Siberia alone, about 150,000 farming families were 'dekulakized'.

In response to the despotism and violence the farmers began massive spontaneous uprisings throughout Siberia. They lasted from 1930 to 1933. Tens of thousands of poorly armed and badly organized farmers took part in them. These uprisings were suppressed with exceptional brutality by the local authorities. In the village Kardoi in the Tulun Okrug in the Siberian Krai the authorities sentenced 58 farmers to death by shooting for taking part in an uprising in March 1930, during which five supporters of collectivization had been killed.

Only through intense labour, at the cost of incredible effort and many victims, using terror, violence and demagogy, were the Communists able to

Table 28.2 The decline in agricultural production in Siberia caused by collectivization*

	1928	1932
Crops (total)	8,500,000 tons	6,000,000 tons
Cows	3,700,000 head	1,900,000 head
Horses	4,700,000 head	1,800,000 head

*Not including the Far East.

achieve the collectivization of the Siberian peasantry. Around 22,000 collective farms and 731 machine tractor stations (MTSs) were organized in Siberia.[5]

Collectivization resulted in the ruin of agriculture; it had not fully recovered by the end of the twentieth century.

The most immediate consequence of collectivization in Siberia was a serious food problem lasting throughout the prewar period, and continuing into the post-war years. In 1933, when the average monthly salary in Siberia was 120 roubles, one kilo of butter cost 30 roubles and a litre of milk cost 2 roubles 30 copecks. After the Second World War, in 1946–7, Siberia become one of the famine zones. This was caused by crop failures and increased food confiscation.

The Cultural Revolution was carried out in Siberia within an all-Union scheme. Most attention was paid to the development of education. Schools, institutes of higher education and scientific institutions were opened throughout Siberia. By 1941 there were over 20,000 schools of various levels and over 70 higher educational institutes. The leading ones were Tomsk University (the oldest), the University of the Far East (formerly the Oriental Institute), and Irkutsk University, plus Tomsk Technological Institute. As a result of these activities, by the late 1930s, the level of literacy among the Siberian population, according to official statistics, exceeded 85 per cent.

Many cultural institutions were also opened: clubs, libraries, theatres, cinemas, museums, etc. The largest of them was the House of Science and Technology in Novosibirsk (now the Theatre of Opera and Ballet). During the Cultural Revolution, literary and artistic life was activated. Several well-known writers began their careers in Siberia during this period, including Vsevolod Ivanov, Lidia Seifullina and Alexander Fadeev, who later became Head of the Soviet Writers' Union.

Particular note should be taken of the cultural development of the Siberian native peoples. The autonomy granted to many peoples in the 1920s–30s created favourable conditions for this process. Autonomous education gradually led to written national languages, national literatures and a national intelligentsia. To assist the smallest and most backward people groups in Siberia a Committee of the North (*Komitet severa pri VTsIK RSFSR*) was established in 1924, which kept its eye on all aspects of life among these peoples.

At the same time, owing to the diversity of its aims the Cultural Revolution in Siberia had both positive and negative effects. Thus, under the pretext of

Figure 28.2 The title page of the journal *Irkutsk Workers' Faculty*

struggling against bourgeois culture and religious superstitions, the cultural heritage of the past was ruined and outstanding cultural monuments were destroyed. The streets of all Siberian towns were renamed to imprint Bolshevik dogma on the minds of the people. Many Siberian towns and villages also had their names changed. Alekseevsk became Svobodnyi, Verkhneudinsk became Ulan-ude (Red Ude), Kolchugino was renamed Leninsk-Kuznetskii, Kuznetsk became Stalinsk, Nikolaevsk-Ussuriisk was named Voroshilovsk and so on.

During the period under review the most important events in Siberian life were the purges and the creation of the GULAG concentration camp system. Purges began as soon as the Civil War had ended. In the 1920s they affected participants in peasant uprisings and protests against *prodrazverstka*, the so-called 'former people',[6] the nepmen and 'kulak saboteurs'. Tens of thousands of Siberians had even then become victims of repression to one degree or another.

The late 1920s and early 1930s brought a new wave of purges to Siberia. The dispossessed farmers and so-called 'wreckers' (*vrediteli*) became their victims. At that time large numbers of dispossessed peasants from the west arrived in Siberia for the first time. They were called 'special relocatees' (*spetspereselentsy*). These forcibly relocated people were deprived of their political and civil rights. They were settled in special settlements, guarded and watched by organs of the OGPU.[7] In 1932 there were around 400,000 of them in Siberia. It was at this time that the GULAG began to be set up.

In the early 1930s a wave of struggle against 'wrecking' swept through Siberia. It was a means used by the authorities to explain their economic blunders. Both the old engineers and other professionals who had begun their professional career before the Revolution and people taken at random were accused of being 'wreckers'. The scale of the struggle against 'wrecking' was quite substantial. For example, during 1932 alone the West-Siberian regional OGPU arrested over 4,000 alleged 'wreckers', more then half of whom were sentenced to death by shooting. The most infamous case in Siberia was the fabricated trial of the 'Peasant Party' in 1931. The world-famous economists A.V. Chaianov and N.D. Kondratiev were accused of 'wrecking'.

The Great Terror of 1936–8 turned Siberia once more into a 'land of prison and exile'. The largest and most horrendous GULAG structures – 'Siblag', 'Dallag', 'Bamlag', 'Yeniseilag', 'Ozerlag' and others were located here. In these camps hundreds of thousands of prisoners from the whole country were held in inhuman conditions. It was their labour that created the majority of Siberia's vast industrial plants: the Norilsk copper-nickel factory, the works in Komsomolsk-on-the-Amur, Novosibirsk, and many other Siberian cities and towns. Hundreds of thousands of Siberians from various social strata also became victims of the Great Terror. The entire party-state leadership in all Siberian regions were purged on more than one occasion; among them were the former high-ranking leaders I.N. Smirnov, S.V. Kosior, C.I. Syrtsov and **R.I. Eikhe**.

During and after the Second World War the scale of repressions even increased. In 1937 one million people were prisoners in the GULAG; by 1945 this figure had grown to 1.5 million and by 1950 it had leapt to 2.6 million. A considerable number of these detainees were in Siberia. In the post-war period the prisoners built new industrial giants such as the Angarsk Oil

Figure 28.3 Irkutsk Cathedral before and after destruction by the Communists

Robert Idrikovich Eikhe (1890–1940) was born into a working-class family in Latvia. He in turn became a factory worker in the city of Mittava. He became a Communist in 1905 and took part in the revolutionary struggle. In 1908 he emigrated to Great Britain. In 1911 he came back to Russia and lived in Riga. He was one of the leaders of the Latvian Social-Democrats. In 1915 he was arrested and exiled to Siberia, but soon escaped and returned to Riga. He was involved in the revolutionary events in Latvia in 1917. He was one of the leaders of the Bolshevik underground in Latvia (1917–19). He worked in the Ministry of Agriculture of the Russian Federation (1920–4) and became the chairman of the Siberian Regional Executive Committee (1925–7). He was the first secretary of the Siberian Regional Committee of the Communist Party (1929–30), then first secretary of the West-Siberian Regional Committee of the Communist Party (1930–7) and then an alternate member of the Communist Party's Central Committee (1925–30) becoming a full member (1930–7), as well as an alternate member of the *Politbureau*. He led industrialization, collectivization and the cultural revolution in Siberia. He became the USSR Minister of Agriculture, but was arrested soon afterwards and then shot as an 'enemy of the people'.

Refinery, the Taishet-Lena Railway and others. After the war, an additional 700,000 *spetspereselentsy* from the western part of the USSR were exiled to Siberia. They were from Latvia, Lithuania, Estonia, the Ukraine, Germany, etc. In Siberia there were also prisoners of war from former enemy armies: over 600,000 Japanese, 250,000 Germans, plus others, all of whom worked on Siberian construction sites.

Over the period of the Second World War (1941–5) Siberia became one of the chief centres in the USSR for military production. Some 322 defence industries and about one million people were evacuated here from the west. Most of them were relocated in west Siberia and went into production during a single three-month period. New industrial enterprises were constructed during the war. For instance, in 1942 the Kuznetsk Aluminium Works was completed. It produced metal for the aviation industry that had previously been in short supply. By the middle of 1942, the reconstruction of Siberian industry to comply with the demands of war had been fully completed. Large quantities of almost all kinds of military machinery, weapons, ammunition and equipment were produced here. Also in 1942 the Altai Tractor Factory was constructed in Rubtsovsk. This works was built in a very short time and was equipped with machinery from a series of evacuated factories. It was the only factory producing tractors for use at the battle front and on the home front during the war.

During this period, at the price of an enormous amount of sacrificial labour, the Siberians managed to achieve significant increases in electricity production, coal mining, the extraction of ferrous, non-ferrous, rare and precious metals and many other types of production needed for the war effort. Since so many men were absent at the front, women and children were used for very heavy work. It was extremely difficult for them but they shouldered the burden.

By the middle of 1942 the conversion of industry to a war footing had been completed. A whole series of factories played a key role in working for victory. For instance, the Kuznetsk Metallurgical Combine produced a very significant amount of steel and tank armour. Some 50,000 tanks were produced from metal smelted here. During the war years the factories of Novosibirsk alone manufactured 15,000 fighter planes (13 per cent of the USSR's total production) and 125 million shells of various calibres.

Besides factories and their machines, valuable cultural items were evacuated to Siberia. The collections of the Hermitage, the Tretiakov Gallery and other museums, the contents of the USSR State Library, as well as Moscow and Leningrad theatres, famous all over the country, were housed in Siberian towns.

Siberians aided the front considerably, making voluntary contributions towards the production of military machinery, equipment and munitions, as well as clothing for the soldiers. A network of hospitals was opened throughout Siberia, where badly wounded soldiers were able to convalesce.

And, finally, Siberians took a most active, direct part in military actions themselves; several million men were called up. At the front they were characterized by bravery, endurance and determination to achieve their goal, characteristics of the Siberian mindset that German generals commented on more than once: they were a most discomforting opponent. It was Siberian divisions that contributed decisively to the defeat of the German Nazi troops in the battle of Moscow. Over 70 new divisions, which covered themselves with glory on the battlefield, were formed in Siberia. Over 1,000 Siberians received the eminent title of Hero of the Soviet Union, and the war ace pilot A.I. Pokryshkin became the first person to receive three such awards.

There is no doubt whatever that Siberia made a significant contribution to the victory of the USSR in the Second World War.

After victory in Europe, Siberians took an active part in the preparation for war against Japan in the east. The areas near the Manchurian border became a base for military operations and the population helped with preparation and supplies. A particularly hard lot fell to the railwaymen, who had to ensure the transport of huge quantities of matériel and troops from west to east. This work took place under extremely difficult circumstances, demanding colossal effort. During the war the rolling stock, rails, sleepers and, even in places, the railbed, which became decrepit through overuse, needed to be replaced. This was particularly the case in the section skirting the southern end of Lake Baikal where 11,000 rails needed to be replaced. The State Defence Committee ordered 30,000 qualified railwaymen, 800 locomotives and a great deal of other necessary equipment to Siberia from other parts of the country. During the three- to four-month period, when war with Japan was being prepared, 116,000 wagons transported various types of loads including 400,000 people, more than 7,000 guns and mortars, over 2,000 tanks, more than 17,000 lorries and 36,000 horses. This provided significant assistance to the army, ensuring swift victory over the Japanese troops.

29 Socio-economic and cultural development, from the 1950s to 1985

The second half of the twentieth century became a time of intensified development in Siberia. Absolutely new industries, which now form the backbone of Russia's economic strength, came into being. They include petrochemicals (oil and gas), the aluminium industry, hydro-power, military-industrial complexes (particularly producing nuclear weapons), diamond production and many others.

Industrial giants emerged in almost every industry in Siberia. These include the world-famous Bratsk, Krasnoiarsk, Ust-Ilimsk and Saiano-Shushensk HEP stations, the Bratsk, Krasnoiarsk, Irkutsk and Saianogorsk aluminium factories, the west Siberian metal production combine in Novokuznetsk, the Bratsk and Ust-Ilimsk timber works, the Omsk and Tobolsk petrochemical plants, machine building giants in Novosibirsk and Krasnoiarsk, the west Siberian oil and gas industries, as well as diamond production facilities in Mirnyi and Udachnyi and many, many others.

A large number of new cities and towns were built in Siberia, such as Angarsk, Bratsk, Lesosibirsk, Mirnyi, Nazarovo, Neriungryi, Nizhnevartovsk, Strezhevoi, Tynda, Ust-Ilimsk and others.

As a result, Siberia ceased to be a predominantly rural economy; it became an urbanized, industrial region. The proportion of urban dwellers reached 50 per cent as early as 1959. During the last few years of the Soviet era this process accelerated. Several major urban complexes emerged: Novosibirsk and Omsk each had populations over a million strong. The overall population also grew substantially: during the 30 years separating the 1959 and 1989 censuses the figures grew by nine million from 23.5 to 32.5 million. This growth was mainly due to migration from other parts of the country to the burgeoning industrial centres.

During the second half of the twentieth century industrial output figures increased dramatically. In 1950 slightly more than ten billion kilowatt/hours of electricity, 70 million tons of coal and 100,000 tons of aluminium were being produced. By the end of the century this had reached 200 billion kilowatt/hours of electric power, almost 190 million tons of coal and 2,360,000 tons of aluminium.

Figure 29.1 Construction of the Bratsk HEP plant

By the 1980s Siberia's share in the gross national output of the USSR exceeded 10 per cent. The export of Siberia's natural riches provided over 50 per cent of the USSR's foreign currency income. Today, Siberia remains one of the backbones of Russia's economy and finances. The region produces:

- over 40 per cent of all Russia's electrical energy;
- over 70 per cent of the country's coal;
- nearly 100 per cent of the gold;
- over 95 per cent of the diamonds;
- over 70 per cent of Russian oil;
- over 90 per cent of the gas;
- almost 85 per cent of the aluminium production; and
- over 50 per cent of the cellulose.

Intensive industrialization of this vast territory required further development of communications. Railways remained the chief means of transport. In the

Figure 29.2 Omsk oil refinery

second half of the twentieth century several important railway lines were built: the South Siberian, the Baikal Amur (BAM), the Tiumen-Nizhnevartovsk, as well as many minor lines. Siberia's railways themselves changed dramatically. All of the major lines were electrified, powerful electric traction units and large-capacity rolling stock replacing the previous steam trains. Shipping underwent similar developments. A new generation of riverboats, powered by diesel engines, appeared on Siberian rivers. New, more powerful icebreakers enabled the inauguration of continuous traffic along the full length of the Northern Sea Route.

Relatively new means of transport appeared, including air and road transport and pipelines. Thus, it was in Siberia that the world's first passenger jet airline appeared, travelling between Irkutsk and Moscow. The airports in Novosibirsk,

Figure 29.3 Construction of the ill-fated BAM Railway

Krasnoiarsk and Khabarovsk are among the largest in Russia. Hard-surfaced roads began to be built in Siberia. It was here, too, that the biggest oil and gas pipelines in the country originated.

Developments in the transport system, in turn, accelerated Siberia's economic exploitation.

At the same time, however, this extensive economic development was characterized by a predatory, reckless approach to natural resources and gave rise to a large number of complex ecological, economic and moral problems. Among these were:

- excessively concentrated ecologically harmful production, which gave rise to the appearance of cities unpleasant to live in such as Angarsk, Bratsk, Kemerovo, Novokuznetsk and others;
- disproportion in the development of different branches of the economy (most attention being given to the development of extractive industries such as metallurgy, timber and petrochemicals, military-industrial complexes and electrical energy), which turned Siberia into a resource colony of Russia dependent to a large extent on the import of industrial and particularly consumer goods;
- wastage in the Siberian economy, low production quality, a fall in investment and a growth in material and labour capacity in the last third of the twentieth century; and
- a standard of living inferior to that in European Russia (for instance, in the late 1980s Siberia was lower down in the supply of food products – half as much per person was budgeted for provisions – but 1.5 times the amount per person of harmful products was expelled into the atmosphere).

The agricultural situation in Siberia in the second half of the twentieth century remained difficult to deal with. The blow inflicted on it in the 1920s and 1930s was too heavy. Yet, during this period the authorities made a series of attempts to revive this vital sector of the economy.

The first of these was the Virgin Lands Campaign, inaugurated between 1954 and which came into being 1957. In these years over ten million hectares of grassland were put into cultivation, predominantly in Western Siberia. At the beginning, the campaign had some effect and the grain crop in Siberia increased, but by the middle of the 1960s soil erosion had reduced it to nothing.

In the mid-1960s the authorities made a new attempt to revive agriculture but this time the measures were country-wide. The agricultural reform of 1965 provided for stricter accounting, but at a lower level (*khozrashchot*), the formation of developmental funds for collective and state farms, and the regular payments of salaries and pensions to collective farmers. At first, these measures had a positive effect. However, inconsistencies and delays in fulfilling them markedly reduced their effectiveness. During the 1970s the nature of the reform was gradually changed in many respects, and agriculture in the USSR, Siberia included, began to revert to the state it had been in before reform.

Furthermore, the flooding of Siberia with new agricultural machinery, carried out on a large-scale throughout the second half of the twentieth century, did not have any pronounced beneficial effect either. Although the volume of agricultural machinery delivered was continually increasing, the poor quality of some types of machine and inefficient usage reduced the results to zero.

Thus, notwithstanding the authorities' attention to the problems of agriculture and their persistent efforts to change the situation for the better, it steadily degenerated during the second half of the twentieth century. The farming population of Siberia was steadily decreasing in numbers. The 1926 census showed that 87 per cent of the 11 million inhabitants of Siberia lived in the countryside; by 1959 only around 50 per cent of the 23.5 million Siberians lived in rural areas, and by 1989 only about 30 per cent of the 32.5 million population were still in the villages. Between 1960 and 1970 the number of villages in Siberia decreased by 50 per cent.

The amount of cultivated land also decreased. By the middle of the 1980s about 25 per cent of previously cultivated land was no longer in use. Ironically, it was often the most fertile soil that ceased to be cultivated, flooded to provide reservoirs for the new HEP stations.

As a result, Siberia was no longer fully supporting itself with food, and in many regions there were food supply problems. Moreover, from 30 per cent to 50 per cent of all agricultural products (except grains) were produced on private subsidiary farms which testified to the ineffectiveness of the collective and state farm system.

In the second half of the twentieth century education, science and the arts continued to develop. The number of secondary/high schools and vocational schools increased and new colleges and universities continued to open. New cultural institutions continued to emerge: clubs, palaces and houses of culture, theatres and cinemas, libraries and museums.

In 1957 the Siberian branch of the USSR Academy of Sciences (*Sibirskoe otdelenie AN SSSR*) was established to develop Siberian science and to coordinate research projects throughout the region. The decision was taken jointly by the Communist Party's Central Committee and the USSR Council of Ministers. Novosibirsk became the centre of this branch, and a special town, Akademgorodok, was built about 25 kilometres from the city to house both institutions and people. At the end of the century the Siberian branch comprised

Figure 29.4 Akademgorodok, near Novosibirsk

63 academic research institutions. Its research is world renowned. For example, the archaeological investigation of ancient Siberia, organized under the leadership of academician A.N. Okladnikov, has become very widely known.

The largest Siberian cultural, educational and research centre is Novosibirsk, where the biggest research library in Siberia, the State Scientific-Technical Public Library (GNTPB), the headquarters of the Siberian branch of the Academy of Sciences, and one of the best universities in the country, Novosibirsk State University, are located. Besides Novosibirsk, Tomsk, Irkutsk, Vladivostok and other large Siberian cities play a similar role.

The emergence of a number of talented writers, V.P. Astafiev, A.V. Vampilov, V.G. Rasputin and V.M. Shukshin, whose literary achievements have gained world recognition, has been a significant feature of Siberian culture during the second half of the twentieth century.

30 Siberia from 1985 to the early twenty-first century

At the beginning of the Gorbachev era and *perestroika*, Siberia was reasonably well-developed in economic terms with a population of over 32 million. However, in common with the rest of the Soviet Union by that time Siberia had come face to face with the problems created by the socialist economy. The most characteristic of these issues were: a decreased tempo of growth in productivity; a decline in efficiency in the use of productive capacity (for example, in Irkutsk Oblast this indicator was only 40 per cent of the 1960 figure in 1985); obsolescence in the agrarian sector; and disproportionate reliance on raw material resources in industrial development, leading to pollution of the environment including the dumping of harmful substances around many industrial plants.

A direct consequence of this situation was a steady increase in economic difficulties and dissatisfaction among the population. Even in the first half of the 1980s most regions of Siberia were experiencing interruptions in the supply of certain foodstuffs. In particular, resort was made to equalizing the supply of meat products and butter by the introduction of special ration coupons (the average norm for each person was one kilo of meat products and 300 grammes of butter per month).

Therefore, Gorbachev's announcement of the policy of *perestroika* and the renewal of society in general was greeted with hope by the Siberians, hope that their lives and economic situation would improve. At first Gorbachev's policies received popular support in Siberia as in the rest of the USSR.

However, as we all know now, these ill-considered reforms led the country into a profound economic crisis, which gradually turned into a socio-political crisis. During the *perestroika* years the economic situation in Siberia grew markedly worse. The authorities were obliged constantly to widen the range of rationed products. Thus, coupons for sugar (one kilo per person per month), vodka (one bottle per adult per month), soap, washing powder and other products were added to the rationing of meat and butter. Many products, in particular clothes, shoes and furniture, were distributed within large enterprises. These measures caused popular dissatisfaction and led to disillusionment both with the policy of *perestroika* and with Gorbachev himself.

Siberians first made loud complaints about their problems in the summer of 1989, when the famous miners' strikes spread throughout the USSR. Signs of open disaffection began to appear in the spring of that year. Spontaneous local strikes with demands for higher wages, improvements in working conditions, reductions in the administrative apparatus and so on began to occur in a series of workplaces, including several coal mines in the Kuzbass. At the same time small organizations and groups of radically inclined members of the intelligentsia opposed to Communist policies began to develop in large cities, notably Novosibirsk and Tomsk, under the influence of the Interregional Deputies' Group (*Mezhregionalnaia deputatskaia gruppa*) at the First USSR Congress of People's Deputies in Moscow. They concentrated on disseminating material critical of the Communist Party, its policies and leadership.

In July 1989 a massive upsurge in the workers' movement took place specifically in Siberia. This played a significant role in the weakening and collapse of the Communist system. A general strike among the Kuzbass miners began on 10 July in the Sheviakov Mine in the town of Mezhdurechensk. Very swiftly the strike spread throughout the Kuzbass. By the third day of the strike, 12 July, 18 pits and opencast sites with around 20,000 workers were on strike; however, a week after it had begun there were 166 enterprises in the coal industry with 180,000 workers involved. At the same time the workers began organizing themselves spontaneously. Strike committees were formed in all the towns in the Kuzbass. The first one emerged in Mezhdurechensk on 11 July, headed by V. Kokorin, a master miner from the Sheviakov pit. As early as 16 July, an 'All Kuzbass Strike Committee' was formed at the first regional conference of strike committees. These strike committees took upon themselves various power functions: the maintainance of order in the towns with the help of workers' detachments (*druzhiny*), the prohibition of the sale of alcohol during the strike, etc. They also conducted negotiations with the authorities and the government. Initially the strikers demanded pay rises, improvements in food supply and the solution of transport problems. The local authorities and, above all, the leaders of the coal industry in the Kuzbass, after experiencing the first shock, and realizing that they did not have the means to suppress the movement, hastened to support the strikers before the central authorities. As a result the local bureaucracy in the Kuzbass managed to establish partial control over the workers' movement and to represent them in negotiations with the government. For instance, the Kuzbass Strike Committee was led by T. Avliani, a USSR People's Deputy and Deputy Director for Capital Construction at the 'Kuzbassugol' combine. The directors of the coal mining enterprises and local authorities tried to advance their own interests through the strikes. They made demands for economic independence for the enterprises (transforming them into self-financing units) and for increased coal-prices, demands not made earlier by the strikers. In the end it was these demands that became central during negotiations with the government.

The broad mass nature of the miners' strike was totally unexpected by the Soviet leadership. As is known, in earlier times the Communists had decisively and mercilessly suppressed any mass social protests. However, Gorbachev's announcing of the policy of *glasnost* in 1987 added to the very scale of this strike and would have made the use of force extremely unprofitable and dangerous. The complete confusion within the country's central leadership had quite a substantial effect on the spread of the strike throughout the whole Kuzbass, and from 16 July to many other coal-mining regions in the USSR (the Donbass, Karaganda, Vorkuta and so on). Only on 17 July did a delegation from the government arrive in the Kuzbass for negotiations with the strikers. The delegation included the secretary of the CPSU Central Committee, N. Sliunkov, the deputy premier of the USSR Government, V. Voronin, and the chairman of the All Union Trades Union Congress (VTsSPS), S. Shalaev. The next day an agreement with the strikers was signed which envisaged the fulfilment of their basic demands and the dissolution of the strike committees at all levels. After this the strike movement in the Kuzbass declined.

The miners' strike in the Kuzbass and other regions of the USSR in 1989 played an important role in the country's political life. It was the first event during decades of Communist rule to show the real strength and power of the workers' movement. The meetings of strikers, many thousands strong, in the main squares of the towns in the Kuzbass became *real schools* for the political and social struggle, teaching workers how to organize themselves. After the strike independent workers' committees began to be formed in many enterprises in the USSR. In the Kuzbass a Regional Council (Soviet) of Workers' Committees was formed. This soviet began publishing its own paper, *Nasha gazeta* (*Our Paper*), which became the most significant and influential means of disseminating democratic ideas in Siberia between 1989 and 1991. As a result of the strike the Kuzbass (Kemerovo Oblast) was transformed into a real 'island of freedom' in Siberia. It provided great support to democratic forces in Russia during the period of struggle for power between 1989 and 1991. The consolidation of democratic forces throughout the country occurred precisely as a result of the July strike.

The 1989 miners' strikes, the conditions of *glasnost*, the activities of the Interregional Deputies' Group (IDG) of USSR People's Deputies plus the example of actions by democratic forces in Moscow and Leningrad led to the establishment of so-called 'people's fronts' in a series of regions in Siberia (Irkutsk, Novosibirsk and Tomsk *oblasts* and others), which united all proponents of democratic change irrespective of their political convictions. These 'fronts' generally supported the policies of the IDG and advocated that Boris Yeltsin should become the leader of the democratic forces. However, these organizations did not have much influence in the regions and were too few in number. Nonetheless, their activity was partly responsible for Yeltsin's convincing success in the elections for the presidency of the Russian Republic in June 1991. The majority of the Siberian electors supported his candidacy, whereas A.G. Tuleev, the chairman of the Kemerovo Oblast Soviet, only came fourth out of the six candidates.

The policy of *perestroika*, with all its pluses and minuses, incontestably revivified the nationality movement in the various peripheries of the USSR. Siberia was no exception. *Perestroika*, especially with the onset of *glasnost*, made it possible to clarify and discuss many hitherto forbidden themes. One of these was the issue of relations between the nationalities and nationalities policy in the 'socialist epoch'. Nationalist sentiments began to grow among the national minority intelligentsia in the autonomous *oblasts* and republics of Siberia. In some places the propagation of nationalist ideas led to a worsening of relations between the nationalities. In particular, beginning in the spring of 1986 and continuing to the early 1990s there were sporadic episodes of large-scale fighting between Yakut and Russian students.

The most serious and aggressive nationalist outbursts occurred in the Tuvan ASSR which, as we learned earlier, was incorporated into the USSR as late as 1944. The Tuvinians had retained their traditional culture and way of life to a greater degree, and had been less subject to the influence of Russian culture than the other Siberian peoples. According to data from the 1989 population census only 60 per cent of Tuvinians understood Russian. This indicator was far lower than in the other autonomous Siberian regions, in which the figure was between 80 per cent and 90 per cent. Apart from which, Tuva was the only Siberian autonomous region where there was a significant proportion of the indigenous people group. In 1989, 64 per cent of its inhabitants were ethnically Tuvan. A severe decline in their standard of living compared with that of the Russians, who as a rule worked in the Republic's industries, led to the development of nationalist feelings, an increase in inter-ethnic tension, and finally to aggression against the Russians. On 28–29 June 1990 a wave of anti-Russian pogroms spread throughout the whole of Tuva, as a result of which 88 people died. To restore order in the Republic a detachment of OMON[1] was sent there from various regions of Siberia on 1 July. With their help it proved possible to stabilize the situation temporarily. However, after the OMON were brought into Tuva a second wave of anti-Russian pogroms occurred. In 1991–2 similar events continued sporadically in various parts of Tuva.

The outburst of aggressive nationalism led to mass out-migration of Russians from the Republic. In the early 1990s several tens of thousands of Russians quitted Tuva, leading to an almost total paralysis of its industry. Many industrial enterprises were left in a state of neglect, among them the strategically important 'Tuvacobalt' complex. Well-appointed workers' settlements became ghost towns. The Tuvan economy has still (2004) not recovered from the consequences of these events. The Republic of Tyva (Tuva) is the poorest and most problem-beset region of Siberia.

However, with the exclusion of Tuva, from the late 1980s to the early 1990s and beyond nationalist sentiments have not become widespread in the Siberian autonomous regions. Attitudes of the aboriginal population to the Russians have remained normal. This is largely explained by factors such as the three-centuries-long experience of peacefully living and working together, the adoption of Russian culture and language by the majority of the titular nationalities, urbanized living, and finally the low level of the indigenous population compared with that of the Russians. In Siberia, apart from Tuva, the 1989 census showed that the titular nationality did not exceed one third of the population in any republic.

A significant landmark in the country's development was the 'August affair' (an attempted anti-Gorbachev *putsch*) of 1991. It led to the rapid demise of the Soviet Union and the development of a separate Russian state during the next few years. In Siberia, as in the country at large, these events were not greeted with unanimity. The vast majority of the population, wearied by the difficulties of *perestroika*, greeted them on the surface with indifference. There were no mass actions in support of the leaders of the *putsch* anywhere in Siberia. On the other hand, opposition to the attempt to seize power from Gorbachev was also expressed relatively weakly. Apart from the general apathy this is explained by the 'information vacuum' organized by the authorities at various levels.

The most noticeable reaction to the 'August *putsch*' occurred in the Kuzbass. As soon as news of the creation of the anti-Gorbachev State Committee on the Extraordinary Situation in the USSR (GKChP) reached Kemerovo on 19 August, a special meeting of the Kemerovo Oblast Council of Workers' Committees was summoned. It adopted a resolution calling for all necessary measures to be taken against the *putschists*. Workers' detachments began to be formed with this in mind; communication was established with the White House, the centre of Yeltsin's Russian government in Moscow. On the same day a special edition of the Kemerovo newspaper *Nasha gazeta* published an appeal to Yeltsin, as president of the Russian Republic, to oppose the GKChP. On the evening of the same day Kemerov television broadcast Yeltsin's message to the people, his Decree (*Ukaz*) on opposition to the GKChP together with a declaration by the chairman of the Kuzbass Council of Workers' Committees, V. Golikov, about the decisions adopted. At the same time, no large activities in support of democracy were organized owing to the opposition of A.G. Tuleev. This popular regional leader and erstwhile rival of Yeltsin in the elections for the presidency, who at the time headed both the legislative and executive arms in Kemerovo Oblast, was effectively supporting the *putsch*. With his declarations to the population on television, on the radio and in the newspapers calling for the maintainance of order he caused a certain amount of confusion in the workers' movement.

The other Siberian regions reacted more calmly to events in Moscow. There were a few meetings in support of democracy in a few towns on 20 August. For instance, there was a pro-democracy rally in Irkutsk; several thousand people took part in it. The meeting adopted a resolution condemning the GKChP and supporting Yeltsin.

The authorities in the regions also reacted to the events in a variety of ways. Some of them, notably in the Altai Krai and Magadan Oblast and others openly supported the GKChP, and were sooner or later removed from their posts in consequence. In particular A.G. Tuleev was removed from his positions for a while on 27 August by a decree from Boris Yeltsin. By contrast, the authorities in some other towns openly supported the Russian leadership. For example, the Novosibirsk Soviet supported Yeltsin on 20 August, and the Mayor of Irkutsk, B.A. Govorin, spoke at a pro-democracy meeting in the city. In the majority of places the authorities demonstrated real 'bureaucratic wisdom' and lay low, making no remarks in support of either side in the conflict. This course of action allowed many regional leaders to retain their posts. Even such an avid opponent of Yeltsin as the head of Novosibirsk Oblast, V.P. Mukha, who was also first secretary of the Communist Party's Regional Committee (*Obkom*) and chairman of the Oblast Council of People's Deputies, sat on the fence. Only at the very end, when the outcome was clear, did the soviets of several Siberian regions support the White House.

After the collapse of the Communist system and the end of the USSR, the extremely complex process of reforming the economy, which became known as the 'Gaidar-Chubais Reforms' or 'shock therapy', began within the Russian Federation. Siberia experienced in full all the difficulties entailed by this new government policy.

As is known, the basis for this policy lay in freeing up the pricing mechanism and the privatization of state-owned property. In Siberia the share of private and corporate ownership had already risen to 50 per cent, and the share of state, public and municipal ownership had slid to 45 per cent. However, these measures did not provide the expected rapid boost to the economy. The process of forming efficient ownerships interested in the development of production dragged on. In the beginning the most profitable enterprises went into private hands. In early 1990s Siberia this mainly meant the export-orientated oil, gas and aluminium sectors. However, at first, even in these sectors the new owners did not pay much attention to the development and modernization of production and the social protection of their workers. Liberalization of prices led to hyperinflation. The lack of a clear aim in government economic policy, which was subject to strong influence by political opportunism and the lack of an effective state regulatory mechanism, led the Russian economy, including its Siberian element, into deep crisis. During the crisis hundreds of enterprises were closed down in Sibera and the volume of industrial production plummeted. The machine building sector suffered particularly severely. The decline in industrial production continued until the 1998 devaluation. By 1998 the level of production stood at only 50 per cent of the 1990 level. However, the oil and gas industries, non-ferrous metallurgy and a few other sectors suffered less from the downturn. The crisis had the unintended effect of improving the ecological situation in Siberia.

The crisis of the 1990s was caused not only by a continuation of Russian government policy, but it also resulted from a concatenation of a series of objective and subjective factors. More than anything else, it resulted from the disproportion in industrial development which took place during the 'socialist epoch', the incapacity of existing industries to satisfy market requirements, the low technological level of many industrial goods, the severing of previous economic links after the end of the USSR and the elimination of the planning and distribution system habitual for the majority of industrial executives in those years, who found it impossible to adapt to working in market conditions.

Finally, the massive, unprecedented and desperate struggle that occurred during the division and distribution of state property worsened the phenomena present in this crisis. During this process the use of bribery, blackmail, threats, corruption and even murder contracts and other similar things became common. Often directors would deliberately weaken the value of their products and then pick up shares or vouchers from their workers for a song and end up owners of the enterprises. Others interested in privatization did not lag behind the directors in this regard. With the help of corrupt officials, enterprises would artificially 'cut off' the inflow of raw materials and supplies, placing the enterprises in a hopeless situation, after which the shares could easily be bought up from the workforce. One example is the finance company Trans World Group (the Ruben and Chernyi brothers), registered in Great Britain, which by the use of such methods managed to seize control of most of the aluminium works in Siberia (the Saian, Krasnoiarsk, Bratsk and Novokuznetsk works) through stooges.

The economic crisis, unemployment, hyperinflation and chronic nonpayment or delay of wages and salaries, the constant price rises and the enrichment of the directors of Siberia's factories caused tension and discontent with the reforms and confusion within Siberian society. The workers' response to a severe diminution in an already poor standard of living was a strike movement. Throughout practically the whole of the 1990s Siberia experienced a struggle through strikes which flared up, only to die down again. The leaders of the strike movement, as before, remained the Kuzbass miners, who from time to time managed to draw the whole country's attention to themselves (this was particularly the case when they stopped traffic on the Trans-Siberian Railway in 1994 and 1997) and forced the government somehow to address the problems of the miners and the coal industry.

Representatives of various political parties, especially the Communist Party of the Russian Federation, tried to utilize the strikes by the Siberian miners and other categories of workers in the early 1990s (especially before the October events in Moscow in 1993 and the elections for President of Russia in 1996) for their own ends. They supported any strike in every possible way and tried to include political elements, from the resignation of the country's president to amendments to the constitution and a return to the Soviet system, in the strikers' demands.

However, the political parties did not manage to extract much benefit from their use of the strike movement. Although the striking Siberians sometimes included the need for government concessions in their demands they remained politically loyal to the president and the government. This was very clearly demonstrated in the so-called 'October events in Moscow' in 1993, when despite all their efforts Yeltsin's opponents did not manage to drag the Siberians into the opposition or to persuade them to organize any events in their support. In Siberia, in September and October 1993, political indifference reigned.

Only later, in 1995–6, when the strike movement in the coal industry was going through a more tense period, did the Communists in the Kuzbass manage to gain control of the miners for a limited time. In the elections to the State Duma in 1995 the Russian Communist Party received 51 per cent of the votes here, and in the summer of the following year the Kuzbass and a few other regions voted against Yeltsin in the presidential elections. This Communist success was short-lived. It came about, above all, because of the concrete socio-economic situation.

In the 1990s, after the collapse of the USSR and the downfall of the Communist system of power in Siberia, the formation of a regional ruling elite took place as elsewhere in Russia. In all the Siberian regions subject to the Russian Federation (*subekty*) close links were gradually formed between the regional authorities and the new owners of industry and those representing financial, industrial and commercial capital. This process was not at all simple. In addition, the regional elites gave stability to the power structure and served as a support for the local bureaucracy in their relations with the population and the central authorities.

The important role of the regional elite in Siberia was clearly shown in October 1993 and the events following it, which provided a serious test for the local power system. Overall the authorities in the Siberian regions maintained a neutral position or supported President Yeltsin. In certain areas, however, namely Kemerovo and Novosibirsk oblasts, they openly supported Yeltsin's opponents. In response to this, immediately after the storming of the White House, the Russian president prorogued the rebellious Kemerovo soviet and once more removed its chairman, A.G. Tuleev, and the governor of Novosibirsk Oblast, V.P. Mukha, from their positions. In the December 1993 elections, to the federation's soviets Tuleev gained over 80 per cent of the votes cast, and in April 1994 he was once more in leadership, heading the Kemerovo Oblast Parliament (the Legislative Assembly), and in 1997 he won the elections for governor of Kemerovo Oblast. In 1995 Mukha was victorious in the elections for governor of Novosibirsk Oblast.

To coordinate the activities of and cooperation between the elites and local authorities, two interregional associations were formed: *Sibirskoe soglashenie* (Siberian Agreement) and *Dalnevostochnoe soglashenie* (Far Eastern Agreement). All political entities in Siberia joined one or the other.

Gradually leaders emerged from among the Siberian governors, people who enjoyed great authority not only in their own region, but in Siberia as a whole and beyond. Particularly prominent governors were Tuleev from Kemerovo Oblast (1997–present), V.M. Kress from Tomsk Oblast (1991–present), V.I. Ishaev from Khabarovsk Oblast (1991–present) and A.I. Lebedev from Krasnoiarsk Oblast (1998–2002). Their elevated, independent position and their defence of the interests of their regions gained them a deservedly strong respect among Siberians. The central authorities, including the national president, carefully listened to their opinions.

In the 1990s in Siberia, as throughout Russia, an unusual phenomenon which went by the name of 'parade of sovereignties' took place. The regional authorities tried to make their local legislation superior to federal laws and also attempted to obtain exclusive privileges for their regions. From the beginning of 1992 the authorities in the Siberian republics, *krais*, *oblasts* and autonomous *okrugs* made extensive use of Yeltsin's famous thesis: 'Grab as much sovereignty as you can swallow.' But the regional laws often contradicted the Russian constitution and federal legislation, sometimes severely infringing the rights of Russian citizens. For instance, the Sakha-Yakut republican constitution stated that only someone knowing the Yakut language could become its president. Since over 50 per cent of the population were ethnic Russians this violated not only the Russian constitution but the rights of a large proportion of the citizens.

Sometimes the attempts of the regional authorities to strengthen their sovereignty reached ridiculous proportions, as when the leadership of the Buriat Republic, an economically weak region, adopted a decision to erect customs posts on its borders with its neighbours and take customs dues on imports into Buriatia. True, the decision lasted for about a week and was never acted upon; its complete absurdity clearly became obvious even to those who had initiated the idea!

Actually, the 'parade of sovereignties' presented quite a serious problem for President Yeltsin and the Russian government. Despite all their efforts to limit the phenomenon, they did not succeeed in making any substantial progress in opposing it. Only after the new millennium had dawned was the new president of Russia, V.V. Putin, able to overcome it. In 2000 federal *okrugs* were created in Russia headed by plenipotentiary representatives of the Russian Federation's president. They began to establish control over all entities subject to the federal government. They were able to put a stop to the 'parade of sovereignties'. The territory of Siberia was subdivided into three federal *okrugs*: the Far East, Siberia and the Urals, which were headed by K.B. Pulikovskii, L.V. Drachevskii and P.M. Latyshev respectively.

The 'shock therapy' reforms and the economic crisis of the 1990s had an extremely deleterious effect on the Siberian population. For the most part Siberia became an unpleasant place to live. From a region in which the population had steadily grown during the course of 400 years, mainly through in-migration from the European part of the country, it became a region from which people began to migrate to other places. In the early twenty-first century the population of Siberia declined by roughly 1.5 million in comparison with 1989, now forming 21 per cent of the nation's total population. According to the 2002 Census it amounted to slightly over 31 million, whereas in 1989 the total had been 32.5 million. In Russia as a whole the population had diminished by almost two million during that period, from 147 to 145 million, Siberia accounted for 75 per cent of this decline. Population decline was particularly severe in the eastern regions which formed part of the Far Eastern Federal Okrug. Here there was a loss of over a million inhabitants. For instance, the population of the most distant and furthest east region, the Chukotka Autonomous Okrug, diminished drastically from 157,000 to 54,000. Magadan Oblast lost almost half its people. Out of 30 Siberian subdivisions of the Russian Federation the population declined in 21 and grew in only 9, and even here the growth was insignificant. Only the Khanty-Mansi Autonomous Okrug, where the majority of the oil and gas industry is located, did the population rise by a hefty 30 per cent.

Apart from this general reduction, the diminution of the rural population as against urban dwellers continued. In the early twenty-first century 72.5 per cent of the population lived in towns and cities. There were over 39 urban locations with more than 100,000 inhabitants. Out of these seven, Krasnoiarsk, Barnaul, Irkutsk, Vladivostok, Khabarovsk, Novokuznetsk and Tiumen, had over 500,000 inhabitants. Omsk and Novosibirsk had over a million each, the latter being the third city in size in Russia. The most urbanized regions of Russia are Magadan Oblast and the Khanty-Mansi and Yamalo-Nenets autonomous *okrugs*, where 90 per cent of the population are urbanized. Khabarovsk Krai, the Kamchatka and Sakhalin *oblasts* have more than 80 per cent of their populations living in towns.

Against this background of an overall decline in population, the indigenous peoples increased their numbers in the 1990s. The increase was more than 200,000, topping 1.5 million (an increase of 13 per cent compared with 1989). Almost all the Siberian peoples grew in numbers. The most numerous are the Buriats (445,000) and Yakuts (444,000).

Legal and illegal Chinese immigration began to be a serious problem for Siberia in the 1990s. According to some figures hundreds of thousands of Chinese immigrants (most of them illegal) are now living in Siberia. They are involved in trade, craft industries, agriculture and poaching. Many of the media regard this phenomenon as dangerous for the region, fearing a gradual Chinese colonization, leading to Russia's loss of Siberia, particularly the Far Eastern regions.

To some degree the August 1998 devaluation has been the key event in Siberian economic development. Lowering the cost of the rouble against the American dollar simultaneously created the preconditions for the development of Russian industry. After devaluation a series of industrial sectors began to benefit from serious capital input aimed at long-term development, having previously suffered from all sorts of dubious owners aiming for the highest possible profits. Serious capital investment was placed not only in the oil and gas sectors, which remained viable and profitable throughout the 1990s, but in Siberian ferrous metallurgy, the aluminium industry, forestry, electical energy, coal mining, and the gold and diamond sectors. The concentration of Siberian productive capacity in the hands of large-scale owners began. In particular, the dubious TWG Company was replaced in the early twenty-first century by a powerful Russian company 'Russian Aluminium', which became one of the largest producers of this metal in the world. It now owns a very significant stake in the largest Siberian aluminium works (Bratsk, Krasnoiarsk,

Saianogorsk and Novokuznetsk) and many allied industries in Siberia, Russia and abroad. Today, over 80,000 people work in their factories and their annual turnover is 3.5 billion US dollars. The company is paying considerable attention to technological modernization and new types of products. Analogous processes are taking place in the other sectors of Siberian industry outlined above.

These reforms have served to stimulate and somewhat enliven the Siberian economy, particularly in the above sectors. For example, gold production rose by 50 per cent between 1998 and 2002, from 99,700 to 148,400 tons. The annual increase in Siberian oil production is on average 10 per cent. Today, Siberia provides Russia with:

- 93.5 per cent of its total gold production;
- 83 per cent of its aluminium;
- 72 per cent of its coal output;
- over 50 per cent of the cellulose;
- over 90 per cent of the gas;
- over 70 per cent of the oil;
- over 95 per cent of diamond production; and
- over 40 per cent of Russia's electrical energy.

As the name of a mountain range in the Far East suggests, Siberia remains the backbone (*Stanovoi khrebet*) of Russia's economy and budget.

At the same time, many socio-economic problems remain. Many sectors of the economy have still not managed to lift themselves out of the crisis. There is a markedly resource-based orientation in the economy and reliance on the export of primary products. For instance, though being responsible for producing over 50 per cent of Russia's cellulose, Siberia is obliged to purchase almost all its good quality paper abroad or from different regions of Russia. The standard of living for the majority of Siberians remains fairly low, leading to continued out-migration.

Nonetheless, since the overwhelming majority of Russia's raw material resources are still to be found in Siberia, the Russian government must inevitably, sooner or later, devote greater attention to its development. Without Siberia and its resource potential Russia and its economy would be condemned to a permanently backward place in the dynamically modernizing contemporary world.

Glossary of Russian terms

Where both are used in the text the singular form of the word is followed by the Russian plural. Anglicized plural 's' is not indicated.

Akademgorodok Campus-style branch of the Russian Academy of Sciences built in the countryside about 20 miles from Novosibirsk.

Amanaty Hostages taken from an indigenous group to ensure future payment of the fur tribute.

Artel Traditional form of Russian cooperative labour group, often craftsmen, builders, etc.

Ataman/-y Cossack military rank: commander.

Bania Traditional Russian sauna.

Boyar son Honorary rank given to reward state servitors.

Chernozem Rich black earth, a belt of which extends from western Ukraine into western Siberia.

Chornosotnye 'Black hundreds': extremist right wing gangs.

Chum See Yurta.

Cisbaikalia Area to the west of Lake Baikal.

Dalbiuro Communist Party bureau for Far East.

Desiatina Old Russian measure of area (2.7 acres; 1.09 hectares); also tithe.

Diak/-i Clerk, administrator.

Duma Council (regional, urban or among indigenous inhabitants).

Dvoriane Noblemen.

Etapy Overnight resting places established for prisoners being marched from European Russia to Siberia.

Gimnazii Secondary schools, usually with classical curriculum.

Gorodnichii/-ie Urban police chief.

Gorodskoi golova Mayor.

Guberniia Province.

Gubernskie vedomosti Official government-owned provincial newspapers.

Guliashchie liudi Vagrants.

Inorodtsy 'Natives'; term for non-Slavic indigenous peoples.

Izba Russian peasant cottage.

Kadetskii korpus 'Corps des pages': elite male educational establishment.

Kaznacheistvo Treasury.

Kibitka/-ki Family-sized indigenous dwelling; nomad tent.

Komsomol Young Communist League.

Konnye Cavalry.

Kormlenie System by which non-salaried medieval Russian tax collectors obtained income, by 'feeding' off the population.

Krai Large administrative unit equivalent to province.

Kulak/-i Derogatory term for a richer peasant; means 'fist'.

Kuptsi Merchants.

Kurgan/-y Tumulus or burial mound erected by nomadic peoples as a memorial to dead leaders; see Chapter 5, note 4.

Lgoty Tax incentives; remissions of dues to facilitate settlement.

Malodvorka Small hamlet.

Masterovye Skilled artisans; factory workers.

Meshchane Petty bourgeois urban population.

MTS Machine tractor station to share scarce mechanized equipment between collective farms; see Chapter 28, note 5.

Namestnichestva Viceregencies.

Novosyoly Homesteaders; fresh peasant settlers.

Oblast Large administrative unit; province; see Chapter 16, note 3.

Oblastnichestvo Regionalism; a political movement for Siberian autonomy.

Obshchiny Village communities.

Okrug Federal district.

Ostrog Russian frontier fortress, usually wooden.

Peshie Infantry.

Pisary Scribes.

Podiachie Clerks subordinate to the *diak*.

Polittsentr 'Political Centre'; radical organization in Far East Republic.

Posad Urban settlement not yet designated as a town.

Priamurie Region adjacent to the River Amur.

Prikaz Administrative department, such as '*Sibirskii prikaz*': Siberia Office.

Prikazchik Official working in a *prikaz*.

Primorie Maritime region adjacent to the Siberian Pacific littoral.

Pripisnye 'Assigned'; that is, peasants or workers directed to settle in a certain place by authorities.

Priuralie Area adjacent to the Ural Mountains.

Prodotriady Bolshevik detachments sent to seize grain from peasants.

Prodrazverstka Grain requisitioning; that is, forcible seizure from peasants.

Promysly Crafts; artisan-type production.

Promyshlenniki Russian hunters and explorers, sometimes in state service, sometimes self-employed; see Chapter 11, note 3.

Pud/-y Old Russian measure for weight (16.38 kg).

Ratushy Town halls.

Revvoensovet Bolshevik Revolutionary Military Soviet.

Sazhen/-i Old Russian measure of length (2.13 metres).

Sezhaia izba   County hall; a body for administering the county.

Sibrevkom   Supreme Bolshevik revolutionary organ in Siberia.

Sloboda   Smallish urban settlement.

Sovnarkhoz   A regional council to direct economic development.

Sovnarkom   Council of Peoples' Commissars; the first Bolshevik cabinet.

Spetspereselentsy   People forced to settle in Siberia during the 1930s purges.

Stantsii   Cossack villages.

Staroobriadtsy   'Old Believers': members of a traditionalist Russian Orthodox sect.

Starosty   Village headmen; elders.

Starozhily   'Old timers'; descendants of early Russian settlers in Siberia.

Stola   Literally 'tables'; title given to administrative sub-departments.

Streltsi   'Musketeers': early regular Russian troop formations.

Syski   Investigations into official corruption.

Taiga   Coniferous forests extending throughout central Siberia.

Tamozhni   Customs posts.

Tiaglo/-ye   Literally 'burden'; refers to those subject to payment of dues to the state in money or kind (not nobility).

Trakt   'Trail'; early Russian road.

Transbaikalia   Area to the south and east of Lake Baikal.

Tsentrosibir   Central Executive Committee of Siberian Soviets.

Uchilishcha   Educational establishments.

Uezd/-y   Territorial administrative subdivision equivalent to county.

Ukaz   A binding decree issued by the government.

Vedro   Old Russian liquid measure equivalent to 15 litres.

Voevoda/-y   Russian territorial military governor.

Volost/-i   Intermediate administrative and legal unit including several villages.

Yarmarki   Trade fairs, often held annually.

Yasak   Fur tribute exacted from indigenous tribes by the Russians.

Yurta   Indigenous dwelling like a tepee; see Chapter 5, note 2.

Zakupsbyt   Centralized cooperative purchase and distribution organization.

Zemleprokhodtsy   Russian hunter-explorers.

Zemstvo   Elected rural regional government body; see Chapter 21, note 4.

Notes

1 General information

1 The natural borders do not coincide with political subdivisions.
2 A landscape zone is a homogeneous piece of land with natural boundaries, within which natural components (rocks, relief, soil, climate, vegetation and wildlife) form an interrelated unity.
3 The names given in parentheses are older forms used before the Soviet era.
4 This group is merely a matter of convenience. It comprises the peoples that do not belong to any of the other groups, but their languages do not belong to the same family.

2 The study of Siberia's history

1 Not only the historians were to blame: sources were regarded as classified information, and were thus inaccessible to researchers.

3 Siberia in the Stone Age

1 Contemporary knowledge of the Stone Age is incomplete. It has been changing and becoming more specific as more and more new archaeological finds are made. It is possible that there will be discoveries radically changing our view of the entire epoch.
2 This classification of periods refers only to Siberia. It is quite generalized since the Stone Age lasted different lengths of time for differing Siberian peoples. Some tribes were still living in the Palaeolithic era, while others were already in the Mesolithic and Neolithic, and yet others were entering the Bronze or even Iron Age.
3 There are current theories that humankind emerged in Siberia about one million years ago.
4 The Inuit were still constructing dwellings of this type in Chukotka and Alaska as late as the early twentieth century.

4 Siberia in the Bronze Age

1 The Bronze Age is a period in human history associated with the use of non-ferrous metals.
2 'Archaeological cultures' in this sense of the term consist of a time- and space-limited group of relics left from ancient human activity and characterized by common features, represented by tools, decorations, ceramics, weapons, etc.
3 Experts do not know whether earlier people could produce dairy products.
4 Shamanism is a specific form of religion (as a rule preceding the inauguration of other, more sophisticated religions). The basis of Shamanism is a belief in spirits and souls, coupled with a spiritualization of nature. Characteristic features are shamans

and a special ceremony of *kamlanie*. The shaman (the word is of the Tungus origin) is a person capable of communicating with spirits using special sacred attributes (garments, a tambourine or a staff) and through the ceremony of kamlanie. Kamlanie is a special ceremony during which the shaman communicates with spirits, by going into an ecstatic state (either the spirits enter his body or his soul goes into the world of the spirits). Through the medium of kamlanie, shamans healed people and asked the spirits for the protection of people in particular circumstances, etc.

5   Siberia in the Scythian period

1   Ancient historians gave this name not only to the tribes of the northern Black Sea coastal area, but also to all the peoples inhabiting the steppe and wooded-steppe zone from Hungary to Transbaikalia (the area beyond Lake Baikal) and Manchuria.
2   *Yurta* – a movable dwelling of Asian nomads, circular in form, consisting of a collapsible wooden lattice frame which was covered with thick felt and cloth.
3   The 'Scythian-Siberian animalistic style' is an ancient form of applied art associated with the depiction of animals and fragments of their bodies. This style was widespread among the peoples of the Eurasian steppes and wooded-steppes.
4   *Kurgan* – a barrow or tumulus built over an ancient grave, generally made from earth, occasionally from stones.
5   At present the Pazyryk saddle is the earliest one ever found (the ancient Greeks, Persians, Assyrians and other peoples did not use saddles at this period).
6   The *sestertius* was an ancient Roman bronze coin weighing 27 grams.
7   Other peoples of south Siberia also used similar weapons.

6   Siberia in the period of the Huns

1   *Shan-yü* was the title given to the supreme chief of the Hunnic military tribal confederacy. The *shan-yü* was elected for life at a meeting of all the chiefs of the Hunnic tribes, being chosen from among the relatives of the preceding *shan-yü*. Most commonly the eldest man in the family was elected (the ancestral principle).
2   The Huns' continuous attacks forced China to begin the Great Wall in the 3rd century BCE.

7   The Turks in Siberia: the Yenisei Kirghiz State

1   Kaghan (Turkic for ruler) is the title which was used by Tumyn, the chief of the Tu-Gyu tribe. Later this title was used by many Turkic speaking peoples.
2   The ancient Turkic written languge was deciphered at the end of the nineteenth century by the Russian scientist V.V. Radlov and Danish scientist V. Tomsen.
3   The east Turkic Kaghanate was subjected to Chinese rule for about 20 years in the mid-seventh century.
4   At the same time (eighth to tenth centuries) some territories in the Far East (Primorie, Priamurie) were part of the ancient state of *Bokhai* with its centre in Korea and Manchuria. This state was founded in 698 by the Tungus speaking tribes of Mokhe. Its structure was, in part, modelled on that of the Tang Dynasty in China. In 926 the state of Bokhai was destroyed by the Kidany nomadic tribes (Liao Dynasty).
5   Kirghiz (Turkic) means red-faced.

8   The Mongols in Siberia: the Siberian Khanate

1   There is an assumption that Transbaikalia was Genghis Khan's native land.
2   According to some sources, the date was 1155 or 1167.
3   Siberian Tatars is a collective name for the Turkic nomadic and semi-nomadic tribes inhabiting the steppe and wooded-steppe regions of west Siberia.

9   The peoples of Siberia on the eve of Siberia's annexation to Russia

1   All names here are those used by the Russians in the seventeenth century. Modern names are given in parantheses.
2   The Turkic speaking *Yakuts* (Sakha) who lived in the Lena River Valley were also cattle breeders.

11   The Yermak expedition: the subjugation of Siberia

1   Yermak's expedition to Siberia was previously believed to have started in September 1581 but studies carried out by Siberian historians in the late twentieth century established that it started one year later.
2   Russians use the terms 'right hand' and 'left hand' to distinguish the different banks of rivers, as if viewing the river in a downstream direction.
3   These explorers (*promyshlenniki*) were Russian hunters and serving men who investigated Siberia partly under government orders and partly as a result of private initiative.

13   The administration of Siberia

1   The state had a monopoly on fur trade.
2   Clerks and deputy clerks were state officials who served in Russian government institutions of the fourteenth to seventeenth centuries. They were paid salaries. Besides their salaries they could be paid by the grant of estates.
3   Unrest mainly took the form of petitions to the tsar, public gatherings and mass migration to other areas.

14   The exploration of Siberia

1   In the seventeenth century in Russia prisoners of war were often not allowed to return to their countries, but kept in Russia where they had to start a new life.
2   *Pud* is an old Russian measure of weight, one *pud* equalling 16.38 kilos. If a serving man accepted a grant of land, the wage was reduced.
3   *Chetvert* is 'a quarter', a dry measure used in Siberia until 1679, equivalent to four *pudy*, later eight *pudy*.
4   One *desiatina* (an old Russian unit of land area) was equal to 1.09 ha.
5   The indigenous population went sable hunting as individuals carrying bows and arrows.
6   *Sazhen* is an old Russian measure equal to 2.13 metres.
7   Up to 100 boats were built annually in Verkhoturie alone.

15   Siberia's foreign policy situation

1   The Chinese government prohibited their merchants to visit Russia except for Kiakhta.
2   The Russian Church Mission in Beijing was inaugurated in 1715.
3   'Up' indicates southwards in this case: the main Siberian rivers flowed northwards towards the Arctic Ocean.
4   The company organized 13 round-the-world trips mainly to supply provisions to the settlers.

16 The administration of Siberia: the Siberian reforms of 1822

1   As a rule the governors general lived in St Petersburg and visited Siberia only occasionally.
2   The 'Siberian satraps' was the unofficial name commonly used to refer to the Siberian bureaucracy in the eighteenth and nineteenth centuries.
3   The *oblasts* were headed by a military governor who combined civil and military administrative duties.
4   Each of these zones was headed by a commandant who combined civil and military duties.
5   *Ratman* was a term used for an elected member of a municipal body of self-government.
6   The only significant change in procedure for urban self-government during the second half of the nineteenth century came as a result of the 1870 Municipal Reform.

17 Socio-economic development

1   *Kibitka* was a term used for a family-sized nomadic dwelling.
2   Taxes were collected from every male peasant of military serving age.
3   It ranged from 5 to 120 roubles per year depending on a worker's skills.
4   No more than one third of this total was cultivated every year.
5   Rye remained the principal crop.
6   Sometimes they were held more frequently.

18 Cultural development and Siberian scientific expeditions

1   This method of support was applied to all other types of schools in Siberia.
2   Hieromonk is a monk who has been ordained priest.

19 Siberia's foreign policy situation

1   The actual work of the expedition commenced in 1849 at Muraviov's initiative.
2   At the end of eighteenth century the French naval explorer La Pérouse had come to the conclusion that the mouth of the Amur was not navigable and that Sakhalin was a peninsula.

20 Socio-economic development

1   Kwangtung Province was set up on the island of the same name which Russia leased from China for 30 years.
2   Poor peasants were most uncommon among the 'old timers'.
3   The Chinese Eastern Railway was built between 1896 and the early 1900s by agreement with the Chinese government across Manchuria from the station at Karimsk in Transbaikal to the station at Nikolsk-Ussuriiskii in Primorie. It made it possible to shorten the distance from Vladivostok and served as a weapon of Russian expansion in Manchuria.
4   The section from Yekaterinburg to Tiumen had been built at the end of the nineteenth century.
5   The specific import dues were reconsidered a number of times, in 1906 they were considerably reduced.
6   A small absolute increase in the Siberian aboriginal population – less than 100,000 people over 50 years – was achieved through the south Siberian peoples.

21 The development of culture and science

1 During the First World War some extra military schools and colleges for ensigns were opened in Siberia.
2 The first educational institution for women in Siberia, E.I. Medvedkova's Orphanage, was opened in Irkutsk as early as 1838.
3 This figure includes girls attending elementary schools.
4 The *zemstvos* were elected local self-government bodies introduced to European Russia in 1864 as part of Alexander II's reforms. They were not introduced in Siberia owing to the lack of gentry there.
5 Originally published in St Petersburg.

22 Siberian social life: Siberia in the Revolution of 1905–7

1 Probably the first political organization in Siberia was a Populist (*Narodnik*) Circle in Irkutsk, led by a *gymnasium* teacher, K.G. Neustroev, in 1881–2. The circle set itself the task of helping political exiles. It was soon suppressed and its leader was executed.
2 The legal code, which introduced European-style practices to Russia, was implemented in Siberia only in the 1890s, and then only partially. Siberia was divided into two Court Districts: Irkutsk and Omsk, both of which cities had courts (*sudebnye palaty*). Lower level courts (*okruzhnye sudy*) were also established in provincial and regional centres and in Barnaul.

23 1917 in Siberia

1 All dates during 1917 are given according to the 'old style', i.e. the Julian calendar used in Tsarist Russia, as opposed to the Gregorian calendar, used everywhere else in Europe. The Julian calendar, 12 days behind the Gregorian by 1917, was phased out in 1918.
2 Another source gives 182 delegates.
3 Bolsheviks gained 25 per cent of the votes in Russia as a whole.

24 Reds and Whites in Siberia, 1918–21

1 All of the dates from 1918 onwards are given according to the new style Gregorian calendar as opposed to the old Julian calendar.
2 Elections to the Siberian Regional Duma and the Constituent Assembly were held simultaneously.
3 In 1917 there were around 400,000 prisoners of war in Siberia: Germans, Austrians, Hungarians, Czechs, Slovaks, Turks, etc.
4 The White Siberian Army units were formed from volunteers on the basis of the anti-Bolshevik underground.
5 The Vladivostok Group of the Czechoslovak troops maintained neutrality until 29 June.
6 Kolchak considered the Constituent Assembly of the 1918 type too leftist.
7 A former general of the Tsarist Russian Army.
8 'War Communism' involved:

   • the total nationalization of industry and transport;
   • universal labour conscription;
   • an embargo on trade and the introduction of centralized food supply with strictly fixed norms;
   • the introduction of forcible seizures of agricultural surpluses (*prodrazverstka*);
   • the abolition of money and money circulation; and
   • the introduction of universal centralized planning.

9   The 'Red Terror' was a system of total repression of the slightest opposition to the authorities and involved:

- massive use of hostage-taking;
- preventive arrests and executions;
- the imprisonment of suspicious persons in concentration camps;
- a simplified procedure of trials and repressions beyond conventional legal procedures;
- repressions; and
- forced mobilization.

The 'Red Terror' gave rise to massive violations of the law, but it helped the Bolsheviks to maintain power. Tens of thousands of people became its victims in Siberia.

25 The Far Eastern Republic of 1920–2

1   The Japanese troops occupied Transbaikalia, Primorie and the Amur areas; in February 1920, under pressure from America and guerrillas, they left the latter.
2   Cooption to the FER Government was permitted.
3   In fact it predominantly consisted of the White troops that had withdrawn from Transbaikalia to Manchuria in 1920, while retaining their organized structure.
4   The Washington Conference was held from 12 November 1921 to 1 February 1922. The following countries took part in it: America, Great Britain, France, Japan, China, Italy, Belgium, Holland and Portugal. The conference discussed issues of international cooperation and the division of spheres of influence in the Asia-Pacific region. The FER delegation was present at the conference and presented documents on the Japanese intervention.
5   The Corps des pages was an elite boarding school for children of the Russian higher aristocracy aged between 9 and 20 years.

26 Siberia's foreign policy situation

1   The Communist International (1919–43) was a centralized union of Communist parties. It was created in Moscow to spread Communist ideas in the world, to foment World Communist Revolution and to support Revolutionary Russia. In 1920 at the 2nd *Comintern* Congress, its leader, the Bolshevik chieftain (*vozhd*) V.I. Lenin, came to the conclusion that the World Communist Revolution could be promoted through the national liberation movement in Asia which would cause the colonial empires and European capitalism to weaken.
2   After the October Revolution, China annulled Mongolia's autonomy and the Russian protectorate over Tuva and stationed troops there.
3   The Mongolian People's Republic was inaugurated in 1924.
4   The Yalta Conference took place on 4–11 February 1945 between the leaders of the USSR, the USA and Great Britain, Joseph Stalin, Franklin. D. Roosevelt and Winston Churchill. The conference discussed the problems of restructuring the world in the post-war era. The USSR agreed to enter the war with Japan on condition that the southern part of Sakhalin and the Kuril Islands would be handed over to her, plus the restoration of the right to use Port-Arthur and the control of the Chinese Eastern Railway (CER), which the USSR had sold to Japan in 1935.
5   The Chinese government was displeased with the fact that the borderline ran along the Chinese bank of the rivers and all the islands belonged to the USSR.
6   Japan insists on the division of the islands, considering the southernmost an inherent part of Japan.

28 Socio-economic and cultural development in the 1920s–40s

1   During the NEP period foreign capital was permitted to take on businesses on a concessionary basis, provided they undertook their technical reconstruction, restoring pre-revolutionary production levels and observing Soviet laws.

2   The average pay for Siberian workers was about 40 roubles per month, whereas a box of matches cost 14 copecks, a cake of soap cost 28 copecks, a roll of thread cost 20 copecks, one litre of paraffin cost 6 copecks and a kilo of sugar cost 36 copecks. There are 100 copecks in a rouble.

3   These developments involved the following: the elimination of private ownership of the means of production; restrictions on trade and an increase in planning; rapid acceleration of industrial development, especially in defence-related industries; the abolition of private farms and forced collectivization; the development of education and science geared towards the needs of industrialization, embedding the major dogmas of Bolshevism in the minds of the populace through education and culture; and finally the personality cult.

4   Apart from this, the construction of a line between Achinsk and Abakan (460 kilometres) had been completed in 1925.

5   The MTS was a centralized mechanized base for several collective farms, enabling sparse machinery to be shared between the farms, and facilitating Communist political control over the peasants and grain collection. In 1937 the Siberian MTS had 42,000 tractors and 15,000 combine harvesters, less than two tractors and one combine per farm.

6   OGPU (political police, forerunner of the NKVD and KGB) documents used the term 'former people' for members of the bourgeoisie, landowners, participants in the White movement, Tsarist army officers, members of political parties, clergymen, etc.

7   In 1934 the *spetspereselentsy* were renamed *trudoposelentsy* (labour settlers), and from 1935 their political rights began to be returned to them, but in 1937–8 a new wave of repressions engulfed them.

30 Siberia from 1985 to the early twenty-first century

1   OMON are special police detachments trained to combat civil disorder, organized crime and terrorism.

Editor's suggestions for further reading

English language books about Siberia are many and varied. An idea of their extent may be gained from my bibliography *Siberia and the Soviet Far East* (vol. 127 of the World Bibliographical Series, Clio Press, 1991), continued in several issues of the journal *Sibirica* (vols 2–3, 2002–3). The books I have included below are chosen for their abiding interest and relatively easy availability.

A really splendid example of documentary sources is *To Siberia and Russian America* (vol. 1, ed. Basil Dmytryshyn and E. Crownhart-Vaughan for the Oregon Historical Society, Western Imprints, 1985). The translations of sixteenth- and seventeenth-century explorers' reports provide insights into the minds of Russia's *conquistadores,* cataloguing new discoveries and their daring and sometimes cruel exploits. The Hakluyt Society's edition of the chronicles glorifying Muscovy's first foray beyond the Urals in 1581–2, *Yermak's Campaign in Siberia* (vol. 146, second series, ed. Terence Armstrong, Hakluyt Society Publications, 1975), includes reproductions of the original illustrations as well as texts.

From a much later date is Alexander Dmitriev-Mamonov's *Guide to the Great Siberian Railway.* Originally published in English in 1900, this fascinating illustrated guide, not only to the railway but to the geography and peoples along its 5,000-mile course, was reissued in 1971 (David & Charles). A new reference guide, compiled by Ye. Akbalyan and complete with CD-ROM, is *Practical Dictionary of Siberia and the North* (European Publications and Severnye Prostory, 2005).

Travellers' tales can be extremely absorbing and readable, even if their content is not always reliable. A good start would be to look at some of the 12 volumes reissued under my editorship as *Siberian Discovery* (Curzon, 1999). I also edited a four-volume *Collected Works* of a pioneer anthropologist from Oxford, Mariya Czaplicka. The set includes an account of her 1914 expedition to study aboriginal reindeer herders living in the remote northern Yenisei region, *My Siberian Year* (vol. 3), as well as the academic result, *Aboriginal Siberia* (vol. 2). Articles in vol. 1 also have considerable Siberian interest (Curzon, 1998).

Other particularly noteworthy travellers' tales from the pre-revolutionary period include: Richard Bush's *Reindeer, Dogs and Snowshoes*, an account of a telegraph surveyor's visit to mid-nineteenth-century eastern Siberia (Arno Press, 1970); the playwright Anton Chekhov's *A Journey to Sakhalin*, an account of a trans-Siberian trip to investigate conditions on the infamous prison island, when he was already dying from tuberculosis (Faulkener, 1993); the revolutionary Leo Deutsch's experiences in exile, *Sixteen Years in Siberia* (Hyperion Press, 1977); and the perceptive account of a 1774–6 tour by Hans Fries, *A Siberian Journey* (Cass, 1974).

Although they do not include all the truth about Siberia under Stalin, I include here several of the harrowing accounts written by victims of the GULAG system. Among the more noteworthy are: Eugenia Ginzburg's *Into the Whirlwind* (Collins Harvill, 1967) and its sequel, *Within the Whirlwind* (Collins Harvill, 1981); Rachel and Israel Rachlin's *Sixteen Years in Siberia*, translated from the Danish (University of Alabama, 1988); and Karlo Stajner's *7000 Days in Siberia* (Farrar, Straus & Girous, 1988). Andrei Amalrik's *Involuntary Journey to Siberia* (Collins Harvill, 1970) demonstrates that the system still existed, though on a far less monumental scale, under Brezhnev. Solzhenitsyn apart, one of the most touching evocations of life in the camps is Varlen Shalamov's *Kolyma Tales* (Penguin, 1994).

Secondary accounts written by Western observers offer a variety of approaches, emphases and depths of scholarly insight. An easy read, indeed a suitable companion to Naumov's book, is Bobrick Benson's *East of the Sun* (Heinemann, 1992). A somewhat more scholarly survey from a prolific American academic, Bruce Lincoln, is *Conquest of a Continent* (Cape, 1994). Victor Mote offers a geographer's perspective in his well-researched *Siberia: Worlds Apart* (Westview, 1998). John Stephan of the University of Hawaii, as well as producing erudite books on the Kurile Islands and Sakhalin, wrote a comprehensive history, *The Russian Far East* (Stanford, 1994).

Western scholarship on Siberia continues to develop. The British Universities Siberian Studies Seminar, a forum for researchers far beyond the UK, has generated many publications, including essays edited by Alan Wood, such as *History of Siberia* (Routledge, 1991) and several incarnations of the journal *Sibirica*. Research in Europe is represented by a series of historical essays, *The Siberian Saga: A History of Russia's Wild East* (ed. Eva-Maria Stolberg, Peter Lang, 2005). The vitality of similar scholarly endeavours in the USA is attested to by Steven Marks' *Road to Power* (Cornell University Press, 1991), a study of peasant resettlement and the Trans-Siberian Railway; by the widely focused *Between Heaven and Hell: The Myth of Siberia in Russian Culture* (ed. Galya Diment and Yuri Slezkine, St Martin's Press, 1993); and by the high standard of many of the essays in *Rediscovering Russia in Asia* (ed. Stephen Kotkin and David Wolff, Sharpe, 1995).

Contemporary research into the region's indigenous peoples is vigorous. An essential introduction is James Forsyth's *A History of the Peoples of Siberia* (Cambridge University Press, 1992). Post-Communist studies include: Marjorie

M. Balzer's *The Tenacity of Ethnicity* (Princeton University Press, 1999); Andrei Golovnev's *Siberian Survival* (Cornell University Press, 1999); and a helpful guide, *The Small Indigenous Nations of Northern Russia*, (ed. Dmitry Funk and Lennard Sillanpää, Vaasa, 1999). Natural history works range from Richard Stone's *Mammoth: The Resurrection of an Ice Age Giant* (Perseus, 2001) to Peter Matthiessen's fine photographic record, *Baikal: Sacred Sea of Siberia* (Thames & Hudson, 1992).

The intrepid traveller enticed to visit Siberia by reading Naumov's history or any of the above could make great use of either Thomas Byrn's *Trans-Siberian Handbook* (5th edn, Trailblazer, 2001) or Simon Richards' *Trans-Siberian Railway: A Classic Overland Route* (Lonely Planet, 2002).

Finally, I must just mention, so that the reader may contrast it with Naumov's approach, the quirky romantic view of Siberia offered by one of the region's most avid literary patriots, Valentin Rasputin: *Siberia, Siberia* (Northwestern University Press, 1996).

Index

People groups and cultures